AF557809

CULTURE OF SANITATION

CULTURE OF SANITATION

FROM INDUS VALLEY CIVILISATION TO SULABH

V. BASIL HANS

RUPA

Published by
Rupa Publications India Pvt. Ltd 2021
7/16, Ansari Road, Daryaganj
New Delhi 110002

Sales Centres:
Allahabad Bengaluru Chennai
Hyderabad Jaipur Kathmandu
Kolkata Mumbai

ISBN: 978-93-90547-13-5

First impression 2021

10 9 8 7 6 5 4 3 2 1

Printed at Thomson Press India Ltd., Faridabad

Contents

Foreword

The book *Culture of Sanitation: From Indus Valley Civilisation to Sulabh*, authored by Dr V. Basil Hans is a welcome and commendable addition to the literature on sanitation. Sanitation though an issue of critical significance often takes a backseat in discourses on environment. But its role in not only creating an ecologically sound physical ambience, but also setting a stage for healthy and sustainable livelihoods is invaluable. Sanitation is a subject that needs to be understood and analysed from a multi-dimensional perspective and this book by Dr Hans, which gives a comprehensive account of sanitation, is a critical input for creating a clean-green social space. Each of the nine chapters in the book has brought up a very important issue that is not only a useful data source but also provides room for further research in that area.

Sanitation assumes critical significance in an age in which tremendous harm is being done to the environment by waste generated both by human negligence and a development process that is insensitive to human well-being. The unprecedented growth of human population in many parts of the world, coupled with problems associated with providing safe living conditions, has resulted in sanitation emerging as one of the major challenges of our times. Growing inequalities between the rich and poor, leave the poor with no choice but to live under extremely hazardous conditions. How can those who cannot afford a 'safe roof' to live under, actually think of providing "safe sanitation" for themselves. It is in this background that sanitation has emerged as one of the major challenges of our times.

The book has engaged in a discourse on sanitation that gives critical inputs for understanding sanitation from multiple perspectives. The discussions in this book clearly point to the fact that sanitation is a subject which is inter-disciplinary in nature. It has a sociological dimension, a political economy angle, a cultural context and of course economic implications.

The book assumes importance because it discusses the issue

of sanitation both as a "theory" and a "practice". It also has policy implications in that it has provided an "action model" through the Sulabh initiative to work out replicable strategies. In a multi-group society like that of India, any change initiative has to take into consideration the local cultural practices, which play a major role in deciding peoples' attitudes to adopting hygienic sanitation practices. The fact that notions of "purity" and "pollution" determine the mindset of people vis-à-vis sanitation stands out as an example of how, in spite of being a human necessity, there is no universal model of "safe sanitation practices".

The book provides a very useful framework for understanding sanitation as a very key component of creating an ecologically sustainable environment. The author has shown that there is evidence to prove that India is heading towards a major sanitation crisis in the coming years. Efforts made to meet sanitation challenges have yielded limited results, as about 65 per cent of the population does not have access to toilet facilities and even the condition and usage pattern of existing toilet facilities in many places is unsatisfactory. A matter of grave concern is that a large number of families, especially in marginalised groups consider a "mobile phone" a greater necessity than a toilet! It is needless to say that many health hazards are directly linked to absence of safe sanitation facilities, especially in economically vulnerable groups both in rural and urban areas. The book has brought out the ramifications of the absence of safe sanitation very effectively with the help of appropriate examples. The stress on the "culture of sanitation" is a value addition to this work, which examines "sanitation behaviour" in the context of culture. In fact the notion of culture of sanitation is examined in a historical context and hence gives new insights for further work in the area.

The book refers to the Swachh Bharat Abhiyan, a programme that is making a conscious effort to make India free of various sources of dirt and remove the obstacles to the mission of creating a pollution-free India. His observation that the complexities inherent in this mechanism must be understood from a holistic perspective brings to the fore the multiple issues that need to be addressed if safe sanitation practices have to be implemented by people across the country.

Ensuring universal access to sanitation in households and institutional settings such as healthcare facilities and schools must be prioritized over other infrastructural needs. Even today there are buildings on which colossal expenditures have been incurred but little or no attention has been paid to the provision of clean drinking water, safe toilets or living and working spaces with proper air and light. It may be recalled that in many schools across the country girls did not go to schools because there were no separate washrooms for them, and it took a long time for the governance mechanism to accept this truth. Today there is an increasing realization that unless safe campuses, which include secure washrooms, are provided both enrolment and attendance of girls and women would be seriously affected.

Innovations in the field of sanitation need to be introduced with vigour today. The author has noted that we need "Toil-o-preneurs", and an effective system of sanitation marketing in India. Dr Hans discusses the notion of toilets of the future too. E-sanitation is well on its way, but there is a long way to go. There is a need to innovate "appropriate technologies" to address the needs of different social settings, based on their location, nature of water resources available. The most important factor is making it cost effective. Environmentally sustainable policies and practices using indigenous knowledge must form the basis for designing sanitation programmes.

The author has chronicled the journey of Sulabh, a civil society group, that has been relentlessly working for setting the stage for creating sustainable sanitation practices. He brings to the fore the challenges the agency faced in inculcating safe sanitation practices, and shows it has been able to make a mark over a period of time. The organisation is engaged in multiple tasks such as information dissemination, awareness building and has virtually emerged as a movement for inculcating the practice and culture of safe sanitation in many regions. By using the historic methodology framework the book profiles the efforts made by Sulabh. It also makes a reference to the Sustainable Development Goals (SDGs), which have set the agenda for creating a "liveable world".

I appreciate the effort that has gone into the preparation of this work and wish that it leads to further research and activism in the area of sanitation.

Dr R. Indira
Formerly Professor and Chairman
Department of Sociology
University of Mysore

Preface

Culture brings the concept of sanitation practice and philosophy into the realm of sociology in general and action sociology in particular. Cleanliness and sanitation practices are both cultural and developmental. Hence the need to study sanitation with a multi-disciplinary approach. This book is one such attempt.

As far as cleanliness is concerned, Mahatma Gandhi's message and mission were of creating a clean and healthy environment alongside the emancipation of the so-called untouchables like manual scavengers. Today, this message and mission are carried forward with real fervour by individuals like Hon'ble Prime Minister Narendra Modi and institutions like Sulabh International.

The Swachh Bharat Abhiyan is the latest sanitation programme in a long line of programmes, going back to the First Five Year Plan in 1954 when the rural sanitation programme was introduced. It was announced on 2 October 2014 with the objective of achieving universal sanitation and making India open defecation-free by 2019, the 150th birth anniversary of Mahatma Gandhi.

The abhiyan offers a promising solution to address the issues of sanitation and water in languishing rural areas and rapidly urbanising ones. Many districts and states of India have been progressing fast towards that goal but much still needs to be done. Though sanitation was historically and culturally rooted in India, today 48 per cent of the country's population defecates in the open.

Evidence indicates that India is heading towards a major sanitation crisis in the coming years. Efforts made to meet the sanitation challenges have been found to have very limited results, with as much as 65 per cent of the population not having toilet facilities along with very low use of existing toilets in urban and rural areas. It is perhaps the right time to critically evaluate and move beyond the excessive focus we have on "provision" and pay attention to the underlying complexities of the "mechanisms" that influence sanitation behaviour among people. If we don't do so, we stand the risk of "missing all the trees for the forest", i.e., missing the social and economic dimensions of the sanitation needs of the people, in the hurry to count the number of toilets provided. It is with this earnest desire that this book is brought out. It is a small but sincere effort to cherish Gandhian principles and to reinforce them in a fast changing socio-economic environment. I hope this is one of the crucial steps in social engineering today. I recall here one of the most famous quotes of Gandhi: "You must be the change you wish to see in the world." It is also in keeping with one of the objectives of Sulabh to promote PEACE in the developing world by enriching:

- Poverty alleviation;
- Environmental sanitation;
- Awareness and motivation;
- Children as agents of change; and
- Education for all in environmental sanitation, as "safe water and basic sanitation" are the foundation of life and health, and personal hygiene is the key to happy living.

I thank Dr Bindeshwar Pathak—the crusader for the lowly untouchables in India—for inviting me to his office in New Delhi in July 2017 for a discussion on action sociology in general and sanitation in particular. I am grateful to him for providing me an opportunity to pen my thoughts on the culture of sanitation.

I am deeply indebted to Dr Richard Pais, my friend, for his constant academic support and assistance in this endeavour. I thank Dr Manohar V. Serrao, the principal of my college, for always encouraging my pursuits in higher and inclusive education, and social concern.

My sincere thanks are due to Rupa Publications, for bringing out this book.

I sincerely hope that the book will be useful for people across disciplines and regions.

Dr V. Basil Hans

Chapter 1

Introduction to Sanitation

1.1 INTRODUCTION

The aim of this chapter is to examine the nature, scope and importance of the subject of the book, i.e., the culture of sanitation. It will trace such a culture from both global and local (Indian, indigenous) perspectives along with its growth and challenges.

Water, like sanitation, has a religious basis. Culture brings the concept of sanitation practice and philosophy into the realm of sociology in general and action sociology in particular. When people, irrespective of regions and religions, develop habits in their lives regarding food and nutrition, health and hygiene, etc., a sense of community culture also develops. Feeling for cleanliness slowly becomes in-built and transforms itself into behaviour, incorporating the mind and body together. Developing and using systems and institutions for personal and public health and hygiene brings forth behavioural models (e.g., toilet use). In the process, however, there will be constraints–misuse of the systems and mechanisms, refusal to accept and adapt, or resistance to change, say, being happy with the old ways of doing things.

Sanitation and culture are, thus, interlinked. An analysis of culture, language and communication patterns can provide clearer ways of explaining and understanding human behaviour. To inculcate positive sustainable sanitation practices in the community we need to understand community culture in the context of defecation as well as clean environment and personal hygiene practices. Values, attitudes, assumptions, behaviour and beliefs people harbour about themselves and others and about the natural world they live in make up community culture. In India, for instance, the use of clean toilets in homes and public places from the time of addressing the issue of scavenging to modern awareness of closed-door cleaning activities under the Swachh Bharat Abhiyan (Clean India Mission) shows the evolution of sustainable sanitation in keeping with the larger concept of sustainable development. So does the growth of Sulabh from toilets to toilet museum, and research publications on sanitation and action sociology.

Source:

Swastika Tripathi opines, “The idea and possibilities of what India can do if there is no open defecation are tremendous....”

It’s always refreshing to see water and sanitation approached in fun ways (in cartoons, movies, ad campaigns, etc.), especially if they change the world more effectively. In 2014, United Nations International Children’s Emergency Fund (UNICEF) asked citizens of India to have a “poo party” in an attempt to reduce open defecation levels. The highly comedic approach—incorporating Facebook, Twitter and YouTube videos—is an example of one public health campaign that is trying to encourage individuals to construct and use toilets.

On 11 August 2017 a Hindi film propagating the toilet message—*Toilet: Ek Prem Katha* (Toilet: A Love Story)—was released.[1] With or without humour, toilet is the best armour for a clean habitat and a hygienic livelihood.

Over the years the Government of India along with many international organisations has made efforts to bring about changes in rural communities by improving sanitation services through various projects, but the achievements are not up to the mark. This is because human factors related to social, economic, cultural, political and ecological determinants of health which also impact sanitation practices are not understood. Therefore, the objectives of this book are:

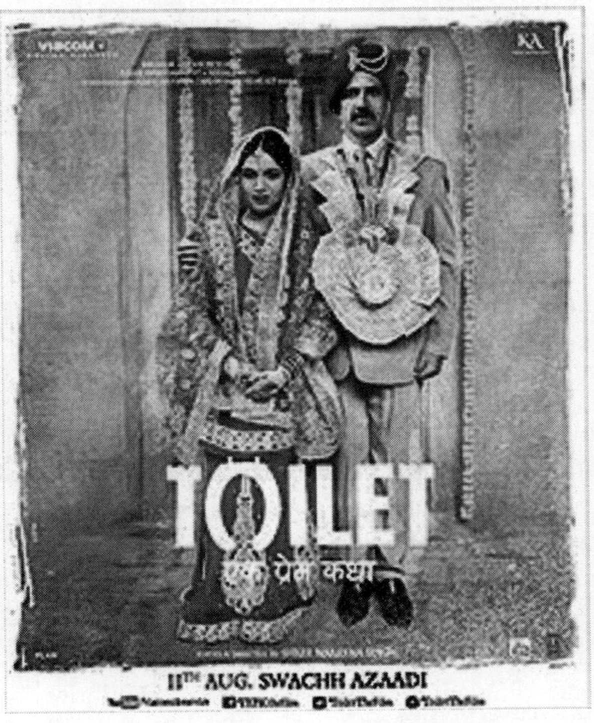

Source: https://www.imdb.com/title/tt5785170/mediaviewer/rm442837248

- To understand "community culture" in the context of open defecation practices
- To understand the connection between values, attitudes, behaviours, beliefs and assumptions that people have about both a clean environment and sanitation practices, especially defecation
- To analyse sanitation as part of learning and doing in sociology, economics and other social sciences
- To reflect on stakeholders' action to tackle some of these challenges based on the experience in some states and elsewhere in the world
- To examine the evolution of sanitation-related activities through

networking, training, technology, and research both during normal times and during crises e.g., disasters including earthquakes, floods

- Promote sharing of strategies and activities through work in sanitation by governments and NGOs
- To support sustainable approach to improve sanitation conditions through the Sulabh Movement and Model
- To facilitate a reflection on the challenges of sanitation practices in the coming years and our preparedness to face them adequately
- To generate a discussion on strengthening the sanitation network at national level and plans for the future.

1.2 FUNDAMENTALS OF SANITATION

Basic human needs are food, clothing, shelter, good environment, including clean air and water and sanitation facilities. The overall purposes of sanitation are:

- to provide a healthy living environment for everyone, to protect the natural resources (such as surface water, groundwater, soil), and
- to provide adequate safety, security and dignity for people when they defecate or urinate.

We also have a human right to sanitation: In September 2010, the United Nations Human Rights Council adopted a resolution recognising that the human right to water and sanitation are a part of the right to an adequate standard of living.

Effective sanitation systems provide barriers between excreta and humans in such a way as to break the disease transmission cycle (for example in the case of faecal-borne diseases). This aspect can be visualised with the F-diagram where all major routes of faecal-oral disease transmission begin with the letter F: faeces, fingers, flies, fields, fluids, food, and floods.

Basic sanitation means protecting the health of communities, and consists of sewage collection and treatment, urban cleaning, solid waste management, and pest control as well as control of any type of pathological agent. Drinking water supply and rainwater management also fit into basic sanitation activities.

1.2.1 Types of Sanitation

Sanitation is the practice of sterilisation, or making sure that microbes or germs do not get into contact with humans, animals, food or water, causing infectious and sometimes fatal diseases. There are different types of sanitation:

Filtration

Filtration involves sterilising water and filtering away waste products, so that it is safe for use. According to the Sanitation Training website, this process involves passing water through a filter, which separates solid and liquid waste products. After adding oxygen and ozone, the water passes through a smaller filter. Once this process is complete, a water handler adds chlorine to the water, killing any leftover bacteria.

Landfills

Carrying waste products to a landfill is another type of sanitation service. According to the Sanitation Training website, city garbage workers transport waste to a temporary holding place, or landfill. The purpose is to isolate the solid waste from residential areas to avoid spread of disease. Sanitary landfill differs from ordinary dumping in that the material is placed in a trench or other prepared area, adequately compacted and finally covered with earth at the end of the working day.

Landfills and dumps have been popular methods of waste disposal since ancient times. Landfill operation refers to waste disposal by burying waste such as paper, glass and metal between layers of dirt and other materials in such a way as to reduce contamination of the surrounding land. Modern landfill (sanitary) sites are often lined with layers of absorbent material and sheets of plastic to keep pollutants from leaking into the soil and water. Unused quarries and mining voids also serve as landfill sites. Care should be taken to avoid generation of leachate (water that collects contaminants as it trickles through waste, pesticides or fertilisers) and greenhouse gases. The people and area around and the vehicles going to and near these sites should also be managed for possible dangers and health hazards.

Dumps are just a big hole or a big pile of garbage and other possibly dangerous things. They do not prevent the waste from coming into contact with the ground, they are full of rats, roaches and other vermin, and they stink.

Treatment

There are several treatment techniques for waste, including hazardous waste. They include biological treatment, carbon adsorption, reverse osmosis, chemical treatment, distillation, electro-dialysis, etc. By using various technologies (e.g., electrochemical cells for water and odour treatment systems) we can clean the wastewater and the entire environment. Waste treatment techniques seek to transform the waste into a form that is more manageable and reduce the volume or the toxicity of waste making it easier to dispose of. Treatment methods are selected based on the composition, quantity and form of the waste material. In Sao Paulo, Brazil, wastewater is treated and reused to offset dwindling water sources. In Oman, golf courses are big consumers of treated effluents. Indian water consumers are also getting the benefits of various points-of-use (PU) treatment devices like ultraviolet technology, ultra filtration, nano technology, etc. It is good to note that several organisations (e.g., Water and Wastewater International) and individuals (e.g., Robert F. Kennedy Jr) are contributing their mite for clean water, clean environment and growth with a future. Besides Acts, we need public-private participation supported by the media and civil society for the purpose.

Source:

Reuse and Recycling

Sanitation also includes recycling. Trained workers at recycling plants sort paper, plastic and other recyclables from a general conveyor belt to one specifically for each. According to Attilo Bisso and Sharon Boots, recycling is a method of materials management wherein discarded materials are separated from waste and processed to acceptable standards to re-enter the economy as usable products. Thus, by this definition recycling occurs in three phases: first, the waste is sorted then the recyclables are collected, and finally the recyclables are used to create raw materials. These raw materials are then used in the production of new products.

Some recyclable items:

- Plastic
- Glass and ceramics
- Paper
- Old cans
- Old clothes and diapers
- Broken furniture

Source:

The "economics of recycling" is becoming popular these days. Rag-pickers or garbage/trash workers—now called waste entrepreneurs—sort leftover trash on the general conveyor belt into piles arranged by type. Separated recyclables are crushed and reprocessed, thereby preparing them for reuse. Separated trash goes to the landfill. The Sanitation Training website cites paper, glass, plastic and metal as materials that are easily recyclable.

Economics of Recycling

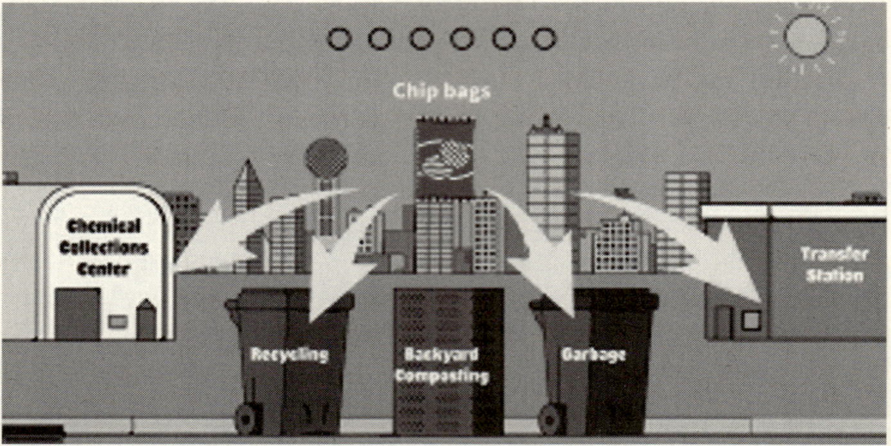

Source:

If recycling industries replace mining industries, the flow of pollutants will be greatly reduced. We must redesign the materials industry (as done in Japan, Germany, etc.).[2] Today's waste is tomorrow's raw material; waste is wealth; and trash is cash. At a supermarket check-out counter "Paper or plastic?" should be replaced by "Do you have your canvas shopping bag with you?" We need to detoxify the earth.

Ecological Sanitation

This concept involves the installation of toilets, especially in developing countries where open defecation takes place. The construction and maintenance of safe, clean toilets is paramount, according to the World Health Organization (WHO). Also part of ecological sanitation is teaching proper handwashing techniques before handling food and after handling excrement. According to the Centers for Disease Control and Prevention website, you should wash your hands with soap and water for at least 20 seconds, or to the tune of "Happy Birthday" twice!

Emergency Sanitation

Emergency sanitation refers to the management and technical processes required to provide access to sanitation in emergency situations such as natural disasters (e.g., earthquakes, hurricanes, floods, landslides, wildfires and droughts), man-made accidents, technological hazards (e.g., chemical spills, disruption of infrastructure), complex situations (produced by conflicts and outbreaks), and during relief operations for refugees and internally displaced persons (IDPs). This involves three phases: immediate, short–term, and long-term. Emergency sanitation needs support from precautionary measures i.e. safety protocols and checks.

Depending upon the nature of the event, vulnerability of the people affected and capacity of local and national systems, deterioration in environmental conditions often results in a steep increase in WASH-related diarrhoeal disease. In particular, in emergencies the World Health Organization (WHO) has the mandate to work with the Ministry of Health to ensure water quality and minimise water-related health risks and support provision of WASH in healthcare facilities. In the immediate phase, the focus is on managing open defecation, and toilet technologies might include very basic latrines, pit latrines, bucket toilets, container-based toilets and chemical toilets.

The short-term phase involves technologies such as urine-diverting dry toilets, septic tanks and decentralised wastewater systems. In emergencies, the use of normal plastic bags or peepoo bags is advisable for immediate intervention at the household level until community or proper toilets can be built, when settlements experience chronic space or land-use limitations, where de-sludging is difficult, or where certain (vulnerable) groups prefer to defecate in personal shelters.

Whatever the type of waste collection and sanitation arrangement, problems and challenges do arise. We know the infamous instance of Bengaluru being called the "garbage city" recently (see Box 1). Hailed first as the country's Garden City and then its Silicon Valley, drawing in multinational IT firms and their monied executives, today Bengaluru is paying a heavy price for its success—it's a city overflowing with garbage, its infrastructure and waste collection services unable to keep up with decades of unchecked growth. "If you are talking about dumping garbage on the roads and littering in public then let me tell you, my friend, that happens in almost every city in India. Take Delhi, Kolkata, Mumbai, Hyderabad, and Chennai, for example", says Shadab Khan, resident of Bengaluru.

Note: This urine-diverting emergency toilet kit uses biodegradable plastic bags and weighs four kilogrammes. By diverting, urine handling becomes easier. Many similar solutions for "sitters" (opposed to squatters) can be applied, if available.

Source:/content/immediate-and-short-term-emergency-sanitation

Raised latrine kit with container tanks as constructed by the IFRC during the Haiti earthquake response in 2010.

Source: IFRC (2011)

A floating sanitary toilet (FST) introduced in Bolinao, Philippines.

Source: PEN (2010), https://www.sswm.info

1.2.2 Sanitation Service

There are various types of sanitation services implemented by cities and countries all over the world. They not only provide convenience for citizens, but also make societies cleaner and healthier to live in.

Municipal waste, also known as solid waste, requires the use of one type of sanitation service. This involves the storage, collection and transportation of this waste. Generally, this type of service is provided by the city.

Landfills also fall within this type of sanitation service because they provide a safe area for garbage to be stored until it can be properly disposed of.

Recycling centres are another variety of sanitation services. It still involves the management of solid waste, but instead of storing or destroying the garbage, it is cleaned, milled and reused.

BOX 1.1 WASTE DISPOSAL IN A CITY

BENGALURU

HOW IT DISPOSES OF ITS WASTE: After protests from locals, attempts to dispose waste in landfills have stopped and waste is now taken to processing units

DUMPS: After the Mandur site was abandoned, two more sites were identified at Bingipura and Lakshmipura. These are not operational because of protests from local people

TREATMENT OF WASTE: The state government has set up seven "state-of-the-art" waste processing units, which can together turn 2,200 tons of toxic garbage into compost

3,500

PEEVE POINTS: Civic body says only 40 per cent of garbage sent to processing units being treated. Despite HC orders, complete segregation at source is not happening. Bulk generators like hotel yet to process own waste SUDIPTO MONDAL

Source::

Another type of sanitation service involves the filtration, cleansing and reuse of water. Human waste, contaminated rainwater and industrial polluted water must all be cleaned and purified so that it can be reused for drinking, bathing and watering crops.

Additionally, there are specialised facilities used for the disposal of hazardous waste products. Chemical agents such as cleaning solutions and oil, medical supplies and radioactive materials must all be separated and treated differently than other waste materials. For this reason, special facilities are available that are used to neutralise and destroy these environmentally harmful agents.

1.2.3 Water for Sanitation

Two sources of water for sanitation are "self-supply" and "supported self-supply" with the first term referring to naturally occurring processes of people improving their water and sanitation services, whereas the second term refers to a deliberately guided process, usually by a government agency or an NGO.

Self-supply of water and sanitation (also called household-led water supply or individual supply) refers to an approach of incremental improvements to water and sanitation services, which are mainly financed by the user. People around the world have been using this approach over centuries to incrementally upgrade their water and sanitation services. The approach does not refer to a specific technology or type of water source or sanitation service although it does have to be feasible to use and construct at a low cost and mostly using tools locally available. The approach is rather about an incremental improvement of these services. It is a market-based approach and commonly does not involve product subsidies.

Some researchers have found that people in rural India do not use latrines because of lack of water. However, in the SQUAT (Sanitation Quality, Use, Access and Trends) survey,[3] only 3 per cent of people who defecate in the open mentioned lack of water as a reason for not using a latrine. Indeed, in rural India, where about 70 per cent of households defecate in the open, 90 per cent of people have access to what the WHO-UNICEF Joint Monitoring Report calls "an improved water source". In contrast, in sub-Saharan Africa, less than half of people have access to improved sources of water (49 percent), but far fewer people (35 percent) defecate in the open. Additionally, variation in access to water within India suggests that water is not an important constraint regarding latrine use.

Family provided with buckets and chlorine and taught how to wash hands properly at home during an ebola outbreak. Photo UNMEER /Martine Perrot Picture courtesy: http://www.unwater.org

In the 2005 India Human Development Survey, rural households with piped water are only 9 percentage points less likely to defecate in the open than rural households without piped water, a difference which can be completely accounted for by differences in socio-economic status between households that have piped water and those that do not.

1.2.4 Sanitation Training

Sanitation training does not have to be difficult to teach or learn once you get the basics down. The basics are applicable to nearly all situations and must have information that is transparent and accessible to all, starting from the concepts and factors:

- Clean—free of visible soil or other unwanted substances
- Sanitise—reduce the number of bacteria to a safe level
- Sterilise—make free of bacteria
- Contamination—the presence of harmful substances in food, water, etc.

In order to tackle poor sanitation, we need to ensure that professionals are trained in the required skills and knowledge, including the design of toilets, technology, building toilets, cleaning and maintenance, eco-sanitation, waste management and setting up sanitation social enterprises. In late 2015 the World Toilet Organization teamed up with the Global Interfaith WASH Alliance (GIWA) and Reckitt Benckiser (RB) to launch the World Toilet College (WTC) in India. The World Toilet Organization started the world's first WTC to build capacity in toilet design and maintenance, cleanliness and sanitation technologies in both urban and rural contexts. The objective of the training, whether at the school/college or village/city level, must be:

- To understand the global context of sanitation and hygiene
- To review the major problems due to lack of sanitation
- To learn about the consequences to children's health, development and well-being
- To consider some of the options for improving sanitation and hygiene

Ideal training programmes and modules must include staff/officials (central, state, district and village/city) and the general public (e.g., toilet users). Besides extensive literature review, there must be field surveys, consultations with field level experts and practitioners, and review and consultation with a panel of policymakers, etc. The training sessions' outcome must focus extensively on capacity building of skills and competencies of people involved in planning, designing and implementing communication and field level interventions (delivery and demonstrations included).

Toilet training, use, making and marketing of modern e-toilets must also be themes in training modules.[4]

1.2.5 Barriers

There are several barriers to accessing and using sanitation facilities:

1. Policy and institutional barriers: Lack of political will and budgetary priority; poor policy on sanitation at the country level; fragmented institutional framework and poor co-ordination; and inadequate and poorly used resources.
2. Implementation barriers: Inappropriate approaches; weak demand for sanitation services; ineffective promotion and low public awareness; inequity in service provision: low importance given to women and children and other marginalised groups; methods/technology ill-suited to context; low involvement of users: neglect of user preferences and top-down approaches.
3. Barriers to improving sanitation:
    - Inappropriate approaches: Frequently, the approach used to provide sanitation services is not in line with the local culture, technical limitations or affordability criteria.
    - Weak demand for sanitation services, ineffective promotion and low public awareness: Often, both the potential users of sanitation services and those responsible for policy and decision-making are not aware or convinced of the importance of good sanitation for health.
    - Inequity in service provision: (i) low importance given to women, children and other marginalised groups; and (ii) neglect of women as potential agents of change in hygiene and education
    - Low involvement of users: sanitation programmes should

consider user preferences for affordability, cultural aspects, etc.

1.3 SANITATION IN SOCIAL SCIENCES

Social sciences, like sociology and economics, have been making huge contributions to the challenge of providing access to sustainable sanitation services and infrastructure for billions of people in both the over- and under-developed parts of the world. People write and discuss a great deal about the inevitability and availability of sanitation. Sanitation is indeed a major concept to talk or write about. Social sciences such as sociology, psychology, anthropology, economics, ethics, political science, geography, etc., provide useful insights into and multifaceted approach to dealing with problems of waste, ill health, etc. Societal needs and economics of sanitation (e.g., costs) will become clear to us. We will be able to make a cost-benefit analysis in this regard. Community latrines and toilet complexes in both rural and urban areas are examples.

Dr Bindeshwar Pathak, social scientist

What is sanitation? Many ideas or meanings emerge:

- Safe collection, storage, treatment, and disposal, and reuse/recycling of faeces and urine, i.e., human excreta
- Management of household wastes, hospital and hazardous wastes, etc.
- Drainage of stormwater
- Conditions relating to public health, especially the provision of clean drinking water and adequate sewage disposal
- Any system that promotes proper disposal of human and animal waste, proper use of toilets and avoiding open space defecation.

The key words here are waste and hygienic. Waste can be hazardous causing health problems. They include human and animal excreta, solid waste, domestic waste, water (sewage or grey water), industrial and agricultural waste. Hygienic means of prevention can be implemented by using engineering solutions (e.g., sanitary sewers, sewage treatment, surface run-off management, solid waste, excreta management and simple technologies like pit latrines, dry toilets, urine-diverting dry toilets, septic tanks) or even simply by behavioural changes in personal hygiene practices such as handwashing with soap.

Sanitation is a primary need and necessity for humans. The WHO defines sanitation as, "The provision of facilities and services for the safe disposal of human urine and faeces". A set of diverse factors have made the availability of these facilities and services hard to provide, thus leading to open defecation. Open defecation has adverse impacts on the economy as well as on tourism, with productivity and risk of disease being the major pinch points. Lack of proper sanitation gives rise to a number of diseases such as diarrhoea, especially in children, having adverse long-term health effects. Other diseases include schistosomiasis, trachoma and helminthiasis.

According to Bas J.M. Van Vliet and Gert Spaargaren there are three particular social scientific topics relevant for the sanitation challenge: the nature of socio-technical change, the issue of multilevel governance and the role of the citizen-consumer. It is argued that sanitation is as much a social as a technical issue, and that the role of social scientific knowledge needs to be strengthened and given more attention in this context. The key contribution from the social sciences is to be found in its capacity to help widen the narrow, technical definitions of sanitation by including actors and their needs and belief systems, and by highlighting the alternative socio-technical tools and governance arrangements that are instrumental in moving beyond some of the dead-end roads of traditional water engineering and sanitation provision.

As far as sociology is concerned, it enables us to study man's behaviour in society as a web of social relationships. It examines human behaviour and actions in a social setting with regard to food and dress habits, housing and health, social institutions like the family, religious and other practices, etc. The problems of access to toilets and latrines, scavenging, night soil carriers, gender and sanitation, environmental issues in sanitation, race, ethnicity, untouchability and culture of sanitation, role of institutions in sanitation are all the subject matter of sanitation sociology. Sanitation as personal and societal practice and public policy is therefore part of sociology.

There are structural reasons which make it imperative to bring in the economic status of households and habitations. In parts of Andhra Pradesh, toilets were used for storing grains as they happened to be the best parts of the habitation that the residents had. Besides, there is the impact of general corruption on issues of sanitation as they are perceived as less important, and so less likely to raise public eyebrows. In many cases, toilets are just built on paper in active connivance with the state officials and municipal and school authorities, and do not attract much public scrutiny. Likewise, issues of sanitation are intimately linked with our notions of human dignity. Construction workers across the country may erect huge buildings but their worksite would hardly have any toilet facilities. Very few households allow domestic workers to avail of toilet facilities. In fact, some housing societies proscribe the use of such facilities for outsiders like maids, milk wallahs, and newspaperwallahs. We have to fight the deep-seated notion of the differing human worth of different groups of people which gets reflected in the facilities for sanitation that they may avail of or are provided with. In sociological jargon, we have to probe the implications of social stratification for an understanding of the complex sociology of sanitation.

The sheer untranslatability of ritual cleanliness and purity into everyday practices of hygienic upkeep of public places poses great challenges. The conditions in pilgrim places such as Varanasi and dharamshalas are cases in point. Interestingly, in the so-called secular places like universities and colleges, shopping complexes, etc., one finds toilets under lock and key to discourage visitors from using them. At times, even in places where hundreds throng on a regular basis for work, authorities display great insensitivity regarding arrangements for toilet facilities. Toilets in some of the village schools are exclusively meant for teachers while students are left to use open spaces in full public view.

Clean Toilets

Ideas about dirt and hygiene vary from culture to culture and have changed from century to century. What is dirty in one place is clean in another. What was seen as clean by our forefathers was unacceptably dirty in the late 20th century. The explanation offered by anthropology for dirt is that it is matter out of its proper place. As each society has rules that create order, violations of that order constitute a threat to society. As each individual makes sense of reality by ordering and classifying, so anomalous or disordered phenomena threaten that structure.

Source:

Source:

In a bid to better understand how the division between the sacred and the profane works out among social groups in India, a group of academics has recommended that the "sociology of sanitation" be studied at colleges and universities. Their opinion is that the sociology of sanitation could be a sub-discipline within sociology at undergraduate, postgraduate and research levels, and promoted as a branch of academic study. "The inclusion of this subject as an academic discipline will not only enlarge the scope of sociology, but also be helpful in solving the problems of society in relation to sanitation, social deprivation, water, public health, hygiene, poverty, gender equality, welfare of children and sustainable development," says Dr Bindeshwar Pathak, founder of Sulabh. That takes us from sociology per se to action sociology. To provide clean and hygienic sanitation facilities to the people, especially to meet the needs of women, girls and children and thereby provide them human dignity, Sulabh International Centre for Action Sociology (SICAS) has maintained nearly 50 public toilet complexes on "pay-and-use" basis in various low-income localities of New Delhi such as Madipur, Mangolpuri, Sultanpuri, Yamuna Pushta. This was done in close co-operation with local bodies after signing an agreement with them.

The action has to start from the base of the pyramid: the schools and homes of children. More so in the case of those who come from a background of families who stand marginalised and deprived in the social structure of society. The school does so by providing an opportunity to them of learning along with the children of families who fall in the category of "haves" in terms of economic and, more important, social criteria. In the minds of the wards, of those who are at the lowest rung of the ladder of society, is inculcated a feeling of equality which in turn gives them confidence to intermingle, to play, to compete, to share joys on par with others. This prepares them to face life as others do. In the school they learn the three Rs, the languages, the rudiments of new technologies which are basic ingredients of modern-day life. The foundations are laid not in terms of visible buildings but invisible essentials of character and uprightness. It is not that there are no shortcomings; it is not that there is nothing wrong, but, in the balance it is the positives which outweigh the negatives. It is an established fact that proper sanitation facilities considerably reduce school drop-out rates and absenteeism and delays in work. Proper sanitation means economic and environmental sustainability.

Studying Sanitation

Source: https://www.amazon.in/Economics-Sanitation-Kavitha-Suresh-Lal/dp/8183877710

SICAS as an institution covers large numbers and a range of activities. The Sulabh Public School is a crucible of the nobility and ideals which are the essence of the process of education. The school also has input of the practicality of commerce. There is a blend of the loftiness of learning with mundane earning. Result: Vocational training. The carefree ambience of learning in lower classes evolves into the anxiety in higher classes of acquiring skills with economic orientation in order to fend for oneself in the future. Courses are conducted in 10 trades. It is, though, difficult to single out which are of greater or lesser importance. SICAS also runs Slum Children Welfare Programmes and a vibrant School Sanitation Club which from the beginning creates awareness among children about the importance of sanitation. It teaches how to lend a helping hand to members of families who live in the shadows and are covered by the penumbra of social ostracisation and neglect by society. This programme is the social upgradation programme. Thus, sociology meets economics.

One of the earliest theories of international trade is that of comparatives advantage—a country must produce that which it can at comparatively lower cost and export that surplus to get something that it can produce at a comparatively higher cost with its trading partner. Going by this classical theory, think about the following:

India has the second biggest population in the world and will move to first position, overtaking China, very soon. Thus, India will also produce the maximum amount of human waste in the world daily, which means that this will be a factor of India's comparative advantage vis-à-vis the rest of the world! It is in the interests of India to exploit this output, namely, human waste, which is most freely available in India and not frittered away into centralised sewer systems as in Western countries.

Poor sanitation is a societal problem and is bad economics. According to the World Bank, poor sanitation, hygiene and water are responsible for about 50 per cent of the consequences of childhood and maternal underweight, primarily through the synergy between diarrhoeal diseases and undernutrition, whereby exposure to one increases vulnerability to the other. With 4.2 million deaths each year (1.6 million among children under five years), acute respiratory infections are the leading causes of mortality in developing countries. Health and labour productivity will be more if there is good sanitation and therefore economic resources invested for promoting sanitation is a good investment. Also, such a thing is supported as a cause of providing basic, minimum facilities and becomes part of the human development index, and its absence a part of the human poverty index. For all these reasons, sanitation can be treated as a critical sector.

In addition to its impact on health, improved sanitation generates both social and economic benefits. Householders understand these wider benefits but scientists have only recently begun to study individuals' motivations for improving sanitation and changing sanitation behaviour.

While the main goal of agencies' sanitation programming is to improve health, householders rarely adopt and use toilets for health-related reasons. Instead, the main motivations for sanitation adoption and use include the desire for privacy and to avoid embarrassment, wanting to be modern, the desire for convenience and to avoid the discomforts or dangers of the bush (e.g., snakes, pests, rain), and wanting social acceptance or status. Furthermore, for women, the provision of household sanitation reduces the risk of rape and/or attack experienced when going to public latrines or the bush to defecate, and for girls, the provision of school sanitation facilities means that they are less likely to miss school by staying at home during menstruation. And in these days when campaigns are launched to increase the rate of female literacy or level of education, the impact of education to promote sanitation culture cannot be sidelined. A study by Arabinda Ghosh says that literacy and public education rather than economic growth are integral to eradicating open defecation. This study was based on sanitation practices in three districts of West Bengal and nine bordering districts of Bangladesh. While the number of households with a latrine on the premises grew by 15.1 per cent in West Bengal from 2001 to 2011, Bangladesh made more rapid progress, highlighting the importance of "shame vs subsidy" as a social marketing programme employed at the grassroots to improve sanitation coverage. A regression analysis was conducted on 615 Indian districts to identify the impact of literacy and population density on the open defecation rate. The regression indicates that a 1 per cent gain in literacy would reduce the open defecation rate by 0.591 percent, holding population density constant. On the other hand, every 1 per cent rise in population density would reduce open defecation by 0.067 percent, holding the literacy rate constant. The relative importance of literacy in reducing open defecation was very high, and the p-value indicated its statistical significance beyond the 1 per cent level, while the population density coefficient was significant only at the 5 per cent level.

The economic benefits of improved sanitation include lower health system costs, fewer days lost at work or at school through illness or through caring for an ill relative, and convenience time saving (time not spent queuing at shared sanitation facilities or walking for open defecation).

The United Nations in its report highlights that every dollar spent on sanitation in developing nations typically yields nine dollars' worth of benefits. This estimation, in itself, highlights the economics of sanitation and its importance to the local as well as national economies. The report also goes on to say that the merits associated with improved sanitation come from reduced direct and indirect health costs, increased efficiency and productivity, increasing returns on investment in education and safeguarding of water systems. These factors clearly demonstrate how the problem of sanitation is in fact deeply interrelated with other major economic, societal and environmental issues.

Understanding an environmental issue from a political economy aspect involves the study of both the economic conditions along with the political scenario of the region itself, as well as the regions surrounding it that directly affect the basic functioning of the region. The political and economic conditions govern and alter the environment we live in. The problem of sanitation too depends immensely on these factors. The origin and rise of social inequalities that are a feature of post-Neolithic society play a major role in the pattern of sanitation in prehistoric and contemporary populations. In fact, there is an issue highlighted about governments at many levels not devoting enough attention and resources to sanitation services, particularly when compared to spending on water supply and other infrastructure services. Additionally, existing sanitation investments and service provisions are not often pro-poor. Efforts to increase access to sanitation infrastructure often benefit better-off urban residents at the expense of the urban poor, slum-dwellers, or rural populations. However, even within the context of competing demands and limited resources, there is an increasing awareness that government decisions regarding sanitation expenditures are determined largely by political rather than technical or economic constraints. As Karl puts it, there are four factors or four wheels on which a modern-day economy runs: labour, accumulation, crises and contradiction. Sanitation being a basic necessity of every human today, and hence a facility every modern economy must cater to, depends holistically on these same four parameters.

The Economics of Sanitation Initiative (ESI) was launched in 2007 with a WSP study from East Asia, which found that the economic costs of poor sanitation and hygiene amounted to over US$9.2 billion a year (2005 prices) in Cambodia, Indonesia, Lao PDR, the Philippines, and Vietnam. The groundbreaking study was the first of its kind to quantify in dollars a country's losses from poor sanitation. The report sparked public awareness and government action in several countries. The ESI was born as a response by WSP to address major gaps in evidence among developing countries on the economic impacts of sanitation. Following the success in East Asia, ESI studies were completed in Africa and South Asia, with a study currently underway in Latin America. Report for India: The total economic impact of inadequate sanitation in India amounts to a loss of US$53.8 billion in 2006. These economic impacts were the equivalent of about 6.4 per cent of India's gross domestic product (GDP) in 2006. This means a per person annual impact of ₹2,180. In 2016, the *Down to Earth* magazine reported that due to poor sanitation on a national level, in terms of total cost, India suffered the most, with US$106.7 billion wiped off the GDP in 2015. It is almost half of the total global losses and 5.2 per cent of the nation's GDP.

From an economic point of view, again, many sanitation advocates now place the affordability of toilets at the centre of the planning process. A common strategy is to encourage people to start with the simplest type of improved pit latrine and then to progress over time towards higher-specification and higher-cost toilets the "sanitation ladder". The critical and most cost-effective step on this ladder, for both health and social reasons, is the first step from open defecation to fixed-location defecation; the subsequent steps up the ladder may yield smaller incremental benefits. Recently, there has been a shift away from centrally planned provision of infrastructure towards demand-led approaches that create and serve people's motivation to improve their own sanitation. Although sound technological judgement about appropriate solutions remains essential, appropriate programming approaches are now more important and contribute most to the success of sanitation work. Regarding the costs of these demand-led approaches, there are few published comparative studies, but sector professionals estimate that they cost less than traditional infrastructure provision. For example, the Water Supply and Sanitation Collaborative Council's Global Sanitation Fund allows average costs of US$15 per person for demand-led approaches, whereas governmental provision of infrastructure typically costs tens to hundreds of dollars per person.

Sanitation marketing uses a range of interventions to raise householders' demand for improved sanitation. The approach involves understanding householders' motivations and constraints to sanitation adoption and use. These are then used to develop both demand- and supply-side interventions to ensure that appropriate sanitation products and services are available to match the demand.

Although macroeconomic analysis shows that sanitation generates economic benefit, the benefit does not necessarily accrue to the person who invests in the improved sanitation. So the economics at the household level remain a constraint to success in sanitation—many people are simply unable or unwilling to invest, given all the other competing demands on their money. This under-researched topic is currently under investigation by the WASH Cost Project 2, which is studying the life-cycle costs of water, sanitation and hygiene (WASH) services in rural and peri-urban areas in four countries.

Spending on health and sanitation, both at the federal and municipal levels, have been the most effective in reducing poverty in Brazil in recent years, reveals research by the Luiz de Queiroz College for Agriculture (Esalq) of the University of São Paulo in Piracicaba. This is followed by state-level spending on both education and culture, and federal social security and welfare assistance. The study was conducted by economist Martha Hanae Hiromoto, as part of her master's dissertation in applied economics, supported by Professor Ana Lúcia Kassouf from the Department of Economics, Administration and Sociology at Esalq. The study, which was based on bibliographic research stemming from Brazil and other countries such as China and India, demonstrated that the total resources at the federal level for social budgeting selected for this analysis grew from 4 per cent in 1987 to 14 per cent of GDP in 2009, coming to a total of R$432 billion.[5] Within the same period, state budgets increased from 4 per cent to 6 per cent of GDP, totalling R$193 billion. Finally, the capacity of municipal level budgeting selected from 2010 was R$212 billion (8 per cent of GDP). "This, can help understand how to focus future spending or even find ways to improve the efficacy of spending in areas which have been less effective," highlights Hiromoto. The main results show that spending on health and sanitation at both the federal and municipal levels were in accordance with the analysis, the most effective in reducing poverty. Expenditure on state education and culture, and federal social security and welfare assistance follow.

We cannot ignore the role of politics and political science here. The most important strategy for a well-developed sanitation programme is political leadership which is manifested by establishing clear institutional responsibility and specific budget lines for sanitation, and by ensuring that public sector agencies working in health, in water resources, and in utility services work together better. Sanitation is not an inherently attractive or photogenic subject. Before 2008, the International Year of Sanitation, sanitation specialists had failed to persuade politicians, the media and other influential people of the importance of the subject. During 2008, however, there were many political events related to sanitation—notably regional sanitation conferences across the developing world—that resulted in Regional Sanitation Declarations, which have moved sanitation up the political agenda.

Political instability and the indifference of those in power have meant that the projects that are finalised and funded are not implemented or executed and the funds are lost mid-way. The trickle-down effect has been relegated to the sheds since the benefits are reaped by the rich, the affluent and those in a position of power. A survey conducted by Population Service International (PSI) noted that an unbelievable 85 per cent of rural households in Bihar had no access to a toilet. This just goes to show that the facilities are lacking more in the rural and comparatively poorer sections of society.

Geographical factors are also interesting facts in the study of sanitation culture and progress. A case here is that of ecological sanitation (ecosan). The flush toilet system requires a good quantity of water, therefore, the inclusion of techniques which require nil or very little of water seems to be a good solution to the scarcity of water in the hills. Ecosan toilets could be a good choice among such available techniques with low water requirement. Arunachal Pradesh, Manipur, Meghalaya, Mizoram, Nagaland, Tripura, Sikkim, Jammu and Kashmir, Uttarakhand, Himachal Pradesh, which have almost 100 per cent of their geographical area under hilly terrain are of main concern.

The Swachh Bharat Abhiyan aims to ensure access to sanitation facilities (including toilets, solid and liquid waste disposal systems, and village cleanliness) and safe and adequate drinking water supply to every person by 2019. Ecosan would be a better choice to check the open defecation in hilly terrain.

1.4 STAKEHOLDERS IN SANITATION

What is a stakeholder? “Stakeholders are people, groups, or institutions which are likely to be affected by a proposed intervention (either negatively or positively), or those which can affect the outcome of the intervention."

Sanitation interventions in the society and nation involve many stakeholders, including various local, regional and federal government offices; NGOs; community-based organisations; private sector companies; political and religious leaders as well as communities. Religious groups have mainly spiritual goals but they could be considered a potential stakeholder serving as a good platform for discussions and dissemination of knowledge on good hygiene and sanitary practices. Youth groups in a country/community have different goals, ranging from self-help among members to preventing misbehaviour of young people. Not only do the relationships in this large network of actors affect the activities of each stakeholder in their functions, they also influence their interventions as a whole. One can analyse their roles, share of responsibilities, problems and potential for better co-operation. For a long time in India, the involvement of the private sector in sanitation interventions has been neglected.

Participatory planning requires the involvement of concerned stakeholders. This includes identifying public concerns and values, and developing a broad consensus on planned initiatives. It is also about utilising the vast amount of information and knowledge that stakeholders hold to find workable, efficient and sustainable solutions. Also, a stakeholder's analysis must be carried out both before and after the implementation of the specific programmes of sanitation.

The first step of a stakeholder analysis is to identify the key stakeholders, i.e., those who are affected by the outcome, negatively or positively, or those who can affect the outcomes of a proposed intervention, from the wide array of institutions and individuals that could potentially affect or be affected by the proposed intervention (see Table 1.1A and 1.1B). The identification criteria of stakeholders for sustainable sanitation and water management will have to answer the following questions:

- Who are the people/groups/institutions that are interested in the intended initiative? What is their role (polluter, regulator, direct consumer, indirect consumer, etc.)?
- Who are the potential beneficiaries?
- Who might be adversely impacted? Who has constraints about the initiative?
- Who may impact the initiative? Who has the power to influence?

Table 1.1A: List of Stakeholders

S. No.	*Stakeholders*	*Stakeholders* Subgroups*	*Details*
1	National authorities (at all levels)	Governor High commissioner Prefect	Regional Provincial Departmental
2	Traditional authorities		Chief of village
3	Communication	Media	
4	Deconcentrated government services	Health Education Environment Agriculture Hydraulic/Water	Health centres Inspectors of education
5	Opinion leaders	Religious authorities Parliamentarians	Imams, Priests, Pastors
6	Local authorities	Head of Municipal Council	The Mayor
7	Direction of municipal technical services	Environment Sanitation Cleanliness General affairs Hygiene and public health	
8	Education	Universities Institutes, Colleges Professional training centres Government schools	Primary secondary, specific training school (health education)

Source: archive.sswmoinfo

After structuring/grouping of stakeholders, the following questions might help to reflect the findings and avert omitting important stakeholders:

- Have all stakeholders been listed?
- Have all potential supporters and opponents of the project been identified?
- Have gender aspects been factored in to identify different types of female stakeholders?
- Have the interests of vulnerable groups (especially the poor) been identified?
- Are there any new stakeholders that are likely to emerge as a result of the project?

Sometimes it is worth to further group and categorise stakeholders to get a more detailed analysis of influence and importance. For structure and documentation reasons this can be of value to provide a clear overview about the nature and role of the stakeholder.

Table 1.1B : Three Categories of Stakeholders

Primary	*Secondary*	*Tertiary*
• Users/Beneficiaries (male, females, children, elderly, etc.)	• Local authority • Direction of municipality technical services • Traditional authorities • NGO and development projects • Businesses and suppliers • Decentralised government services • Research institutions • School and university • Services providers	• Financial institutions and donors • National authorities (at all levels) • Opinion leaders • Civil society • Foreign cooperation agencies • Media

The identification of possible stakeholders is a precondition for any participatory planning process. If stakeholders are not identified, they cannot be invited to participate! Furthermore, all parts of a stakeholder analysis should not only be done by planners and project managers, but should be repeated with representatives of the involved stakeholder groups. This assures a deeper understanding of the issue by the stakeholders and prevents the exclusion of stakeholders at an early stage.

Advantages

- Planning of stakeholder involvement reduces the avoidance of implementation failures.
- Assures the involvement of all relevant stakeholders.
- Precondition to give people some say over how projects may affect their lives.
- Best practices can be attained.

Disadvantages

- Can be time-consuming.
- Needs expertise and local knowledge.
- Risk of omitting important stakeholders.
- Might not be representative if only done by a few people.

The planned establishment of a multi-stakeholders regional forum that would gather various actors and enable them to share experiences and ideas and cooperate on a regional scale seems to be a good way to start. Any sanitation intervention takes place against a background of complex relationships between different stakeholders. The nature of these relationships inevitably affects the way in which a sanitation project is planned, implemented and managed. Regional and local bodies, say the village panchayats and urban/city corporations play a very important role here. Such institutions are at the bottom of the pyramid of local governance. The advantage of this is that members of these bodies and their special/ad hoc committees live in the intervention area; people respect them and are not reluctant to ask them for information. They work at the household level and carry out preventative and promotional work. Both the main and subcommittees are held responsible for controlling overall sanitation facilities in the area under their jurisdiction, i.e., at hotels, at schools, in the beverage and food industry. Sub-city health and sanitation offices also provide infrastructure in a sub-city, e.g., roads and public toilets. Sub-city offices have their own strategic and action plans for each local unit (taluk/village/city) under their jurisdiction. Each unit has its own strategic and action plans because problems in each unit may vary.

Local service providers are commonly contracted by the local government and NGOs for sanitary supplies and procurement. In the case of Catholic Relief Services in Ethiopia, which went beyond that, local artisans were contracted to develop plastic slabs for arborloos. WaterAid in Ethiopia also appoints private companies to perform baseline studies. The Protestant Church also works with general sanitation issues in this area. They also cooperate with church-based organisations (CBOs) through religious leaders and with CBOs such as Idriss, women and youth organisations. There are many players involved in urban sanitation, which can make it more complicated—city planning and development officers, those who are in charge of roads and drainage, those who are in charge of waste management, revenue collection and so on. To quote the Ethiopian example, again, it has the Community-led total sanitation (CLTS) committee and CBOs. The latter can easily reach out to communities having their trust and respect and they are usually trained by local NGOs.

Cooperation with a variety of stakeholders brings along some challenges, e.g., cross-learning might be difficult, everyone may be keen to defend their own interests and approach limitations may, as a result, become a serious bottleneck. Cooperation with local government on project sites where sanitation coverage is very low and marginalised people live is generally non-problematic. However, in urban settings securing land as well as bureaucracy can become a challenge. The WASH (Water, Sanitation and Hygiene)[6] Programme (UNICEF) and the Swachh Bharat Programme (India) can be successful only if stakeholders move together and towards a better coordinated and more effective approach, understanding each other's strengths and limitations. They must overcome stumbling blocks and have work relationship building blocks. They share their knowledge and skills with regard to policies and strategies, budgets and financing, institutions and capacities, coordination, and monitoring and evaluation within the existing frameworks of the sanitation sub-sector to determine if all the building blocks are in place, what the most critical issues are and the next steps in addressing these issues. At the broader and more technical level, this also needs stakeholders' mapping. The overarching objective of the stakeholders' mapping study must be to contribute to improved coordination and information exchange among stakeholders implementing and/or supporting sanitation and hygiene activities in the country which are relevant to the national sanitation campaign as well as local ones (e.g., rural household sanitation). The vision must translate into a mission.

In principle, the Ministry of Health (MoH) has a key role. However, in developing countries, health sector-implemented school health programmes tend to focus on schools in urban areas and/or elite schools. The health of school-age children is the responsibility of the MoH, but is often given low priority compared to clinical services, and infant and maternal health. Nevertheless, health education delivery by teachers or other agents can only proceed with the explicit permission of the MoH. In addition, health and hygiene messages disseminated through a project for hygiene, sanitation and water in schools must be coordinated with the messages disseminated through the MoH, as well as with messages disseminated through other projects, NGOs, or CBOs. Conflicting messages can confuse beneficiaries and even undermine the sustainability of education activities. Other public sector agencies can play important enabling roles. The ministries of welfare and social affairs can provide mechanisms for the provision of social funds that in some settings should finance part of a project. Where decentralisation processes have been undertaken, the ministries of local government are often the local fund-holders for teacher salaries and school expenditures.

In Tanzania, non-governmental stakeholders have made noticeable achievements that add to government efforts in promoting access to improved sanitation and hygiene in the country, including resource mobilisation. Departments within and between local government authorities (LGAs) have developed qualities of coordination in finance, works and lands. In Temeke Municipal Council, a WASH group known as WAHECO (Water, Health, Education, and Community Development) has been established to provide more support in matters of sanitation and hygiene. NGOs, as one of the stakeholders, have collaboration with at least one LGA department of sanitation and hygiene. This synergy was credited by some stakeholders in the study as being an important step towards a well-organised implementation of WASH activities within LGAs.[7]

In India, in order to synergise the efforts and achieve accelerated sanitation and hygiene promotion at the LGA level, development and implementation of a district-level joint plan of action on sanitation and hygiene among stakeholders is critical. The current practice in all LGAs is that non-governmental stakeholders operate in isolation from the NSC implementation framework and targets at the LGA level. The experience in most of the LGAs is that a government department, for example, the department of education, is involved in the promotion of school toilets; at the same time, one or more NGOs are also implementing school WASH activities. However, these stakeholders might have never met and they do not have a forum for sharing the results and experience. The main reporting channel for some NGOs is their funders. Lack of coordination between relevant LGA departments, with no clear responsibilities between some departments, and in particular, ambiguity about the roles of the departments of health, and environment and sanitation in the national programme implementation has been identified in this study as one of the constraints that hinder efficient implementation of sanitation and hygiene activities. A few technicians and personnel within LGA departments involved in WASH and Swachh Bharat activities also impede effective implementation of sanitation activities.

There is a need to strengthen electronic information sharing systems to support and improve coordination and information sharing among stakeholders involved in sanitation and hygiene issues across the country. Such systems need to be constantly updated and may include a secure portal for information sharing and collaborative working between the ministries, LGA departments and non-governmental stakeholders across the country.

1.5 GLOBALISATION AND SANITATION

Since the late 1970s, globalisation has become a phenomenon that has elicited polarising responses from scholars, politicians, activists and the business community. Several scholars and activists, such as labour unions, see globalisation as an anti-democratic movement that would weaken the nation state in favour of the great powers.

Globalisation is a set of economic processes in which production, marketing and investment are integrated across the borders of nations. The liberalisation and opening up of markets to the global economy is leading to the emergence of a single market for goods, capital, technology, services, and information and to some extent labour. Globalisation is also a socio-political process because of its impact on culture, governance and domestic policy. The process of globalisation is a convergence, though at differing speeds, of many institutional, legal, economic, social, and cultural practices and processes across the borders of nations. Globalisation as an idea is how we are looking at the world and reducing cultural diversity in terms of perceptions and products.

There is no doubt that globalisation, no matter how it is defined, is here to stay, and is causing major changes around the globe. Given the rapid proliferation of advances in technology, communication, means of production and transportation, globalisation is a challenge to health and well-being worldwide.

Globalisation has re-emphasised socio-cultural dualism. Recent census data in India revealed that more homes have telephones than toilets. The figures shed light on the contradictions in a country that is experiencing an economic boom while struggling with poverty. There are thousands who have no option but to head out to the open fields or alongside the railway tracks to relieve themselves. Even in the capital, New Delhi, it is common to see people squatting by roads and openly defecating because there are simply no adequate public toilet facilities and those at heritage and historical sites—where thousands visit every day—are found unclean and poorly maintained.

Globalisation generates new challenges in preparing strategies for urban development because globalisation threatens to exacerbate urban environmental pollution and natural resource degradation. Liveable cities will be needed. Many public health issues have cropped up. The outbreak of Bovine spongiform encephalopathy (BSE) or mad cow disease in several European countries is one example of how trade can promote the spread of dangerous diseases. Mosquitoes that carry malaria have been found aboard planes thousands of miles from their primary habitats, and infected seafood carrying cholera bacteria has been shipped from Latin America to the United States and Europe. The most important ways that infectious diseases with regard to public health are affected by globalisation include:

- Increased global travel
- Increased trade in goods
- Food-borne illnesses
- Urbanisation
- Climate change
- Other environmental concerns

Table 1.2: People Indulging in Open Defecation (% of population): Select Countries and Economies

Country/Income level	*2000*	*2015*
Afghanistan	26	14
Albania	1	0
Angola	51	33
Bangladesh	18	0
Bhutan	11	0
Cambodia	83	41
China	2	2

Denmark	0	0
Egypt	2	0
France	0	0
Germany	0	0
India	66	40
Japan	0	0
Kenya	17	12
Libya	0	0
Malaysia	2	0
Nepal	65	30
Oman	11	0
Pakistan	41	12
Rwanda	4	2
Sierra Leone	26	19
Sri Lanka	0	3
Trinidad and Tobago	0	0
Uganda	15	6
USA	0	0
Vietnam	18	4
Zambia	24	15
Low and middle income	25	14
Low income	41	24
Lower middle income	42	24
Middle income	23	13
Upper middle income	4	2

Source: NETSSAF Participatory Planning Approach: A tutorial for Sustainable Planning, NETSSAF, 2008

Globalisation means open trade, and more places to send goods and ideas. Open defecation amidst all this looks odd and bad. High densities of people combined with unsanitary conditions make for almost perfect breeding grounds for pathogens. Open defecation is reducing but is still a menace (see Table 1.2). Open defecation is defined as defecation in fields, forests, bushes, water bodies or other open spaces.

One answer to open defecation amidst globalisation is globalisation of toilet culture. In many countries, people still do not use toilets and defecate and urinate outdoors. In India, open toilets are a huge problem. The cause of this is not just poverty but culture as well. For instance, between 1997 and 2000, the WHO subsidised the construction of 1.6 million outhouses in India. Today, only 47 per cent are being used in the intended manner. The rest are used for storage. The World Toilet Organization is trying to add momentum to international health organisations to continue promoting hygienic global toilet culture. The reason for promoting toilet culture is to improve sanitation. Without proper sanitation, water bodies are polluted by open defecation. Over one million children die of diarrhoea each year due to lack of proper sanitation practices. In many countries in Asia, the squat-style toilet is used. Health officials are saying that squat-style toilets contribute to osteoarthritis of the knee and should be replaced by regular Western-style toilets known as Thomas Crapper-style sit-down toilets. Twin-pit pour-flush toilets, septic tanks, urine diversion dry toilets, biogas toilets and terra preta are some technologies that can also be employed to improve toilet culture and sanitation.

The Bill & Melinda Gates Foundation's Reinvent the Toilet programme also generated many new technologies for sanitation. However, proper sanitation is largely a behavioural change challenge. Unfortunately, the rational approach of teaching people to use a toilet for health and hygiene has had limited success. As mentioned earlier, many toilets provided to poor people end up not being used. The World Toilet Organization says that the solution is "to raise the social status of toilets as objects of desire and make having toilets a trendy fashion".

Similar to drinking water, there have been very significant improvements with regard to the availability of improved sanitation facilities around the world. However, data availability for this basic service remains quite poor, in particular at country level. In 1990, only one in two people had access to good quality sanitation compared with almost 70 per cent of the world's population today. Since then some 2.1 billion people 2worldwide have gained access to improved sanitation.

According to the UNICEF, "safely managed" sanitation services represent a higher service level that takes into account the final disposal of excreta (see Figure 1.1). In 2015, 2.9 billion people used a "safely managed" sanitation service, i.e., a basic facility where excreta is disposed of in situ or treated off-site. A further two billion people used a "basic" service, i.e., an improved facility that is not shared with other households.

The 600 million who shared improved sanitation facilities with other households count as using a "limited' service.

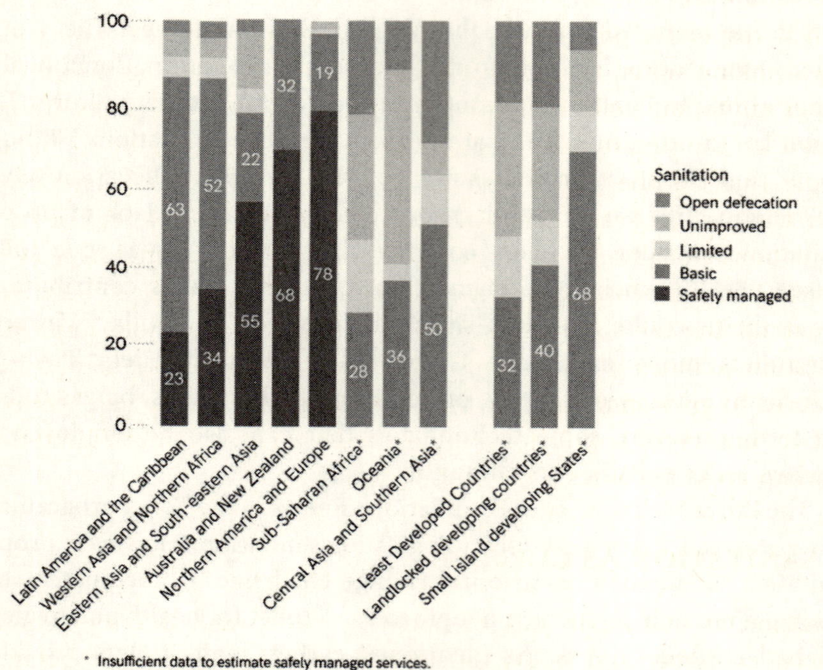

Figure 1.1 : Estimates of Safely Managed Sanitation Services are Available for Five out of Eight SDG Regions

Source: WHO/UNICEF JMP Progress on Sanitation and Drinking Water: 2015 Update and MDG assessment

But progress has been uneven and today approximately 34 per cent of the world's population is still using poor quality sanitation facilities, with almost 950 million people still indulging in open defecation (United Nations, 2015). From an absolute perspective, the improvements may appear modest, as today 2.4 billion people still do not have access to sanitation facilities compared with 2.5 billion in 1990. The growth in the global population, primarily in developing regions, has contributed to this apparent discrepancy between proportion and absolute populations. But for least developed countries (LDCs), the situation has only improved for a third of the population. In urban areas the problem is less acute but nevertheless remains a serious one, with some 705 million people living in unsanitary conditions. This nevertheless represents a sizeable improvement compared with two or three decades ago. Even though for LDCs as a whole, the improvement has been dramatic, almost two-thirds of their respective populations remain without good quality sanitation. Like drinking water, there is a marked difference in the availability of proper sanitation facilities between rural and urban populations around the world. The situation is worse in rural areas where roughly 1.7 billion people (half of the global rural population) live without sanitation. Over the past 25 years, sanitation has only improved for half of rural populations globally. The population of the world is projected to grow by some 2.3 billion people over the next 30 years. This will also contribute to maintaining the absolute number of people living without improved sanitation facilities at a high level. In particular, as urban populations are expected to grow more quickly than rural populations, the gap between the two "unserved" populations is expected to narrow as lack of sanitation in urban areas becomes a growing problem.

1.6 SANITATION AS CULTURE

Sanitation as culture is part of people's growth and development in society, economy and polity. Sustainable development itself being a cultural form, it consists of various ideas, symbols, concepts, theories, explanations, justifications that legitimise actors or stakeholders to engage in actions—including building institutions and infrastructure—to do good and prevent bad. Sanitation is public good with a cultural form with practical efficacy.

As civilisations grow and develop, culture becomes a contributing factor in progress. Culture is considered a system of shared values, beliefs, behaviour, symbols that the members of society groups use to interact with their social surroundings. The way in which cultures manifest themselves is made tangible through different categories, and symbols of or relating to values, norms and beliefs form the core of any culture. They express feelings and affections e.g., towards what is dirty/clean. Often, they are based on historical circumstances, which do not correspond to today's living environment any more. Culture distinguishes human beings from animals. That way art and thought, customs and law, object and learning are part and parcel of culture. These elements, however, evolve in a complex process.

Examples: A river we classify as filthy and unhealthy may not be regarded as such by locals living adjacent to it. They might have adopted the belief that water from that river is healthy from their ancestors, when this was actually the case. Yet today, the perception of the water quality would not any more correspond to the reality. In brief, beliefs about water quality might persist even when one would think it obvious to everybody that it was not so any more. In Islamic countries and many traditional cultures, according to cultural and religious beliefs, water use should be free of charge. This makes it challenging to convince people to pay for water supply services.

India is a land of rich and diverse cultures. Most historians and sociologists trace the cultural origins here back to the Indus Valley civilisation. However, many social conflicts arose due to cultural crises, and clashes occurred especially after Independence.

Understanding the relationship between culture and sanitation requires understanding the social habits of the people. An urban person, for instance, washes his hands indoors, say, in the wash basin, whereas a rural person washes his hands outdoors, say, near a plant or a tree. Similarly, caste, education and awareness, social domination or deprivation, an inferiority complex, exploitation, etc., influence the culture of sanitation.

There are clear differences in attitude towards the use of sanitation facilities and the handling of excreta in diverse cultures. Despite an instinctive repulsion towards excreta, our cultures influence our attitudes towards handling of it. This applies specially to sustainable sanitation as its operation and maintenance have a broader impact on lives' differentiation between people being repelled or not repelled by excreta. India, for example, is commonly referred to as a faecophobic culture, where the Dalit caste (the untouchables), living at the bottom of society, are responsible for excreta removal. On the other hand, experience has proved that by establishing closed-loop sanitation systems, a change towards reducing cultural stigmatisation of faeces is possible too. In areas with predominant cultivation of land and little livestock farming (e.g., some areas in China), people realised the fertilising potential of human excreta and therefore developed a more positive attitude towards it.

Religions vary considerably in addressing excreta. In the Bible the act of elimination is mentioned only once, and it does not address the subject of using excreta for agricultural purposes. The Koran, however, prescribes strict procedures to limit contact with faecal material, including its use in agriculture, because excrement is considered impure. The principal Hindu text that details the code of conduct for rituals, the Artharva Veda, clearly specifies the use of water for personal hygiene. But nowhere do we find excrement included in a more religious context than in Buddhism. An integral dimension of Buddhism is reincarnation, which promotes the harmonious concept of recycling life's treasures; it is therefore not surprising that Buddhist cultures treat earthly resources similarly.

In developing countries, women are promoters, educators and leaders of home and community-based sanitation practices. But in WASH concerns are rarely addressed appropriately due to societal or cultural barriers because the issue of which roles women can play within a social group is strongly determined by the conditions under which they live, their respective culture, the traditions and the education level in the social group.

Any relations between people and their environment are embedded in culture. More precisely, any choices and behaviours related to water and sanitation are deeply rooted in a cultural context. To deal with excreta might often be taboo or water might be connected to beliefs and traditions. Therefore, the respect for assessment and integration of the cultural context of users such as religious or cultural beliefs, gender or generational differences in water and sanitation programmes are crucial to mitigate risks of failure and promote sustainable solutions. The cultural context of the users may act as an enabling factor or as a counteracting force for good water management. By assessing cultural backgrounds of the users, one can raise ownership and increase the potential of success, or, on the other hand, mitigate risk of failure. Failure could mean that systems are not used or, worse, are sabotaged.

To respect the cultural context means taking into consideration not only religious and non-religious beliefs and values, traditional practices, but also how different cultural groups cope with gender and generational differences. Water and sanitation experts nowadays urge taking these contextual aspects into consideration. It should be part of the research in the planning and design phase and also the monitoring phase. It is about not only considering these issues, but also implementing them in the projects or programmes. Cultural competence is crucial for successful and sustainable implementation of projects. Despite investments of

US$15 billion in the WASH sector the Millennium Development Goal (MDG) on sanitation could not be met. This is partially because of lack of sufficient knowledge about the socio-cultural environments of the projects. Socio-cultural aspects have not been investigated sufficiently, if at all, in most project designs, and this leads to behavioural change that is not sustainable. Culture regarding hygiene and sanitation behaviour has changed over time all over the globe. It was, for example, acceptable for the Vikings to squat everywhere and in the 19th century in the countryside of America it was natural to live in a dirty environment. The use of chamber pots that were then emptied out onto the street from the window in England in the late 19th century is another illustration of how the culture surrounding hygiene and sanitation changes over time. What was once acceptable is not any more. In every society there are unwritten rules and taboos regarding sanitation behaviour. Defecating has often had low priority and this can be because of the lack of usefulness and sense of disgust at excrement. Another reason for the taboo can be traced back to the fact that the organs for defecation are positioned close to the genitals and those who dared to write about sanitation behaviour were often seen as vulgar.

Cameroonian communities did not want to adopt latrines at all. As, which is true in a lot of countries, this would alter their traditional defecation practices and would taint the purity of the home if placed in or in attachment to the house. It is also sometimes believed that high hygiene standards can be indicated by the absence of faeces in the toilet. In Kenya, for example, there is a superstition about throwing children's faeces into the latrine as this is believed to be used for witchcraft. So the children's faeces are supposed to be hidden away to prevent being picked up by ill-willed people. There are also beliefs that if people with power and wealth leave their faeces unprotected from their enemies they can risk personal harm. With the caste system in India the lower caste is used for the dirty work in the community, such as collecting human faeces. Even though it is now illegal, the Dalits are still looked upon with disgust by the other castes. The issue of status is discussed as an important consideration along with issues regarding social relations when adopting hygiene practices.

Even today people are not willing to use toilets that smell of faeces,; not mainly because of disgust but because they do not want others to believe that they are responsible for the smell. Studies conducted in slums across the world show that the people prioritise sanitation lower than lifestyle investments such as cell phones and TVs, making open defecation still common. CLTS is another approach that wants to ignite a sense of disgust and shame among the community and to mobilise it into initiating collective action to improve the sanitation situation and respecting nature. Nurture and teaching involve the nurture by parents, teaching in schools, in church and also the teaching and research that is done by government and NGOs.

Poverty apart, open defecation is a social convention—widely practised and reinforced by traditional beliefs which relate not only to the practice itself, but also to latrine use. In many rural areas in West Africa, the practice of open defecation is ritualised and bound in tradition. The behaviour and attitudes of ethnic groups are mostly drawn from traditional beliefs and cultural values which, in certain circumstances, resist the use of latrines. Studies and research must try to identify these beliefs, which act as social and cultural barriers to the adoption of improved sanitation. By mapping the social communication channels relevant to each community, the studies can also aim to find potential ways of encouraging social change and engaging with communities to end open defecation.

It is important to define "socio-cultural factors" and barriers, and how they could explain the practice of open defecation (see Table 1.3). Culture is the particular knowledge, beliefs and understanding of art, law, morals, customs, and other skills and habits that a person acquires as a member of a given society. Beyond their individual differences, the members of a group or society have particular ways of thinking and behaving, and will react to situations in similar ways. Culture is also an instrument; a tool by which we assign meaning to the reality around us and to the events that happen to us. This constant building of meaning involves repetition—reproduction of the ways of doing things and behaving which have been acquired; and renewal—incorporation of new elements that add to or replace what has been acquired. Because of these processes of repetition and renewal, societal attitudes are not unchangeable and communities can choose to give up harmful practices, although there is a need to accept that this process may take some time.

A number of studies and considerable field experience have shown that the introduction of water treatment technology without consideration of the socio-cultural aspects of the community and without behavioural, motivational, educational and participatory activities within the community is unlikely to be successful or sustainable. Therefore, initiatives in water, hygiene and sanitation must include community participation, education and behaviour modification. In the 1990s the WHO said that a number of systems had been developed and successfully implemented for this purpose; one of the most widely used and successful being PHAST, which stands for participatory hygiene and sanitation transformation.

Table 1.3: Some Socio-cultural Barriers in Sanitation

Shame/Embarrassment: Defecation as a private practice	People are ashamed or embarrassed to be seen walking in the direction of a latrine or toilet—even by close relatives such as their spouses or children—as other people will know they are going to relieve themselves. Most people will avoid walking directly towards toilets, and some prefer not to have any at home as they feel that defecating in the bush offers more privacy.
Smell: Offensive and off-putting	Compared to other types of waste, living with human exreta is unacceptable to most people.
Social Status : Obligation to hosts	Only "rich people" should own latrines. For the Bwaba ethnic group in Burkina Faso, if someone gives you food, you are expected to defecate in his field (and fertilise the crops), as the act of giving entitles the giver to receive something in return.
Evil: Fear of being possessed	In Ghana, fear of being possessed by demons or losing your magical powers is the leading cause of open defecation.
Ancestral Practices: Continuing the tradition	In Mali, and for the Idoma people in Nigeria, open defecation is seen as an ancestral practice passed down through generations. Most husbands do not
	allow their wives or daughters to share latrines with them, and will generally refuse to pay to build latrines for the use of female family members.

Other Barriers: Poverty, safety, environmental concerns, etc.	People often say they cannot conceive sleeping in thatched-roof juts, but they adjust. On the other hand they build latrines with cement and reinforcing steel just to defecate. The use of the latrine can be hazardous especially for small children who may easily fall into the pit. The geophysical conditions in some locations make latrine construction more difficult, either because the ground is too hard or because it is too sandy and unstable.
Indiscipline: People who just don't care	Carelessness and disrespect for civil authority—incivility.

Source: Water Aid Report 2009

It is an adaptation of the SARAR (self-esteem, associative strengths, resourcefulness, action-planning and responsibility) method of participatory learning. PHAST promotes health awareness and understanding among all members of a community or society in order to change hygiene and sanitation behaviour. It encourages participation, recognises and encourages self-awareness and innate abilities, encourages group participation at the grassroots level, promotes concept-based learning as a group process and attempts to link conceptual learning to group decision-making about solutions and plans of action for change and improvement of the current situation. It encourages internally derived decisions and both material and financial investment of the community to effect change. Current approaches to participatory education and community involvement in water and sanitation interventions apply behavioural theory and other related sciences to successfully implement control measures.

We can capture good traditional behaviour and integrate it with new improved behaviour that is more likely to be sustainable. For example, using traditional behaviour such as plants or ashes instead of soap where people cannot afford soap is a way to base the intervention on the traditional behaviour, starting from the people's own practices. In order to ensure people are able to adopt the WASH practices, the issue of poverty needs to be tackled. For example, through setting up self-help groups (SHGs) in the communities and creating income generating activity. This should be done either from inside the programme or with outside help. Feeling proud at their clean house or the feeling that when they are clean they can do anything is strong motivation for improvement and are good tools to use for hygiene and sanitation promotion. So social norms can be used through methods like model homes and visiting communities where a specific behaviour is practised to see the change and replicate it back home.

Also, there is need for further research within the area of socio-cultural aspects and their influence in cleanliness behaviour and sanitation practices as, for example, the need to capture the local knowledge and its synthesis with modern education, equipment and practices, say, herbal medicines and organic material. For instance, the government of Uganda is bringing traditional herbs into Western medicine, so there is a need to identify what herbs are effective to ensure people are not at risk. There is also a need to identify if the plant previously used for handwashing sufficiently removes faecal contamination to ensure that it is a safe alternative to soap.

1.7 STUDY AND RESEARCH IN SANITATION

All humans produce wastes of various types; for example, urine and faeces; waste from washing and cooking, and solid wastes produced at homes and in workplaces, schools, hospitals and other public buildings. Then why don't we study about this—its problems and management? Sanitation challenges people as well as administrators, policymakers, scientists and researchers. Sanitation in varying contexts of time and pace of our civilisation was not recognised as an area of academic research and study. Until recently, most academicians shied away from the topic as dirty and no further progress was expected. With Dr Pathak's call for developing "Sociology of Sanitation", a new trend started—quite a number of intellectuals began to devote attention to this ignored subject, said Hetukar Jha, the sociologist, who recently passed away.

Providing water and sanitation for all in an equitable and sustainable way is central to achieving global justice for poor women and men. Despite successive global declarations and efforts, the situation remains appalling with millions suffering from lack of access. Simplistic portrayals of water and sanitation "crises" have often led to misunderstandings about the nature of the problem and how to address it. The result has been a failure to centralise the needs and interests of the poor and marginalised within different solutions. There is a need for intervention to educate individuals about drinking water treatment methods, sanitation and handwashing practices. A number of challenges remain, including important research needs for sanitation. In the past, many water and sanitation intervention programmes took their own designs and implemented them in areas with need. This led to some unsustainable, culturally inappropriate, or irrelevant installations that were not always effective.

New concepts focus on smaller, community-based projects that are chosen by the household and implemented through microcredit. The major research areas mirror these approaches, leading to more social marketing research, health behaviour research, technical and microbiological investigation, and health outcomes, and impacts research. The future of sanitation improvement lies in trying new approaches—creative approaches to technology and delivery, greater dissemination of information on what works and what does not, providing greater training and building capacity in human resources, and greater political and financial commitment.

There are many research and action research initiatives on sanitation at various levels. Many action research activities have been taken up by NGOs and international organisations. The Government of India in collaboration with international organisations like the UN, United Nations Development Programme (UNDP), UNICEF, WaterAid, Plan International, CARE, and multidonor and bilateral institutions like the World Bank, Asian Development Bank, Department for International Development (DFID), etc., has undertaken various studies on sanitation.

The Institute of Development Studies (IDS) UK, conducts research at and within the STEPS Centre. Its work is on water justice critically examining the politics and pathways of water and sanitation policy and practice through interdisciplinary research on access, and rights and control over these key resources. Through this research it asks how future global action on water and sanitation and water resources management can centralise the needs of the poor and most marginalised. Secondly, the IDS has been working on the research, learning and networking aspects of CLTS for close to a decade. During this time, CLTS has become an international movement. The IDS programme on CLTS works around the world to ensure that CLTS goes to scale with quality and in a sustainable and inclusive manner. The aim is to contribute to the dignity, health and well-being of children, women and men in the developing world who currently suffer the consequences of inadequate or no sanitation and poor hygiene.

There is an interesting action research partnership with Participatory Methodologies Forum of Kenya (PAMFORK) in promoting participation through the use of participatory action research (PAR) methodologies, facilitating multi-stakeholder processes that deepen the understanding of the relationship between water, sanitation and hygiene. The study emphasised students' performance, learning in schools, building and strengthening capacities of stakeholders from the district level to implement WASH-related interventions that are evidence-based. The determination of and the relationship between the status of water, sanitation and hygiene in schools and the performance of boys and girls have also been discussed.

At national and international levels, several studies have been undertaken on various facets of rural sanitation. But I found that there were only a few academic studies conducted by universities in India. For the last 50 years, several international development organisations have conducted a number of studies and surveys with an emphasis on rural sanitation and water supply.

A newly published research study by the India WASH Forum in Indian villages has identified and analysed key barriers and motivators of change in sanitation and hygiene behaviour. The WHO-funded study, "Formative Research to Develop Appropriate Participatory Approaches towards Water, Sanitation and Hygiene in Rural Areas", was conducted in Gujarat, Telangana and Jharkhand in 2015 and 2016. Depinder Kapur, a member of the core team of researchers, opines that this is a credible intensive work undertaken by the India WASH Forum on the basic questions of why people are using, not using and not building toilets. These questions need to be asked repeatedly and the deeper motivation and barriers explored and addressed for improved sanitation and hygiene behaviour. The research questions included "Are there barriers to sanitation arising owing to the lack of knowledge and ignorance about the benefits of having and using toilets or from a deeper level of self-perception and barriers of caste, class and gender? Who among village habitants are adopting, building and using toilets and why? At what threshold level are more people willing to adopt or change their behaviours to start building and using toilets? What is the role of behaviour change communication (BCC) messaging and how is it perceived by the people? Why is it not working?"

Universities and research centres have undertaken projects individually and jointly on wastewater management and other related aspects of sanitation, health, and hygiene. Most of the research highlights and analyses several barriers to sanitation and hygiene in those rural areas. Among them are not only financial and physical limitations but also gender inequalities. Low sanitation coverage could be an outcome of material conditions of lack of water and space for toilets as well as a result of subsistence livelihoods. The sanitation situation often varies from one village to another; with growing density of population, the practice of open defecation is shrinking, which promotes people to build toilets. However, where open spaces are plenty, there is often less pressure to build toilets. Even gender barriers have come into the open.

Gender barriers to sanitation uptakes are not as simple as they appear. "Many women, girls and elderly do feel a desperate need for a toilet, but they think that it is unreasonable to make the demand considering the financial crisis of the family and the struggle of their parents or head of the family," explains the report. Although men make most financial decisions including construction of a toilet, women said that they understood and agreed with the men whenever financial stress was a limiting factor. There is an acute agrarian crisis in rural India and its impact on rural sanitation cannot be explained in gender terms alone.

For a huge country like India, with differing social and economic contexts, any research on the topic of sanitation should try to take more than a snapshot of the rural sanitation reality of India. Sanitation behaviour change should not be reduced to selling toilets to people. India faces the challenge of having the most number of people in the world defecating in the open and also has a burgeoning crisis of untreated faecal waste that is contaminating surfaces and groundwater, creating an imminent health crisis. We must break the myth and perception—branding rural people as ignorant and dirty. Research implications, recommendations and messages should begin by honouring and respecting their hard physical labour and their dirty hands and feet. Only then should the handwashing and toilets message follow.

We need more and more research on sanitation—scientific, social science and social-service oriented.

NOTES

1. The film is a satirical comedy in support of governmental campaigns to improve sanitation conditions, with an emphasis on the eradication of open defecation especially in rural areas. The film was financially successful. Akshay Kumar, who starred in it, dug a toilet in Madhya Pradesh to promote the film. Siddharth Singh and Garima Wahal, the writers of the film, hark back to a real incident in which 19-year-old Priyanka Bharti fled her husband's home in 2012 due to lack of a toilet. In the film, before the credits, the makers state that it is based on the story of Anita Narre from Madhya Pradesh who refused to go back to husband Shivram's home due to lack of a toilet.
2. Mangalore city has gone in for source segregation of waste at the time of door to door collection. In 2003, the Government of India initiated the Nirmal Gram Award to promote a clean environment. Similarly, the government of Karnataka initiated the Nairmalya Ratna award.
3. The SQUAT survey was designed to be representative of the rural open defecation challenge in five plains states of north India: Bihar, Haryana, Madhya Pradesh, Rajasthan and Uttar Pradesh. Districts were selected to match the state-level trend in rural household open defecation rates between 2001 and 2011. The survey was specially designed to highlight the sanitation beliefs and behaviour of men and women living in north Indian villages. The respondents were asked detailed questions to understand how people prioritise latrine use, what they think is healthy, where they defecate, why they defecate the way they do, and what they think are the advantages and disadvantages of open defecation versus latrine use.
4. The World Toilet College has uniquely designed training to facilitate effective execution of the Swachh Bharat Abhiyan and motivate government representatives to learn and deliver a holistic programme that aims at using waste as resource, promoting recycling and resource recovery. We must appreciate the Karnataka government for taking the initiative to send representatives to Singapore to learn best practices from the Singapore model and replicate them in Karnataka.
5. R$ is to Brazilian unit of currency.
6. Water, Sanitation and Hygiene (WASH) Project is aided by UNICEF.
7. Universal, affordable and sustainable access to WASH is a key public health issue of international development and is the focus of Sustainable Development Goal 6.
8. However, sanitation league results for September 2014 indicate that Temeke Municipal Council was among the LGAs which were placed in the red band, indicating poor performance in achieving the agreed NSC targets. In the same period, Tanga City Council was similarly placed in the red colour group while Same, Mwanga, and Mtwara were in the green group, indicating good performance of 75 per cent and above.

Chapter 2
Theory and Practice of Sanitation

In this chapter a theoretical explanation will be provided for sanitation in study and practice, linking it with health, hygiene and demographics. Here we concentrate more on "behavioural" models as they are the current phenomena in economics, judging by emerging economic theories and Nobel-winning economists' contributions. Sanitation practices, both individual/household and institutional, with comments on inadequacies and need for interventions will be provided.

2.1 THE PROBLEM

Globally, millions live without sanitary toilets and with food and organic waste rotting in the street. Those health hazards could be resources. Most interventions around sanitation are focused on access to safe drinking water and improving basic hygiene standards. Maxine Perella looks at how toilet waste like faecal matter and urine could not only be segregated and captured more safely, but also put to better use.

Toilet waste is a major part of the bio-cycle yet, because it is almost always handled separately from other resources, it remains underexploited. This is something that the Toilet Board Coalition (TBC) is looking to change. In 2016, the TBC ran a feasibility study to explore the potential role of sanitation in the circular economy—later that year, it published its findings which highlighted ways in which value could be maximised from what it calls "toilet resources", not just at a local level but globally too.

"Let's suppose we address the sanitation issue not by building lots of sewers, but by building a holistic biological waste system," says Sandy Rodger, circular economy project lead at the TBC. "We built sewers a long time ago, but we've never got on top of the rest of the biological waste. To this day, we're complaining about food waste. But supposing you had a system from the start that could deal with all this biological waste, what would happen then?"

Such a system could see low-income countries ultimately leapfrog developed nations, Rodger explains. "Potentially, you could change the resource profile of the economy as these developing countries grow. It's an idea that goes way beyond sanitation, but if you're in the waste management industry, it's a huge idea. But it does require people to think very differently."

Donor agencies, specialised organisations and governments do not invest enough in sanitation and hygiene. They often fail to recognise that such investments are strategic multipliers, or change agents for the host of ills described above.

Millennium Development Goal 7, Target 10, aimed to "Halve, by 2015, the proportion of people without sustainable access to safe drinking water and basic sanitation". A majority of the 2.5 billion people without access to improved sanitation and hygiene facilities reside in developing countries, and progress towards MDG 7, Target 10 lagged far behind many other MDG targets. Trends clearly showed most developing countries missing Target 10 (The Sustainable Development Goals Report 2019, and some more than others (WHO/UNICEF JMP, 2012). Now, in the SDG,[1] we have the sixth goal: Ensure availability and sustainable management of water and sanitation for all. How soon will we reach this goal? Prior to starting an intervention, it is important to assess the cultural practices, systems and beliefs, leadership structures, and other existing drivers of change within the various ethnic groups present in a community. This process should help to identify opportunities or issues specific to that cultural setting that could be drawn on to facilitate or trigger behavioural change. Why has progress in the sanitation and hygiene sector remained sluggish in most African, Asian and Latin American countries?

2.2 THEORIES OF SANITATION

What is needed to maintain proper or at least minimum sanitation and hygiene standards in the region, and to catalyse the gains in sanitation and hygiene coverage that have been made? What are the obstacles to progress? While discussing these questions we must also look into theories and models. Behavioural theories and institutional theories come in handy.

Institutional interventions are no doubt necessary. In order for these interventions to result in meaningful improvements in population health, behaviour and technologies must be adopted and maintained over time. At the time of behavioural interventions the elements of these two sets of theories do inevitably converge.

2.2.1 Behavioural Theories

Behaviour is the way in which one acts or conducts oneself, especially towards others. Its synonyms include: conduct, way of behaving, way of acting, deportment, bearing, etiquette.

Theory aims to understand what variables are most important to behavioural change and how the variables relate or interact. It also provides the potential to explain differences in behavioural change across situations, populations and contexts.

Behavioural change theories are attempts to explain why behaviour changes. These theories cite environmental, personal and behavioural characteristics as the major factors in behavioural determination. In recent years, there has been increased interest in the application of these theories in the areas of health, education, criminology, energy and international development with the hope that understanding behavioural change will improve the services offered in these areas. Some scholars have recently introduced a distinction between models of behaviour and theories of change. Whereas models of behaviour are more diagnostic and geared towards understanding the psychological factors that explain or predict a specific behaviour, theories of change are more process-oriented and generally aimed at changing a given behaviour. Thus, from this perspective, understanding and changing behaviour are two separate but complementary lines of scientific investigation. The ability to compare things and make a choice is a fundamental skill, central to human behaviour and economics alike.

Use of behavioural theories or frameworks in the design and implementation of behavioural change interventions can result in improved behavioural outcomes. A number of researchers have identified factors—which we refer to as behavioural determinants—that influence the adoption of WASH technologies and the continuation of improved practices, and organised these determinants into theoretical frameworks or models (see Table 2.1 and Table 2.2). The Integrated Behavioural Model for Water, Sanitation and Hygiene (IBM-WASH) represents synthesis of these existing behavioural models, by Robert Dreibelbis, Peter J. Winch, Elli Leontsini, Kristyna R.S. Hulland, Pavani K. Ram, Leanne Unicomb and Stephen P. Luby, based on their review of the evidence base for a number of other behavioural determinants not emphasised in those models, and feedback from concurrent formative and pilot research as mentioned in the methods.

Table 2.1: Theory

Sanitation	*Circulation*	*Sterilisation*
Nails	Hygiene	Electricity
Bones	Shop Management	Muscles
Personal Hygiene	Nerves	Vascular System

Source: https://slideplayer.com/slide/10958664/

As we see, therefore, there are three dimensions to sanitation behaviour or expected change in behaviour—contextual dimension, psychosocial dimension and technological dimension. These can be applied or studied in multi-level situations:

1. The societal/structural level broad organisational, institutional, or cultural factors that influence behaviour.
2. The community level the physical and social environment in which individuals are nested, as well as the formal and informal institutions that shape individual experiences.
3. The interpersonal/household level interactions between individuals and the people they intimately associate with, including household members, close friends and neighbours.
4. The individual level socio-demographic factors such as age and gender, individual cognitive factors and attitudes towards the product, hardware or behaviour.
5. The habit level nested within the individual, it reflects the fact that the opportunity and necessity for sanitation behaviour is repeated over the course of the day, and the multiple processes or events that can result in specific behavioural outcomes.

Table 2.2: Theoretical Models of WASH and WASH-related Behaviour included in the Systematic Review

Citation	*Behaviour or outcome of focus*	*Included determinants*
Environmental Health Project et al., 2004	Diarrheal prevention	Access to hardware: water supply systems, improved sanitation, household technologies. Hygiene promotion: communication, social mobilisation, community participation, social marketing, advocacy. Enabling environment: policy improvement, institutional strengthening, community organisation, financing, partnerships.
Rainey and Harding, 2005	Household water treatment (SODIS)	Application of the Health Belief Model, including: individual perceptions: perceived severity and perceived susceptibility to disease (diarrhoea). Modifying factors: demographic variables, socio-economic variables, structural variables; perceived threat of disease; cues to action. Likelihood of Action: perceived benefits of taking action *minus* perceived barriers, perceived efficacy of action and ability to complete it, likelihood of taking action.
Jenkins and Scott, 2007	Sanitation	Preference (motivation): dissatisfaction with current practices, awareness of options. Intention: priority of change among competing goals, absence of permanent constraints to acquiring sanitation.
Curtis, et al., 2009 (elaborated in Curtis, et al. 2011)	Handwashing with soap	Planning: teaching children manners. Motivation: disgust, norms, conforming, nurture. Habit: train children, tips to train oneself. Social norms. Physical facilities: cues, costs. Biological signs of contamination.

Citation	*Behaviour or outcome of focus*	*Included determinants*
Devine, 2009 / Coombes and Devine, 2010	Handwashing (FOAM) and sanitation (SaniFOAM)	Opportunity: access / availability, product attributes, social norms (FOAM), sanction/ enforcement (SaniFOAM). Ability: knowledge, social support (FOAM), skills and self-efficacy, roles and decisions, affordability (SaniFOAM). Motivations: beliefs and attitudes, outcome expectations, threat, intention (FOAM), values, emotional/ physical/social drivers, competing priorities, willingness-to-pay (SaniFOAM).
Figueroa and Kincaid, 2010	Household water treatment and storage	Individual: knowledge/skills, attitudes, perceived risk and severity, subjective norms, self-image, emotional response, self-efficacy, empathy and trust, social influence, personal advocacy. Household: time allocation, family support, resources, decision-making. Community: valuing water quality, leadership, action, resources, cohesion. Environmental/context: burden of disease, WASH technologies, community infrastructure, socio-demographic infrastructure, income inequality.
Wood, et al., 2011	Household water treatment (filters)	Awareness: perceived need, awareness of products, assessing value of products and relevance to lives, Action: trial / initial use, sustained use. Maintenance: purchase, sustained use.
Mosler, 2012	WASH practices (general)	Risk factors: perceived vulnerability, perceived severity, factual knowledge. Attitude factors: instrumental beliefs, affecting beliefs. Normative factors: descriptive, injunctive and personal norm. Ability factors: action knowledge, self-efficacy, maintenance efficacy, recovery efficacy.
		Self-regulation factors: action control / planning, coping planning, remembering, commitment.

Source: Robert Dreibelbis Research Gate 2013 October

Behavioural change is extremely individual-centric. Interventions must be creative and tailored to the individual, which is extremely difficult to do at scale. An important question in behaviour change is, whose responsibility is it to deliver change? Should we plan for change, or continue to plan for inputs and outputs?

Moving from a situation where people practise open defecation as a habit to a new social norm of "no open defecation" requires a change in people's expectations. Follow-up is needed to change initial open defecation-free (ODF) behaviour into a new social norm. Within the UNICEF's programmes there is evidence that social norms are embedded within the processes, although it is not necessarily an explicit part.

It has been found that there are supporting factors required to achieve social norms change:

- Community engagement throughout the process: It needs the whole community in order to create new social norms. A respected leader also needs to be involved throughout the process.
- Children and youth are central to the process: Where schools are the entry point the children not only help to drive the process of social norm change, they also feel differently about how things should be in their community.
- Incentives/sanctions: Sanctions need to be decided collectively by the community and agreed on. For example, in Sudan some communities are not letting their daughters marry into a family without a toilet.

Table 2.3: The Integrated Behavioural Model for Water, Sanitation and Hygiene (IBM-WASH)

Levels	*Contextual factors*	*Psycho-social factors*	*Technology factors*
Societal/ Structural	Policy and regulations, climate and geography	Leadership/ advocacy,cultural identity	Manufacturing, financing and distribution of the product; current and past national policies and promotion of products

Levels	*Contextual factors*	*Psycho-social factors*	*Technology factors*
Community	Access to markets, access to resources, built and physical environment	Shared values, collective efficacy, social integration, stigma	Location, access, availability, individual vs collective ownership/access, and maintenance of the product
Interpersonal/ Household	Roles and responsibilities, household structure, division of labour, available space	Injunctive norms, descriptive norms, aspirations, shame, nurture	Sharing of access to product, modelling/ demonstration of use of product
Individual	Wealth, age, education, gender, livelihood/ employment	Self-efficacy, knowledge, disgust, perceived threat	Perceived cost, value, convenience and other strengths and weaknesses of the product
Habitual	Favourable environment for habit formation, opportunity for and barriers to repetition of behaviour	Existing water and sanitation habits, outcome expectations	Ease/effectiveness of routine use of product

Source: Dreibelbis et al., BMC Public Health 2013, 13:1015

To conclude, the language of social norms is fairly new regarding "behavioural change". It has no specific indicators but can make use of proxy indicators.

2.1.2. Theory of Institutions

The word "institution" is ubiquitous and has no clear-cut definition. In the context of this book, institution is examined as a source of both social order and social change. North considers institutions as humanly devised constraints imposed on human interaction. According to E. Ostrom, the New Institutional economist, institutions are regularised behaviour that has turned into routine.

Institutions are also defined as the "rules of the game" in a society in which individual agents or organisations are the players. Amable adds that institutions are rules that provide information about how agents are expected to act in certain situations, and can be recognised by members of the relevant group as the rules to which others conform in these situations. Agents (i.e., individuals or organisations) embrace institutions as devices for coordination, for reducing uncertainty, and for implementing best response strategies. Thus, institutions must be relevant for all agents, providing them with a common understanding of how the game is played.

One can use the analogy of soccer to further characterise institutions; for example, the rules of soccer can be seen as the institutions, the players as the actors, the team as the organisation, and the referees as the enforcers. Without rules and referees in soccer, fair play cannot be guaranteed. In the same way, without stable institutions life becomes chaotic and arduous.

Institutions are also viewed as equilibrium strategies. As equilibrium strategies, institutions emerge and stabilise through self-enforcement—that is, through endogenous institutional change wherein agents work out new rules. Gérard distinguishes between types of institution that change slowly and continuously, and rapidly and irregularly. He classifies culture (including values, beliefs and social norms) as a slow-moving institution and political institutions as fast-moving. According to Amable, rules that are not socially shared cannot be considered institutions. Therefore, things that are specific to individuals and have no social dimension, such as rules of thumb and habits, do not qualify as institutions.

North separates institutions into two sets of rules or norms, either formal (i.e., devised and designed by human beings) or informal (conventions and codes of behaviour) which actors generally follow, whether for normative, cognitive, or material reasons. Similarly, Scott, Djelic and Quack present institutions as being both structures and formal systems, and normative and cognitive frames which provide stability and meaning to social behaviour. It is worth noting that for designed institutions to function, both the formal and informal institutions must coincide or match each other.

A common understanding of institutions, as well as the enforcement of these institutions, is necessary to make this happen; situations of multiple claims to governance, in which actors other than the State engage with the provision of basic services, the provision of security and settlement of disputes, etc. Enforcement mechanisms need to be part and parcel of the institutional structure to ensure that people abide by it. Firstly, agents must acknowledge rules to be binding for them to be legitimised.

Amable points out that the sanction accompanying non-compliance with formal rules is codified and formal (fines, sentences, etc.) whereas informal rules are not fully codified and non-compliance is not punishable by a formal authority. Sanctions related to informal rules may include social exclusion and impacts on social status, self-esteem, or reputation. Individuals, groups or organisations internalise norms and values, which motivate them to respect and defend the status quo even in the absence of controls or sanctions.

North defines an institution as a set of formal rules and informal norms. Thus, we can focus specifically on the following questions: What are the existing institutions (rules, norms, laws, customs, etc.) pertaining to sanitation and hygiene? How are these formal and informal institutions followed and enforced? What sanitation and hygiene practices actually prevail? How do rules and norms conflict with or complement not only each other, but also actual sanitation and hygiene practices on the ground? Thus there are diverse contributions that a particular institutional theory of cultural biases makes to public administration and policy research.

Sanitation intervention and sanitation marketing require strong institutional frameworks. The term "institutional framework" refers to a set of formal organisational structures, rules and informal norms for service provision. Water and sanitation service providers are one of the key institutional entities that are responsible for delivering the water and wastewater services at different levels of society, based on the law—national, state and local. An institutional framework for sanitation and water management should show integrity, comprehensiveness, and a sound division of roles and responsibilities. Then there will be effectiveness and economies of scale.

In Palestine, institutional water and sanitation framework envisages a clear separation between regulatory and delivery functions. It emphasises that the National Water Council (NWC) is the policymaking body, the Palestinian Water Authority (PWA) is the key regulator, and the service providers, local government units (LGUs) are the major entities that are responsible for delivering the water and wastewater services at different levels of society.

Water and sanitation institutions set the rules and define, thereby, the action sets for both individual and collective decision-making in the realm of development and management. Since these rules are often formalised in terms of three inter-related aspects, i.e., legal framework, policy environment, and administrative arrangement, water and sanitation institutions can be conceptualised as an entity defined interactively by three main analytical components, i.e., water and sanitation law, water and sanitation policy, and water and sanitation organisations as shown in Figure 2.1.

Laws are made by policymakers and regulators do the follow-up action. Organisations include both governments and NGOs and private stakeholders mainly as service providers and user associations. Even civil society should be institutionalised by established user associations and appropriate participation channels. This helps ensure public participation in development and decision-making.

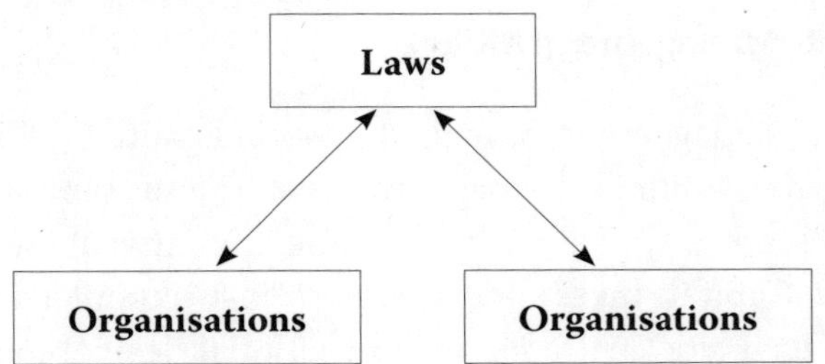

Figure 2.1: Water and Sanitation Institutional Structure

Ideally there can be a four-level institutional framework:

- Decision-making level e.g., water councillor, Sewage Board—responsible for review and approval of sanitation policies to support the work of the higher authorities. Ratifies plans, tariff policy, reports, guidelines and internal regulations.
- Regulatory level—e.g., waste water authority—responsible for water resources management and development planning, monitoring, assessing, licensing, management. Implements water and wastewater projects.
- Supply level—link between civil administration and people.

- Operational and service providers level—responsible for providing water and sanitation services in the city, including water distribution and treatment and associated customer relations.

The management models for water and sanitation service provision can be grouped into two main categories (although there is scope for mergers and amalgamation of organisations):

Delegated Public Management Model

In the delegated public management model, the water and sanitation system is built and operated by a water and sanitation utility. A water and sanitation utility also operates the infrastructure as a permanent concessionaire. In this model, water and sanitation utilities are owned by a group of municipalities (shareholders) and thus it is a public organisation, although it may be operated on a commercial basis. This model was developed in the West Bank during the time of Jordanian rule prior to 1967.

Direct Public Management Model

In the direct management model, the municipalities, village councils or joint service councils manage the water and sanitation services. Municipalities are responsible for funding the current investment and capital cost. Capital investments are almost completely funded by external financial aids (national or international development agencies), and municipalities are the owners of the infrastructure and the operators of the system.

Thus, institutional theories, by explaining the functional, financial and other jobs/roles of the organisations and departments, shed much light on structures and structural reforms, options and strategies, governance and participatory levels and loopholes, strengths and weaknesses, conflicts of interest and resolving modes and so on.

2.3 HYGIENE AND SANITATION

Sanitation is the provision of adequate excreta or waste disposal facilities that effectively prevent human, animal and insect contact with the waste.

Latrines and rubbish or garbage pits have been found to allow for the safe disposal of waste such as excreta and thus reduce the transmission of disease. Although the presence of pit latrines was observed in most of the homesteads, use cannot be guaranteed since this is steeped in beliefs and traditions. In the Nyakach community, pit latrines are majorly constructed by men and sharing them with in-laws and older children is prohibited while children's faeces are thrown out in the open fields as a means of disposal. The norms governing latrine use and beliefs surrounding hygiene practices are observed and any deviation from the norm is considered taboo and attracts chira, a curse.

Sanitation is the effective use of tools and actions that keep our environment healthy. These include latrines or toilets to manage waste, food preparation, washing stations, effective drainage and other such mechanisms. Hygiene is a set of personal practices that contribute to good health. It includes things like handwashing, bathing and cutting hair/nails. Handwashing is the single most important activity we can all do to encourage the stopping of spread of disease. The difference is subtle but important.

Millions lack menstrual hygiene and vital handwashing facilities. Diarrheal disease, largely caused by poor water, sanitation and hygiene, is a leading cause of malnutrition, stunting and preventable child mortality, claiming around 5,61,000 lives of children under five, annually. Inadequate facilities also affect education and economic productivity and impact the dignity and personal safety of women and girls. With so many solutions at hand, the continuing deprivation of too many is a shameful reflection of our society's priorities. In 1840, the "global sanitary revolution" transformed life in Europe and other parts of the developed world. In fact, it actually furthered the economic transformation by making those societies cleaner and healthier. But many countries still await a sanitation revolution.

The WHO/UNICEF Joint Monitoring Programme for Water Supply, Sanitation and Hygiene (JMP) has reported country, regional and global estimates of progress on drinking WASH since 1990. The JMP maintains an extensive global database and has become the leading source of comparable estimates of progress at national, regional and global levels. The 2015 update marked the end of the Millennium Development Goal period and the 2017 update established baseline estimates for monitoring the new SDG targets.

The 2017 update estimated that in 2015, 29 per cent of the global population (2.1 billion people) lacked "safely managed drinking water", meaning water at home, available, and safe; 61 per cent of the global population (4.5 billion people) lacked "safely managed sanitation" meaning access to a toilet or latrine that leads to treatment or safe disposal of excreta. For the first time, the report analysed hygiene. In sub-Saharan Africa, 15 per cent of the population had access to a handwashing facility with soap and water.

Fortunately, in developing the 17 SDGs for the 2016-2030 period, UN member states have recognised that good sanitation and hygiene (SDG 6, Target 6.2) have positive, knock-on effects for eight other goals. Specifically, these are goals to end poverty and hunger, create healthy lives, provide quality education, attain gender equality, foster sustainable growth, reduce inequality and develop sustainable cities.

UNICEF's WASH team works in over 100 countries worldwide to improve water and sanitation services, as well as basic hygiene practices. Last year, UNICEF's efforts provided nearly 14 million people with clean water and over 11 million with basic toilets. In times of crisis children are particularly vulnerable; UNICEF responds and provides emergency relief to those in need.

2.3 1 WASH and Livelihoods

Access to WASH will help drive progress towards the SDGs concerned with poverty, work and economic growth, not least because it will help achieve gender equity. It is women and girls who bear the burden of collecting water and caring for relatives made sick by lack of WASH, and who often miss out on education due to the domestic roles assigned to them. Lack of WASH exacerbates the marginalisation of females by locking them into a cycle of poverty and drudgery, with wider consequences for society and national economies.

2.3.2 WASH and Education

School and childhood should go hand in hand, but many children in low-income communities with no access to WASH are unable to attend class because they are sick with a diarrhoeal disease or, particularly in the case of girls in rural areas because they have to spend large parts of each day fetching water for their family. For children who are in school, the situation may be no better than at home: globally, around a third of schools have no safe water supply or adequate sanitation, leaving children dehydrated and less able to concentrate, and forcing pupils to use inadequate latrines or go to the toilet outside in the school grounds.

For adolescent girls, the presence of a safe water supply and clean, functioning, private toilet facilities can be the difference between dropping out of school and getting an education. Furthermore, hygiene education at school can begin a lifetime of better health for all children.

2.3.3. Wash and Health

The impact of universal access to WASH on global health would be profound. There is the potential to save the lives of the 8,40,000 people who currently die every year from diseases directly caused by unsafe water, inadequate sanitation and poor hygiene practices, and we could also drastically reduce child malnourishment, and help alleviate physical and mental underdevelopment. Today, 50 per cent of child malnutrition is associated with unsafe water, inadequate sanitation and poor hygiene. Women and girls would have the facilities and knowledge to be able to manage their menstrual cycles in safety and dignity. Similarly, during pregnancy, childbirth and post-natal care, medical staff, expectant mothers and their families will be better equipped to ensure newborns are given the safest and healthiest possible start in life.

2.4 SCAVENGING THROUGH THE AGES

To scavenge means to search for and collect (anything usable) from discarded waste. For example, "people sell junk scavenged from the garbage". Scavenging is the practice of manual cleaning of human excreta from service dry latrines. The scavengers crawl into the dry latrines and collect the human excreta with their bare hands, and carry it on their heads in a container to dispose it. Scavenging is both a carnivorous and a herbivorous feeding behaviour in which the scavenger feeds on dead animal and plant material present in its habitat. But here we are referring to scavenging by humans.

In India, as per the 2013 Act, manual scavenger means "a person engaged or employed, at the commencement of this Act or at any time thereafter, by an individual or a local authority or an agency or a contractor, for manually cleaning, carrying, disposing of, or otherwise handling in any manner, human excreta in an insanitary latrine or in an open drain or pit into which the human excreta from the insanitary latrines is disposed of, or on a railway track or in such other spaces or premises, as the Central Government or a State Government may notify, before the excreta fully decomposes in such manner as may be prescribed, and the expression 'manual scavenging' shall be construed accordingly".

Manual scavenging is a caste-based occupation involving the removal of untreated human excreta from bucket toilets or pit latrines that has been officially abolished by law in India as a dehumanising practice. The workers, called scavengers, rarely have any personal protective equipment. The term is mainly used in the Indian context.

It is not that scavenger is a derivative of scavenge; the reverse is true, scavenger is the older word, first appearing in English in 1530; scavenge came into English in the mid-17th century. Scavenger is an alteration of the earlier scavager, itself from the Anglo-French scawageour, meaning collector of scavage. In medieval times, scavage was a tax levied by towns and cities on goods put up for sale by non-residents, in order to provide resident merchants with a competitive advantage. The officers in charge of collecting this tax were later made responsible for keeping streets clean, and that's how "scavenger" came to refer to a public sanitation employee in Great Britain before acquiring its current sense, referring to a person who salvages discarded items.

A caste-based and hereditary profession, which is handed down as a legacy from one generation to the next, "manual scavenging" has been an age-old routine for this community, which is untouched by technological advancement in sanitary practices. Not only does the prevalence of this culture seem antediluvian, what is worse is the fact that those born into this community are considered agents of pollution due to their social hierarchy, based on birth. They are the most oppressed and suppressed class of Indian society—hated, ostracised, vilified, and avoided by all other castes and classes. The appalling hardship, humiliation and exploitation they face has no parallel in human history. The practice started in the Puranic period and continued in the Buddhist, Mauryan, Mughal and British periods.

The practice of manual scavenging in India dates back to ancient times. According to the sacred scriptures and other literature, scavenging by some specific castes of India has existed since the beginning of civilisation. One of the 15 duties of slaves enumerated in the Naradiya Samhita was of manual scavenging. This continued during the Buddhist and Mauryan periods also. Emperor Jahangir built a public toilet in Alwar, 120 km from Delhi, for 100 families in 1556. Scholars have suggested that the Mughal women with purdah required enclosed toilets that needed to be scavenged. It is pointed out that the Bhangis (Chuhra) share some of the clan names with Rajputs, and so the Bhangis are probably descendants of those captured in wars. There are many legends about the origin of Bhangis, who have traditionally served as manual scavengers. One of them, associated with Lal Begi Bhangis, traces the origin of Bhangis from Mehta community or gong farmers.

Municipal records from 1870 show that the British organised municipalities in India which built roads, parks, public toilets, etc. The British administrators organised systems for removing the faecal sludge and employed Bhangis.

Scavenger appears as an occupation in the 1911 census of England and Wales. This job title was used to describe someone who cleans the streets and removes refuse, generally a workman (a modern-day garbage collector, janitor, or street cleaner) employed by the local public health authority. Young people in developing countries revert to scavenging to develop entrepreneurship skills in order to operate in hostile economic contexts. In European history the terms "night soil collectors" or "night men" or "gong farmers" were used. The contemporary term for safe night soil collection is faecal sludge management. Towns with sanitation systems based on pail closets (bucket toilets in outhouses) relied on frequent emptying, performed by workers driving "honeywagons", a precursor to the vacuum truck now used to pump out septage from septic tanks. The municipal emptying of pail toilets continued in Australia into the second half of the 20th century; these were known as dunnies and the workers were dunnymen. In Haiti, this type of occupation is called bayakou.

In India, the term manual scavenging is used for the removal of raw (fresh and untreated) human excreta from buckets or other containers that are used as toilets or from the pits of pit latrines. The excreta is piled into baskets which the workers may carry on their heads to locations sometimes several kilometres from the latrines. The employment of manual scavengers is officially prohibited in India since 1993 but is still taking place to this day.

According to the Socio Economic Caste Census of 2011, 1,80,657 households were engaged in manual scavenging for a livelihood and 7,94,000 cases of manual scavenging were found across India. Maharashtra, with 63,713, tops the list with the largest number of households working as manual scavengers, followed by Madhya Pradesh, Uttar Pradesh, Tripura and Karnataka. The employment of manual scavengers to empty "dry toilets" (meaning toilets that require daily manual cleaning) was prohibited in India in 1993 and the law was extended and clarified to include insanitary latrines, ditches and pits in 2013.

Manual Scavenging

Source: Sulabh

Bhangi, Balmiki, Mehar, Halalkor and the like are caste names of scavengers in north India; Thoti, Pakay, Relli and the like in south India; Barvashia, Jamphoda, Mela, etc., in western and central India. Adi Dravida and Adi Karnataka, Harijan and so on are the new names acquired by some Scheduled Caste groups in Karnataka to obliterate the stigma of untouchability.

Not all forms of dry toilets involve "manual scavenging" to empty them, only those that require unsafe handling of raw excreta. If the excreta is already treated or pre-treated in the dry toilet itself, as in the case of composting toilets and urine-diverting dry toilets, for example, then emptying these types of toilets is not classified as "manual scavenging". Container-based sanitation is another system that does not require manual scavenging to function even though it does involve the emptying of excreta from containers.

Also, emptying the pits of twin-pit pour-flush toilets is not classified as manual scavenging in India, as the excreta is already partly treated and degraded in those pits.

The International Labour Organization describes three forms of manual scavenging in India:

- Removal of human excrement from public streets and "dry latrines" (meaning simple pit latrines without a water seal, but not dry toilets in general)
- Cleaning septic tanks
- Cleaning gutters and sewers

Manual cleaning of railway lines of excreta dropped from toilets of trains is another form of manual scavenging in India. Manual scavenging still survives in parts of India without proper sewage systems or safe faecal sludge management practices. It is thought to be most prevalent in Gujarat, Madhya Pradesh Uttar Pradesh, and Rajasthan. Some municipalities in India still run public toilets using simple pit latrines.

The biggest violator of this law in India is the Indian Railways. Many train carriages have toilets dropping the excreta from trains on the tracks. Indian Railways employs scavengers to clean the tracks manually. In March 2014, the Supreme Court of India declared that there were 96 lakh (9.6 million) dry latrines being manually emptied but the exact number of manual scavengers is disputed—official figures put it at less than 7,00,000.

Manual scavenging is done with basic tools like thin boards and either buckets or baskets lined with sacking that are carried on the head. Due to the nature of the job, many of the workers have related health problems.

2.4.1 Eradication Measures

Legislation

In the late 1950s, freedom fighter G.S. Lakshman Iyer banned manual scavenging when he was the chairman of the Gobichettipalayam

Municipality, which became the first local body to ban it officially. Sanitation is a state subject as per entry 6 of the Constitution. Under this, in February 2013, Delhi announced the banning of manual scavenging, becoming the first state in India to do so. District magistrates are responsible for ensuring that there are no manual scavengers working in their district. Within three years' time municipalities, railways and cantonments were to make sufficient sanitary latrines available. The government of Maharashtra has planned to abolish manual scavenging soon. But by using Article 252 of the Constitution which empowers Parliament to legislate for two or more states by consent and adoption of such legislation by any other state, the Government of India has enacted various laws and the continuance of such discriminatory practices is a violation of the ILO's Convention 111 (Discrimination in Employment and Occupation).

Two important laws are:

1. The Employment of Manual Scavengers and Construction of Dry Latrines (Prohibition) Act, 1993
2. The Prohibition of Employment as Manual Scavengers and their Rehabilitation Act, 2013 or M.S. Act, 2013

Activism

In the 1970s, Dr Bindeshwar Pathak introduced his Sulabh concept for building and managing public toilets in India. The concept has introduced a hygienic and well-managed public toilet system. Activist Bezwada Wilson founded a group in 1994, Safai Karmachari Andolan, to campaign for the demolition of then newly illegal "dry latrines" (pit latrines) and the abolition of manual scavenging. Despite the efforts of Wilson and other activists, the practice persists two decades on.

In July 2008, "Mission Sanitation" was a fashion show held by the United Nations as part of its International Year of Sanitation. On the runway were 36 former scavengers, and top models to create awareness of the issue of manual scavenging.

But the problem still exists. Is it possible that hundreds of thousands of dry latrines across India have been cleaning themselves? That was the embarrassing question senior state government officials had to face at a review meeting attended by secretary and DG-level officials of all the states and the union territories held on 21 July 2016 by the National Commission for Scheduled Castes (NCSC).

Telangana, for instance, reported 1,57,321 dry latrines as of 31 December 2015, but zero manual scavengers. The survey results submitted by Himachal Pradesh, too, showed 854 dry latrines but "nil" manual scavengers. Chhattisgarh reported 4,391 dry latrines but only three workers. "A manual scavenger can at the most clean 30 or 40 latrines. How can three of them clean 4,391 latrines?" asked an official at the meeting. Similarly, Karnataka reported 24,468 dry latrines but only 302 manual scavengers, and Madhya Pradesh's numbers were 39,362 and 36. Bihar reported only 11 manual scavengers, while Haryana reported "nil" for both dry latrines and manual scavengers.

The mismatch between the numbers of dry latrines and those of manual scavengers is considered a serious anomaly as it points to the failure of the state governments to identify the manual scavengers who doubtless exist, as attested to by the existence of dry latrines, as well as by the census data.

Although manual scavenging is prohibited in the country, as per the latest Socio-Economic Caste Census data released in 2015, India still has 1,80,657 households that make a living from manual scavenging. The states, therefore, get funding from the centre for rehabilitation of manual scavengers.

Identification of manual scavengers is the first step towards rehabilitating them. The NCSC observed in a note circulated for the meeting that "expenditure for the last three years is negligible" under the Self-Employment Scheme for Rehabilitation of Manual Scavengers (SRMS). The budgeted amount for SRMS for 2015-16 was ₹470.19 crore. The expenditure was "nil."

Interestingly, Rajasthan, Punjab and West Bengal reported an increase in the number of manual scavengers over the previous year. Union Minister for Social Justice and Empowerment Thawar Chand Gehlot said in August 2017: "When we seek information, most states say there are no manual scavengers. Till July 2017 13 states finally admitted to having 13,500 manual scavengers."

Despite a clutch of laws and strictures from the highest court of the land, the practice of employing human labour to clean sewers continues to this day, claiming the lives of labourers and leaving their families in the lurch. Tragedies, including death, are widely reported (See Box 2.1).

BOX 2.1: PLIGHT OF SCAVENGERS

- A manual labourer lost his life while cleaning a sewer pipeline at Sassoon Docks in Mumbai on 31 October 2017. Ahmed Ansari was cleaning the sewer pipeline in Mumbai's Port Trust area when he fell unconscious.
- Three workers were cleaning the sewer pipeline. When the chamber began to emit gas, they fell unconscious. They were rushed to St George Hospital. However, one of the workers lost his life.
- As the scorching heat of the first month of summer baked the grubby streets of Cuddalore on 20 March 2017 three young men (Jayakumar, Murugan, and Velu)—two below 30 years and one in mid-30s—were called to clear a block in a manhole near Mohini Bridge in Thirupadiripuliyar. When the three reached the manhole near Mohini Bridge, the surface of the road was too hot though it was evening. Velu got into the manhole first, followed by Murugan. When both of them did not surface, Jayaram went in. Shortly thereafter, all the three died of asphyxiation.

Following their death, protests erupted in Cuddalore with relatives and representatives of Social Awareness Society for Youth demanding that murder charges be pressed against government officials concerned and a case booked under the SC and ST (Prevention of Atrocities) Act as two of the deceased were Dalits. Protesters also called for strict implementation of the Prohibition of Employment as Manual Scavengers and their Rehabilitation Act, 2013 (MS Act, 2013) to identify and rehabilitate conservancy workers.

- Just five days before this incident, two conservancy workers died in Vijayawada in Andhra Pradesh and three men died of asphyxiation in Bengaluru on 7 March 2018.

Magsaysay Award winner and national convener of Safai Karmachari Andolan Bezwada Wilson is on record terming the practice of manual scavenging a part of "the dirty Indian culture" rooted in the caste-based society.

Aren't we reminded of Bakha, son of Lakha, an 18-year-old Indian youth, a sweeper and the protagonist of "Untouchable", Mulk Raj Anand's famous novel of 1935? Strong and able-bodied, he is fascinated by the life and ways of India's English colonisers. His position as an untouchable has resulted in high levels of self-deprecation and depression.

Bakha can be judgmental and at times helps perpetuate the very system that keeps him oppressed. Paradoxically, he still questions the status quo and challenges a caste system that is supposedly "set in stone." His is a war against stigma. Anand proves that Bakha is doing the Herculean task of carrying the society's shit. He can clean but will not tolerate. His war against untouchability will continue. However, the question sometimes weighs heavily on his heart when his conscience seeks an answer. "For them I am a sweeper, sweeper—untouchable! Untouchable! Untouchable! That's the word! Untouchable! I am an Untouchable!"

"Posh, keep away, posh, sweeper coming, posh, posh, sweeper coming, posh, posh, sweeper coming!"

This is how Bakha announced his entry into populated areas every morning so that people were alerted and no one knocked against him accidentally.

Anand knew he could not generate a solution to the anathema that had made life hell for Bakha and his people, but he knew that if he could churn some sympathy in Indian hearts for people like him, it could be a partial balm for Bakha's wound. Mahatma Gandhi had tried to lift these underdog castes out of the identity crisis they had been living in by giving them a new identity and by calling them Harijans. Combined with the reservation and special status of backward classes, these castes have been able to slightly emerge out of the depths. However, none of these has proved to be an effective remedy and these castes are still battling the same problems that they faced centuries ago. India has come a full circle but it has not been able to change itself in terms of caste and class.

Subaltern concern is what is revealed in literary pieces like this.

Certified from various sources

2.5 SANITATION PRACTICES

There were two kinds of scavenging, public or outdoor street scavenging and private or house scavenging. The two dominant methods for transporting and collecting night soil were the dry conservancy and the bucket system. The scavenging operations primarily consisted of sweeping and removing dirt from streets, cleaning and removing sludge, flushing drains, and cleaning and removing night soil, which was executed by a huge labour force consisting of men and women scavengers, cart coolies and drivers, bullocks, latrine boys and girls.

In a congested locality, the scavenger has to crawl through a narrow passage, pushing the basket with one hand, resting his body weight on the other to make his way up to the latrine chamber through a narrow opening. In the latrine, where the seat is deep inside, he/she has to stretch his/her hand to the fullest and thrust his/her head into the hole to clean the toilet. The scavenger has to bend forward into the narrow space to clean excreta from the toilet antechambers. In latrines which have no receptacles, human excreta drops directly on the floor, which, with passage of time, wears the brickwork that becomes patchy and uneven. In most cases, the sidewalls are also without cement plaster, so the excreta gets stuck everywhere on the sidewalls and also on the floor. The scavenger, while cleaning, has to scratch the floor and sidewalls to effect maximum cleaning.

It is a common sight to see scavengers, mostly women, moving with excreta on the head, stored in bamboo baskets, or in leaking drums, with the muck trickling down over face and body. Passers-by avoid such persons. If a scavenger comes in close proximity, he or she is showered with a hail of abuse. In many places, latrines are so constructed that the users do not even see their own excreta. They simply squat, perform and go away without even caring to know who cleans their toilets. No human degradation could be more cruel and inhuman than the one suffered by scavengers.

Manual scavenging is not like other professions that have managed to break through the caste system if even a little. It is still firmly set as it was created about 3,000 years ago.

The ministry has estimated there are 2.5 lakh manual scavengers across the country and only 10 to 12 states have sent the details of 12,000 manual scavengers. The ministry provides financial assistance of ₹40,000 to those people who leave manual scavenging. According to some reports a high percentage, almost about 95 per cent of manual scavengers, are Dalit women.

One must also realise that just the government abolishing the practice does not automatically clear away the deep-set prejudice and stigma that comes from being in the profession and caste.

So even if they wanted to escape this profession, other professions would not take them. The way ahead is difficult. Laws are made by policymakers and regulators do the follow-up action. Organisations include both governments and NGOs and private stakeholders mainly as service providers and user associations. Even civil society should be institutionalised by established user associations and appropriate participation channels. This would help ensure public participation in development and decision-making.

NOTE

1 The MDGs declared by the UN were for the period 2010-15. The SDGs are a new, universal set of goals, targets, and indicators that UN member states will be expected to use to frame their agendas and political policies over the next 15 years.

Chapter 3

Sanitation: Global and National Scenarios

Most people feel that sanitation in the world and particularly in urban India is in a crisis (see Box 3.1). The magnitude of India's sanitation crisis may be summed up in one sentence: Two-thirds of urban residents lack toilets and access to the sewer grid, and over 600 million people in rural and urban areas still defecate in the open.

Where the grid does not serve toilets, faeces is periodically collected from unhygienic and unsustainable septic tanks and pit latrines to be discarded in open areas, landfill sites, lakes and freshwater sources. The tragedy of our commons therefore multiplies manifold, as do health consequences. These sanitation solutions are not only undignified, but also cause immense environmental damage. Pit latrines are emptied every few months by poorly trained and ill-equipped service employees. These "frogmen" jump into the pits of human waste, manually empty the pit latrines using buckets, and then haul the overflowing buckets of waste through the settlement community to the nearest waterway or field, where the buckets' contents are released into the environment.

3.1 GLOBAL SCENARIO

Archaeological excavations confirm existence of sitting toilets in Egypt (2100 BC). Though we have been able to mechanise the working of these toilets, the form and basic format of the toilet system remains the same. In Rome, public bath-cum-toilets were also well-developed. There were holes in the floor and underneath was flowing water. When the Romans travelled, they constructed toilets for their use. The pans were key-hole type so that the liquid and solid wastes were separated at the origin and disposal became easier. Excavations in Sri Lanka and Thailand too have uncovered a contraption in which urine was separated and allowed to flow while the other portion was used at the same time for defecation. Every country has contributed to the growth of sanitation.

BOX 3.1: POOR SANITATION IMPACT

- Twenty-five lakh diarrhoea deaths globally and six lakh in India alone. Two thousand deaths in India per day, 60,000 roundworm, 65,000 hookworm deaths.
- Diarrhoeal disease kills nearly 1.6 million children each year. Children under age five suffer more from diarrhoeal diseases than HIV/AIDS, malaria and tuberculosis combined. This affects not only individual families, but entire economies.
- Developing countries lose 2 to 6 per cent of GDP each year due to lost worker productivity from sanitation-related diseases.
- The problem is particularly acute in slums, where over one billion people live. By 2030, this population will double to over two billion people worldwide. The high population density in slums, combined with the lack of physical space, infrastructure and resources, exacerbates the sanitation crisis.
- Kenya's eight million slum residents are forced to rely on unsanitary options such as "flying toilets" (defecating into plastic bags that are then tossed onto the streets) and pit latrines that release untreated human waste into the environment.
- The gruesome rape and hanging of two teenage girls in the populous Uttar Pradesh state again proves how women have become the biggest victims of India's sanitation crisis. The two girls were going to the fields to defecate when they went missing at night.
- A senior police official in Bihar said some 400 women would have "escaped" rape last year if they had toilets in their homes. Women living in urban slums of Delhi reported specific incidents of girls under 10 "being raped while on their way to use a public toilet" to researchers of a 2011 study funded by WaterAid and DFID-funded Sanitation and Hygiene Applied Research for Equity.
- Violence against women on the way to or from public toilets has been reported from countries like Kenya and Uganda too. But for India, a country which aspires to superpower status, lack of toilets is an enduring shame.
- Prime Minister Narendra Modi had promised, "Toilets First, Temples Later".

Certified from various sources

Historical evidence exists that the Greeks relieved themselves out of the house. There was no shyness in using toilets. At dinner parties in Rome slaves would bring in urine pots made of silver; members of the royalty used them and continued festivities at the same time. Whatever little information is available about the history of toilets in India shows they were quite primitive. The practice of covering waste with earth continued till the Mughal era, in the forts of Delhi and Agra where one can see remnants of such methodologies to dispose of human waste.

People in China, like other people around the world, used human poop to fertilise their fields and grow more food. You can see a system where when you wanted to go to the bathroom you climbed up to this hut. The poop fell down through a hole into a cesspool near the pigpen. The pigs ate the poop and converted it into food. This system was efficient, but it sometimes spread diseases.

Around 500 BC, under the Eastern Zhou Dynasty, rich Chinese who lived in cities started to have latrines in their houses. These toilets didn't have seats. They were a hole in the ground with two bricks to squat on. Most people didn't have latrines in their houses. They just squatted right in the street (as in ancient Greece or Rome at the same time). To wipe themselves, they used straw or leaves or broken pieces of pottery.

People in Rome were building public toilets by about 100 BC. By AD 700, as more people lived in cities under the T'ang Dynasty, businessmen in China started to build pay toilets. These toilets were mud-brick shelters for one person the size of a bathroom stall today, with a hole in the floor to squat over. Businesses collected the poop from these pay toilets and used donkey carts to pull cartloads of poop out to the country. Farmers bought the poop to spread on their fields. Businesses made a lot of money by selling poop, but using human poop on fields spread dysentery germs.

Most city people didn't want to pay for toilets. They used chamber pots in their own houses, and then carried the dirty pots to the river to clean them. Sometime around AD 500, rich people in China started to use toilet paper to wipe themselves. Most people could not afford fancy toilet paper and went on using whatever was handy.

In the absence of proper toilet facilities, people had to defecate and urinate wherever they could. Defecating on the road, open spaces, or just easing themselves in the river was very common. While the authorities were educating people to have private places for defecating, and getting them cleaned, in actual practice there was total disorder. Squalor and filth abounded in cities. Social reformers advised people where to defecate, how to defecate in privacy and to control themselves when in company.

Han Dynasty Model of an Outhouse (ca. 100 ad)

Source: Google images

Another Han Dynasty Outhouse Pigsty Model
(Art Institute of Chicago)

Children were taught not to touch human waste. At the same time, there was no hesitation in letting loose pigs to eat human excreta.

A number of enactments, however, could not prevent people from defecating in the open. A delegation led by master weavers protested in front of the French Municipal Building and said: "Our fathers have defecated at the place where you prevent us from doing so. We have defecated there and now our children will defecate there."

The rich used wool or hemp for ablution while the poor used grass, stone, sand or water, depending upon the country or weather conditions or social customs. Use of newspaper was also common. In Russia, to the utter dislike of all, the subordinates even stamped the toilet paper with the imperial arms for use of the Czar. But it was termed sacrilege. The final solution to the problem of ablution was found when in 1857, Joseph Gayetty invented the commercial toilet paper in the US. This invention has enabled human beings to have tissue paper, which is convenient to use, is absorbent as well as compact and within reach while defecating.

According to Hiroshi Umino, European culture blossomed after contact with crusaders from the East. Washing hands before eating also became popular. The social reformers admonished the people by saying, "Suck your fingers, beast, do not wipe them on the wall." In colonial times in India, the British called big cities "vast mass privy" due to defecation by people at all times and at all places. There were also no separate toilets for men and women, till a restaurant in Paris put up separate "Men Toilet" and "Women Toilet" at a dance party in 1739.

It is also around this time that the urinal pot was introduced to enable men to relieve themselves. The facilities for women were meagre and they were taught the virtues of control. Despite technological breakthrough, a lot needed to be accomplished to educate people to use the new technology appropriately, to ensure that the toilet drainage system was not misused by disposal of other household waste. However, at city level the disposal of human waste still remained a problem.

In 1519 the provincial government of Normandy in France made provision of toilets compulsory in each house. The French government also passed a parliamentary decree to make cesspools in each house compulsory. Again a similar attempt was made in 1539. In Bordeaux in France, the government made construction of cesspools compulsory. It was tried again in 1668 when the Lieutenant of Police made construction of toilets compulsory. In England the first sanitation law was passed in 1848.

In 1872 the municipalities in France asked private companies to manage public toilets for a lease period of 20 years. The private companies also offered amounts to the government as they were confident of recovering the same through user charges. Ground-floor owners were also requested to construct latrines for use of passers-by. The owners of the former Palais Royal Hotel in Paris started charging a monthly fee from diners. Condoms were also sold there as part of the facilities.

The 18th century was a century of toilets. Despite the invention of the water closet by John Harington in 1596, which cost only six shillings and eight pence, it was not adopted on a large scale for almost 179 years. Delays in actual use of inventions are common in human history. Alvin Toffler calls this a "cultural lag". It was true for the railway train, the ballpoint pen and innumerable other inventions. During this period, people used the earth closet. In these toilets, instead of water, loose earth was used. So the problem of cleaning remained. The world also saw development of pan closets which was like a cigarette ash tray with the material at the bottom. This too required manual cleaning. At the same time chamber pots, close-stools and open defecation continued. Harington's toilet under the name of Angrez was being used in France, though not introduced on a large scale in England. In 1738 J.F. Brondel introduced the valve-type flush toilet. Alexander Cummings further improved the technology and came up with a better device in 1775. In Cummings' design water was perennially present in the toilet so it suppressed odours. Yet the working of the valve and fool-proof inlet of water needed further improvements.

From 1880 onwards, however, the emphasis has been more on aesthetics to make cisterns and bowls decorative. The bowls became so colourful that some suggested using them as soup bowls. It was in 1880 that toilet curtains made their appearance. The period was called the age of "Belleepoque" in France and Edwardian in England. In 1890 we had the first cantilever-type toilet. Since then the world has not witnessed any significant technical change except some change in shape of toilets and reduction in quantity of water per use. It was around 1900 that the institution of the bathroom came into vogue in Europe.

3.1.1 Some Toilet-related Eccentricities

It was also popular in those days to emphasise the medicinal values of human waste. Urine was supposed to have many therapeutic values. Some quacks even claimed that by studying an urine sample they could confidently say whether a young girl was a virgin or not. Hiroshi Umino reports that a Pharaoh got an eye problem cured by using the urine of a woman, whom he later married. It was also widely believed that the dung of a donkey mixed with night soil removed black pustules and the urine of a eunuch could help make women fertile.

In the Middle Ages, people used to throw excreta from their houses on the roads below. In Europe the period between 500 to 1500 was a dark age from the point of view of human hygiene. It was an era of cesspools and human excreta all around. Rich men's houses and forts in India had protrusions in which defecation was performed and the excrement fell into the open ground or the moat below.

In Europe it was an era of chamber pots, cesspools and close-stools and toilets protruding out of the castles and excrement falling into the

Source: https://www.sulabhtoiletmuseum.org/history-of-toilets/

river or surrounding ditches. It was also an era of "liberty to pee". The French poet, Claude le Petit, described Paris as 'Ridiculous Paris' in the following words:

My shoes, my stockings, my overcoat,
My collar, my glove, my hat.
Have all been soiled by the same substance
I would mistake myself as rubbish.

There was a lot of jest and humour relating to toilet habits and toilet appurtenances. Ballets were performed with baskets of night soil in the form of hoods on the head or a tin plate commode moving around with toilet sounds while the clothes were dotted with accessories from toilets. The characters were Etronice (night soil), Sultan Prime of Foirince (i.e., diarrhoea), and so on. There are stories by Guerrand which depict the mood of Europe at the time. A lady of noble birth requested a young man to hold her hand. The young man suddenly felt the urge to urinate. Forgetting that he was holding the hand of a lady of noble birth, he relieved himself. At the end he said, "Excuse me, Madam, there was a lot of urine in my body and it was causing great inconvenience.," Similarly, Maid of Honour Anne of Austria, owing to excessive laughter, urinated in the bed of the queen. Joseph Pujol (hero extraordinary of French scatology) in his shows demonstrated many types of farts by a young girl, mother-in-law and bride. He could even extinguish a candle, 30 centimetres away, by farting.

BOX 3.2 : HIGHLIGHTS IN THE EVOLUTION OF THE TOILET SYSTEM—2500 BC TO 2001

- 2500 bc: In Mohenjo-Daro, there existed a highly developed drainage system with wastewater from each house flowing into the main drain.
- 1000 bc: In the Bahrein Island in the Persian Gulf, the flush type toilet was uncovered.
- ad 69: Vespasianus, for the first time, levied a tax on toilets/urinals in Rome.
- 1214: Construction for the first time of public toilets manned by scavengers in Europe.
- 1596: John Harington invents the W.C.
- 1668: Edict issued by Police Commissioner, Paris, for construction of toilets in all houses.

- 1738: Architect J.F. Brondel argues that an attached toilet is ideal.
- 1739: First separate toilets for men and women appear at a ball in Paris.
- 1824: First public toilet in Paris.
- 1852: First public lavatory with flushing toilets opened in London.
- 1857: Toilet paper went on sale in the USA.
- 1859: Toilet of Queen Victoria is decorated with gold.
- 1883: First ceramic toilet designed by Thomas Twyford for Queen Victoria.
- 1889: Sewage treatment for the first time in the world.
- 1959: All surface toilets abandoned (Paris).
- 1970: Sulabh International is established by Dr Bindeshwar Pathak, as a non-profit NGO in Bihar, India.
- 1980: Installation of auto control public toilet.
- 1992: The US Energy Act was passed, requiring flush toilets to use only 1.6 gallons of water.
- 2001: The World Toilet Organization is formed.

Source : Tim Lambert, A Brief study of Toilets

3.2 INDIA IN THE PAST

The Aryan code of sanitation ethics has links to the Manusmriti and the Puranas. Before going to the toilet the scripture prescribes an elaborate drill. Before going for defecation one was to chant the following mantra from the Narad Purana:

Gachhantu Rishio Deva
Pishacha ye cha guhyaka
Pitrbhutaganasurve
Karis hye Malamochanam.

It is a request to all invisible souls to leave the place as one will defecate. Before going for defecation it was prescribed that the sacred thread should be rolled to a smaller size and be put on the right ear so that it does not touch dirt. The head was to be covered with a cloth. In the absence of a cloth, the sacred thread was to be brought over the head and was to be hung on the left ear. Then, while observing silence and facing north in the day and south in the night one could defecate. While defecating one was not to touch water. After defecation the water pot was to be held in the right hand, and the left hand was to be used for cleaning.

There was also an ablution code. In the Vishnu Purana some rules are laid down for the post-defecation stage.

Aika Lingagudatrindashabamkaremrid,
Hastdve cha samaranyascharana cha tribhistribhi.

This says that while defecating the orientation of the face should not be towards the "sun", "Brahmin", "fire", or "moon". After defecation the "linga" (generative organ) is to be washed once, "guda" (anus) to be washed three times, the left hand to be washed 10 times, and the right hand seven times, and both the feet to be cleaned with earth and water three times. After defecation the water pot was to be held in the right hand and still to be used for cleaning. The linga was to be rubbed once with earth and the guda three times with earth. Then both had to be washed with water. This was to ensure that there was no odour left on the body. After this one should pick up the water with the right hand. One was advised to pick up a fistful of earth. This was to be divided into three parts. With the first part the left hand was to be cleaned 10 times and with the second part the right was to be cleaned seven times. The third part was to be used to clean the water pot three times. It was also laid down that both feet were to be washed with water. The following shloka gives the philosophy of protecting the environment by adoption of elaborate defecation practices:

Dashasthanparitjaymutramkurya
Jalashay Shathasthan
Purisharthatirthamnadyam Chaturgunam!
Dharashauchnakurvitashauchashudh
Mabhipsta! Chulukairaiv Kartabya
Hashtatshudhi Vidhanta!

Urination ought to be done 10 cubits from the water source and defecation 100 cubits from the water source. At least 40 cubits' distance was to be observed while urinating near a river or a temple while defecation had to be 400 cubits away. Urination and defecation ought not to be done in running water or a river. Water should be taken in the hand and washing done away from the river. For different classes, the Manusmriti also laid down specific rules:

Aitchhouchgrihasthana,
Dvigunbrahmacharyanam!
Trigunavanaprasthanam,
Yatinam cha chaturgunam!

For those who are celibate or have renounced the world, the rules are to be observed differently. The celibate should observe the rules twice more intensely. Those who are in "Vanaprastha" should observe them three times more intensely. Saints should observe the rules four times more intensely.

Separate lenient rules were laid down for those who were sick or infirm, as the following shloka makes clear:

Diva shauchalayanishyardha,
Parthapadovidhiyate!
Aarte Kuryadyathashakti
Shaktaakuryadyathochitam!

The rules are for urination and defecation in the daytime. At night the frequency of washing and so on is reduced by half. If one is travelling the rules are further reduced by half. If one is sick, the rules need to be observed as per capacity.

The perusal of literature brings home the fact that we have only fragmentary information on the subject of the toilet as it is a private secluded place to help one get rid of one's waste. Sitting-type toilets in human history appeared quite early. In the remains of the Harappan civilisation in India, at a place called Lothal (62 kilometres from the city of Ahmedabad in western India), in the year 2500 BC the people had water-enabled toilets in each house which were linked with drains covered with burnt clay bricks. To facilitate operations and maintenance, there were man-hole covers, chambers, etc. It was the finest form of sanitary engineering. But with the decline of the Indus Valley civilisation, the science of sanitary engineering disappeared from India. From then on, the toilets in India remained primitive and open defecation became rampant.

In the Indian scriptures there are stories about the strength of wrestlers. If a wrestler defecates too much, he is relatively weak because he cannot digest all that he eats. Similarly, a perfect saint has no need to defecate, for he eats as much as he can digest or he is able to digest all that he eats. So not to defecate was considered saintly while in other societies not to defecate was considered manly. Bruno Bettelheim states that men of the Chaga tribe blocked their anus during the ceremony of attaining manhood and pretended as if they did not defecate at all. This was also one way of establishing superiority over women. The ancient Greeks, it is reported, had similar beliefs. Swallowing something and not emitting it was considered a source of power and authority.

The forts of Jaisalmer in India and big old houses on the banks of rivers bear testimony to this fact. In India, it is very common to use water for ablutions. However, the hand one uses varies in various parts of India. While in south India people use the right hand for eating food, it is considered disgusting to use the same hand for ablution with water. So the left hand is used for sanitary purposes. In most parts of north India, however, no such sharp distinction exists.

Mughal Emperor Jahangir built a public toilet in Alwar, 120 km from Delhi, for use of 100 families at a time in 1556. Not much documentary evidence exists on the quality of its maintenance but one can well visualise how, with rudimentary technology and with the government managing the operation and maintenance (O&M) functions, it like others must have been in very unsatisfactory condition. As hygienic conditions in public toilets were bad, people preferred open defecation. This was true in most countries.

In India the institution of gusalkhana (bathroom) was established by the Mughal emperor in 1556. Oppressed by the heat and dust of India, the Mughal constructed luxurious bathing and massage facilities. But this was only for the rich. The ordinary citizens, however, lived in insanitary conditions.

In the past, latrines were tucked away in attics to keep them away from the noses and eyes of the family and society. In contrast, the twentieth century has given pride of place to toilets in the home. They are more opulent, more spacious than at any time in the past. While the provision of a toilet in the house solved the household problem of cleanliness, the challenge remained as to how to dispose of human waste at city level. This was solved when the sewer system was introduced. Haussmann in 1858 describes beautifully the sewerage system. He says, "The underground galleries which are the organs of the big city will work in the same way as organs of the body, without being revealed". Around the same time the sewerage system was introduced in Calcutta, the capital of colonial

India. However, its extension in the country was and remains slow as it is capital-intensive and beyond the resource capacity of the economy even today.

In 1970, realising that sewerage facilities would remain out of the reach of society at large, Sulabh International introduced a pioneer twin-pit pour-flush latrine (TPPF) and human excreta-based biogas plants. Sulabh has constructed in the last 40 years over 1.3 million toilet-cum-bath complexes and 190 human excreta-based biogas plants and is maintaining them. This gives an appropriate solution to dispose of and recycle human waste into fertiliser, electricity and working gas.

The Sulabh experiment is a success story and the technology is well-established and has been successfully functioning for the last 40 years and is financially sustainable. At household level, the TPPF latrine, based on the Sulabh model, has also been a success and is in use in 1.3 million households. It is, however, now necessary to replicate it in India on a mass scale with public pay-and-use toilets with biogas plants at neighbourhood level and the Sulabh TPPF latrine at household level.

Though the challenge to provide toilet facilities has been totally overcome in rich countries, it has still to be met in developing countries like India. The journey of the toilet has ended in Europe and North America but continues in the developing countries.

3.3 THE CURRENT SCENARIO IN INDIA

Probably one of the most dismal records that India has relates to sanitation, especially in rural areas. As per the 1991 Census, a staggering 91 per cent of households in Indian villages did not have toilet facilities! As may be seen from Box 3.1, even at the turn of the century, not much change has taken place in the situation.

It is estimated that by 2051, half of the Indian population will reside in urban settlements, the total number of urban centres will be more than 600 and the contribution of urban settlements to GDP will be around 80 percent. It took nearly 40 years for India's urban population to rise by 230 million. It could take only half the time to add the next 250 million. If not well managed, this inevitable increase in India's urban population will place enormous stress on the system. India seems to suffer from an over-urbanisation syndrome. Already, large-scale urbanisation has imposed a severe strain on urban infrastructure like water supply,

Photo courtesy: https://www.google.co.in

Photo Courtesy: https://www.economist.com/news/asia

road and water transport, health and hygiene, sewerage and sanitation, drainage and solid waste management.

India is looking to ride the wave of development and is aiming to do so at breakneck speed. One major part of such development is expanding the cities. On the flipside, one also needs to consider the fact that India perhaps has the largest amount of people in the world who live in urban areas and yet do not have access to private and thus, safe toilets. This has happened in spite of the fact that the government has placed immense priority on sanitation.

As per a report by a global NGO,[1] the number of people who live in urban spaces without private toilets is estimated at around 157 million. The number of people in urban areas who practise open defecation is 41 million. The report states that due to high population density in the urban areas, diseases can spread in a short span of time. This is especially applicable when proper sanitation facilities are lacking (see Table 3.1 and Map 1).

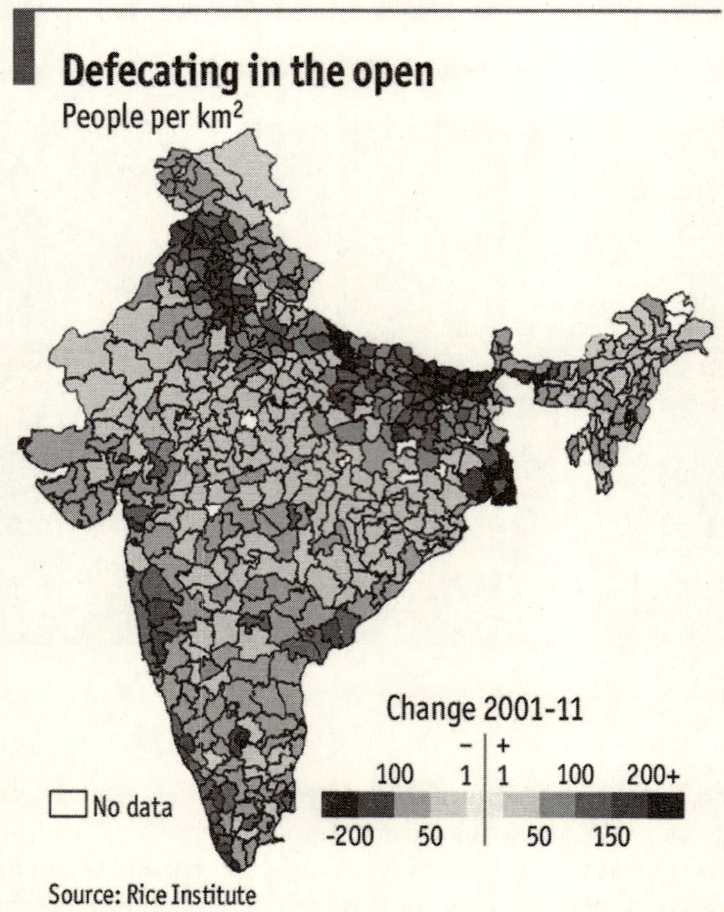

Map 1: Open Defecation in India

The report has mentioned that, at present, India is seeing the biggest migration from rural to urban areas in recent history. In spite of how the government is treating the entire issue of sanitation, the number of people living in urban areas sans sanitation is only going up. Since 2000 this number has increased by 26 million.

It is estimated that approximately 100 million people have no recourse but to relieve themselves in the open. Such people normally use roadsides, plastic bags and railway tracks. "Flying toilets", the infamous euphemism for tying and throwing a poo-filled plastic bag is perhaps the bane of open defecation. The report states that the amount of waste generated through open defecation in the streets of cities and towns in India can easily fill eight Olympic-size swimming pools or 16 jumbo jets every day.

The sanitation ladder

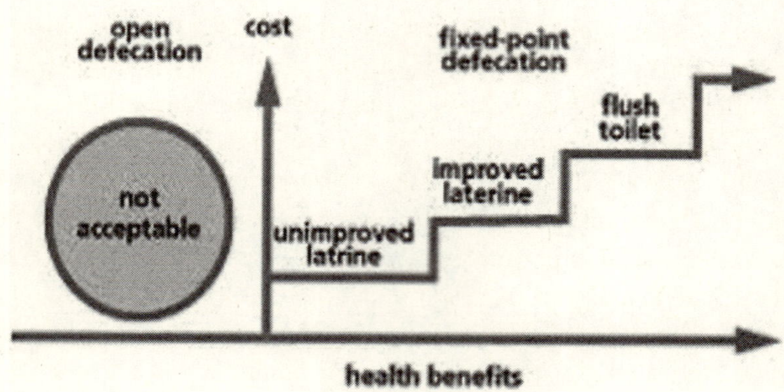

Photo courtesy: https://www.google.co.in/

Table 3.1: India Sanitation Usage

Proportion of population using improved sanitation facilities (%)	40
Proportion of population using shared sanitation facilities (%)	10
Proportion of population using other unimproved sanitation facilities (%)	6
Proportion of population practising open defecation (%)	44

Source: https://data.unicef.org/country/ind/# Accessed 7 December 2017

3.4 WOMEN AND SANITATION

There are strong linkages between access to water, sanitation and hygiene, and gender equality. A gender approach to water and sanitation services refers to assuring that all people, regardless of gender, benefit from and are empowered by improved water and sanitation services and hygiene practices. Due to cultural and historical reasons, women are often the primary collectors, transporters and users of water in developing countries. They tend to have the main responsibility for health, childcare and are managers of domestic water as well as promoters of home and community-based sanitation activities. This division of labour generally results in women's and men's different priorities for water use and management. Yet, in many societies women's views are not systematically represented in decision-making bodies, and gender-based inequalities are often made invisible in debates and cultural norms. Women have accumulated knowledge about water resources, including location, quality and storage methods, as well as insights into common habits and problems within a community, which are important information for programming.

Women experience many motivational drivers for improving sanitation, but it is unclear how women's role in household decision-making affects whether a household opts for better sanitation. Mitsuaki Hirai, Jay P. Graham, and John Sandberg analysed the Kenya Demographic and Health Survey 2008/2009 with a representative sample of 4,556 married and cohabiting women to examine the association between women's decision-making power in relation to that of partners and the type of sanitation facilities used by household members. The independent effects of respondents' education, employment status, and socio-economic status on the type of sanitation facilities were also explored. The direct measurement of women's ability to influence sanitation practice was not available. To address this problem, this study used proxy measures of women's decision-making power in the household. The results of this study revealed that women's decision-making power for major household purchases was positively associated with households having better sanitation ($p < 0.05$). The findings suggest that increased gender equity could potentially have spill-over effects resulting in more households opting to improve their sanitation conditions.

Parimita Routray, Belen Torondel, Thomas Clasen and Wolf-Peter Schmidt conducted a mixed-method study among rural households in

Photo courtesy: http://www.google.co.in

Puri district with 475 randomly selected households. Decisions on the construction of household-level sanitation facilities were made exclusively by the male head in 80 per cent of households; in 11 per cent the decision was made by men who consulted or otherwise involved women. In only 9 per cent of households the decision was made by women. Households where women were more involved in general decision-making processes were no more likely to build a latrine than households where they were excluded from decisions. Qualitative research revealed that women's non-involvement in sanitation decision-making is attributed to their low socio-economic status and inability to influence the household's financial decisions. Female heads lacked confidence to take decisions independently, and were dependent on their spouse or other male family members for most decisions. The study revealed the existence of power hierarchies and dynamics within households, which constrained female participation in decision-making processes regarding sanitation.

Whereas cleaning of toilets is primarily women's responsibility, construction and maintenance of pit latrines (digging, repairing and

Photo courtesy: http://www.google.co.in

exhausting) is primarily done by men. However, in some regions, the task of emptying the latrines falls exclusively on the shoulders of poor women, and the labour conditions under which they do this work are appalling. In many households, women are also responsible for making sure there is sufficient water for sanitation and there are many cases where women have to pay for water from limited household budgets. Despite the role of women in hygiene and sanitation at household level, toilet construction programmes that provide income generation opportunities often presume that only men will be interested in or suited for these tasks. Both women and men need access to cash income and would welcome the potential economic benefits of ecological sanitation and related small entrepreneurships.

Ecological sanitation approaches can only be empowering if both women and men have the possibility to influence the direction of, participate actively in the implementation of, and benefit from these approaches. The chosen solution in most areas of the world is pit latrines. They do not comply with the criteria for sustainable sanitation. Pit latrines tend to be foul smelling and lead to unhygienic conditions. And they pose additional gender problems. In general, women use the pit latrines several times a day whereas men are not similarly dependent on them as they can easily relieve themselves outside. Therefore, men might be less interested in changing the toilet situation.

There is also much disparity between a rural woman and an urban woman as far as sanitation level is concerned. Fundamental knowledge and products for feminine hygiene are still unavailable to women in rural areas. According to a Mumbai-based start-up, 88 per cent of women use unhygienic material such as newspapers, cloth and husk when menstruating; 70 per cent of women suffer reproductive tract infections. However, the notion that sanitation problems are only restricted to women in rural areas is wrong. The average woman living in urban areas disposes of 150 to 200 kg of sanitary napkins, tampons, etc., that eventually find their way into landfills and are burned due to their non-biodegradability. The need for biodegradable menstruation hygiene products is greater than ever. A Pune-based NGO has highlighted the fact that sanitary napkin manufacturers need to include proper disposal measures for used sanitary napkins in order to ensure safety of waste pickers who manually separate waste.

The 2011 Census reveals that only 25.4 per cent households in rural India have bathrooms compared to the 19.7 per cent who do not have a roof over their heads. The remaining 55 per cent has no private bathing space at all, forcing women to bathe in the open. When we study sanitation and hygiene practices, and the health of women in terms of extra workload, we find that 17 per cent of women in rural areas must walk more than half a kilometre to get water from ponds, lakes or rivers for their families and cattle. With so much time and energy spent getting water for basic functions, fetching it for bathing seems like an arduous task. As a result, most women end up bathing at the water source. The situation is worse in areas of Rajasthan, Bihar, Jharkhand and Odisha that are drought-prone or face perennial water shortage. In these states one can realise the multi-faceted problem of bathing in the open. First, hygiene is compromised because when bathing in the open, women end up bathing with their clothes on. Second, the source of bathing water is the same as that for washing clothes, utensils and drinking water resulting in infections and further contamination of the water source. Third, bathing in water bodies has its own dangers in the form of water snakes, quicksand, cattle waste and garbage. Fourth, women become victims of eve-teasing and lewd comments. Even though some communities have ensured dedicated times of the day for women to bathe in public places and are strict about men being spotted around those areas, this is not the case in a majority of communities and does not lessen the need for privacy for women.

While women are tough and find ways to overcome challenges they face due to patriarchal mindsets and neglect for their well-being, they need to have the right to privacy to bathe and use a toilet. In the urban milieu, a 1-BHK is the bare minimum a family should have in terms of shelter. And that unit includes bathroom space, however small. In fact, the government is working to ensure this through multiple schemes of housing for the poor. Under the Swachh Bharat Abhiyan (Gramin), rural families who have access to homes are being motivated to build toilets and use them. Within this gambit, the one aspect that has not received enough attention is private bathing spaces within homes. This is especially a concern from the point of view of women.

During summer, some women carry a bar of soap when they go to work in the fields or to the market. If they find a water body, tap or well, they manage a bath. Some women bathe in groups and catch up on community gossip or share their lives' tales at this time. Some women have a bath at the community well, when the men leave for work in the fields.

This apathy towards the dignity of women regarding access to sanitation and hygiene is more cultural than economic in nature. More rural households have access to mobiles and satellite television today than before. With multiple income generation programmes such as Mahatma Gandhi National Rural Employment Guarantee Act (MGNREGA) and the thrust to improve agricultural output, incomes and consumption are on the rise. A recent report found that rural India spends about three times more on alcohol (₹140) and tobacco (₹196) than healthcare (₹56) each month; and an average of ₹500 (18% of the monthly budget) on fast-moving consumer goods (FMCGs) like food items, soaps, detergents, shampoos and hair oil.

3.5 WHAT NEEDS TO BE DONE?

We, the citizens of India, must examine and explore the situation and needs of sanitation in the country. Also, we need to pay attention to success stories from various regions.

The Swachh Bharat campaign, started by Prime Minister Modi, emphasises the fact that it is only when the cities and towns in India grow in an equitable and sustainable manner that it will help the country be wealthy and healthy in the long run. Planning should be done in such a way that there is absolute priority for providing basic services such as clean water, proper and sustainable management of waste generated through open defecation, and safe sanitation facilities. He also says that in order for this to be achieved popular participation is needed because if people can be made stakeholders by making them understand the importance of all of it, these programmes stand a greater chance of being successful. This is perhaps the sole avenue that can be followed to create a future that is more sustainable and healthier.

The Swachh Bharat Mission offers a 12,000-rupee incentive to below poverty line (BPL) and certain above poverty line (APL) households without a toilet. However, translating the incentive into successful sanitation improvements has been a challenge. Innovative and customisable ways, ideas and processes are needed to ensure community buy-in and achieve greater ownership of the process and high rates of toilet use in an environmentally safe manner.

Chhattisgarh has seen great successes ending open defecation and ensuring usage of toilets. With two districts and over 50 blocks declared ODF, Chhattisgarh has also shown strong commitments to community-led processes and has seen a number of innovations, one among them being the Community Incentive Method. This method has evolved to meet the specific requirements of the state and has shown promise especially in areas where there is a mix of households who are eligible and those ineligible for the incentive. Through this method, Chhattisgarh has paved the path for many more districts, states both in terms of innovations around the incentive as well as to customise solutions for the state.

In April 2015, Nadia in West Bengal was declared the first ODF district in India. The Sabar Shouchagar campaign has been working to achieve this goal since 2013. Sabar Shouchagar has received numerous awards, including the United Nations Public Service Award in 2015. Its approach to realising an open defecation-free district is being hallmarked as "an emerging and inspiring district level model for eliminating open defecation in India". Following public forums with elected representatives and key interest groups, district leadership came together to launch the innovative "Sabar Shouchagar" (Toilets for All) movement on 2 October 2013. The new initiative was developed with the mandate to

- generate mass awareness for adopting improved sanitation and hygiene practices for collective behavioural change and eliminating open defecation
- improve access to sanitary toilets and stop open defecation; and
- improve health outcomes through improved sanitation.

Sabar Shouchagar identifies the complexity of sanitation and behavioural change in strategic priorities. The workplan was developed around strong monitoring and evaluation, mass community mobilisation and participation (particularly of women, children and faith-based organisations), increasing the efficiency of sanitation services with innovation and building capacity, promoting partnerships, creating an enabling environment with policy and advocacy, improving access to sanitation and prioritising equity, and finally, reforming financing for sanitation. Sabar Shouchagar has lessons learnt to share:

- Community involvement is the key to making a programme successful
- Every stakeholder's contribution matters
- Women's participation is a game-changer
- Convergence of available funding resources generates synergy, supports the realisation of basic sanitation, and increases demand

- There is no substitute for intense monitoring! Monitoring helps judge the status of implementation, and is vital for informed decision-making.

3.6 RURAL INFRASTRUCTURAL ISSUES IN INDIA (WITH REFERENCE TO SANITATION)

The new millennium is progressing fast and, almost a decade since the reforms began, a meagre 9 per cent of the rural population has been covered by some form of sanitation. This is infrastructure of utmost urgency and no time can be wasted over such issues as whether there exists a demand for it, whether class and caste factors prevail upon the decision to possess and use such facilities. In a country where the rural infant mortality rate has remained as high as 38 per 1,000 live births (2016 report by the Registrar General of India) and a major cause of mortality is diarrhoeal disease (occurs mostly due to oral faecal infection), sanitation remains the crucial option. It is rather unfortunate that even when Indian scholars and planners debated for decades over rural poverty and its correlates, one hardly comes across a study that has undertaken careful analysis of the pathetic performance in rural sanitation (this despite valuable data being made available in the National Sample Survey Office (NSSO), Census and other rural development data sources).

Notwithstanding the dearth of studies in this field, especially relating to demand for and willingness to pay in the rural Indian context, it will be worthwhile to consider provision of household-level facilities rather than common toilets. In the case of common toilet arrangements in urban and semi-urban areas, mostly through the very successful Sulabh International effort, the facility is mainly used by a non-resident and transient population. However, in rural areas, at a residential level, such a concept will be difficult to operationalise. In fact, maintenance on a regular basis will remain the most ticklish issue to handle.

In an extensive field survey-based study by Das and Visaria in 1998, concerning evaluation of an intervention under the Integrated Rural Sanitation Programme in north Gujarat, it was learnt that most beneficiary households reported the use of the latrine facility by all members of the household. What is interesting to note, however, is that among the reasons given for the use of the facility, hygienic considerations did not receive prime attention. Whereas this could be reflective of laxity in efforts at IEC (information, education and communication), the clear preference for the facility, presumably, indicates that once a facility is created its advantages begin to be recognised and it gets used. This was an instance of hardware-induced change in sanitation practices.

The provision of latrines under this scheme for some households generated a high demand among the non-beneficiaries for them. Nearly 90 per cent of those surveyed indicated their willingness to have latrines constructed. About 40 per cent wanted some subsidy but the rest were willing to pay the full cost themselves, although opting for a variety of modes of payment. The spokespersons of the nodal agency also confirmed this observation and indicated that they had been approached by non-beneficiary households for toilet components, design and possible subsidies. Such demand was articulated by all households regardless of socio-economic status. Also, contrary to popular belief, there was no social inhibition about having a latrine within one's house. However, for some who face the space constraints, provision of community latrines on common village land, although attractive, is not an effective solution because of the problems with regard to maintenance and the sharing of responsibilities.

It seems possible that in future similar projects can be viably implemented on almost self-financing basis. Therefore, creation of a revolving fund or establishment of a sanitary mart, where latrine components can be made available at reasonable price and on instalment basis, may also promote the adoption of sanitary facilities among many segments of the people. However, the problem remains for those poor households who do not have enough land for constructing the toilets. Whether inexpensive or free land provisioning is possible is a matter that needs attention. As private investment would certainly be disinterested in this sphere, the State has to devise mechanisms to address this issue.

- In rural areas each block of villages has a primary health centre (PHC). Each PHC has a male and a female doctor, sanitary inspectors, health visitors, vaccinations, midwives and compounders. Each centre has its own dispensary and three sub-centres in a block. One of its functions: Rural sanitation and hygiene with emphasis on popularisation of sanitary latrines, composting of refuse, etc.

- Community development programmes, being based on the principle of self-help, can be organised without waiting for help from the government. Community health programmes can thus have a quick start. These programmes include improved sanitation, cleaning of drains, prevention of breeding of mosquitoes and houseflies, inspection of food articles sold to the public, keeping the environment clean, involving adolescents and adults, and arranging lectures and talks by specialists on topics pertaining to health and disease. What is positive in community endeavours is that involvement of the people in matters that concern them can be ensured. In Karnataka, most NGOs e.g., The Shri Kshethra Dharmasthala Rural Development Project (SKRDP) in Dakshina Kannada are very active in this regard.

3.7 EVOLUTION OF SANITATION IN INDIA

Most of the technological developments relevant to water supply and wastewater date back more than 5,000 years ago. These developments were driven by the necessity to make efficient use of natural resources, to make civilisations more resistant to destructive natural elements, and to improve the standards of life, both at public and private levels. Major human settlements could initially develop only where fresh surface water was plentiful, such as near rivers or natural springs. Throughout history, people have devised systems to make getting water into their communities and households, and disposing (and later also treating) wastewater more convenient. The historical focus of sewage treatment was on the conveyance of raw sewage to a natural body of water, e.g., a river or ocean, where it would be satisfactorily diluted and dissipated. Early human habitations were often built next to water. Historically, Indian society has given high priority to sanitation. Excavations at the Indus Valley civilisation sites including Harappa (3300-1900 BC) reveal ingenious solutions to facilitate wastewater conveyance through underground drainage systems. The Indus Valley civilisation in Asia (Bronze Age) shows early evidence of public water supply and sanitation. The system the Indus Valley civilisation developed and managed included a number of advanced features. A typical example is the Indus city of Lothal (ca. 2350 BC). Rivers would often double as a crude form of natural sewage disposal. Harappan houses had private toilets and public baths. During the Mohenjo-Daro era, however, only the affluent had access to toilets, while most people would squat over open pits to defecate.

Burnt clay bricks were used to construct drains. The bricks had holes to pass down the waste. For urination people would use small pits dug in the ground. With the decline of the Indus Valley civilisation, these toilets were forgotten and people went back to open defecation.

Sanitary engineering, as far back as 5,000 years ago, was at a developed stage. Such visions on improved sanitary practices continued across the reign of various dynasties like the Mauryas, Guptas and the southern kingdom of Vijayanagara that ruled the subcontinent. Even from an ideological point of view, various social reformers of India propagated the importance of sanitation. From Patanjali's philosophy to the writings of Vivekananda and the Gandhian concept of sanitation, the emphasis on sanitation was integral to India's cultural foundation.

Though built on a history of understanding the relevance of sanitation, marginal concern was accorded to it among human settlements developed in the pre-Independence period under British rule. Issues of governance were dealt with through the lens of Britain's experience in India. For instance, when rampant outbreaks of cholera and plague were affecting the health of British Army personnel, it invoked the intervention of establishing improvement trusts to clean up cities, the first of which was the Bombay Improvement Trust in 1898. The trust was given an institutional mandate, which was lost post-Independence.

It was in 1986 that the government launched the Central Rural Sanitation Programme (CRSP), the first nationwide sanitation programme. Several other major sanitation programmes have been launched since then such as the Nirmal Bharat Abhiyan (NBA) in rural India, and Basic Services to Urban Poor (BSUP), under the Jawaharlal Nehru National Urban Renewal Mission, in urban India. Though sanitation was historically and culturally rooted in India even today 48 per cent of the country's population defecates in the open. Open defecation is not a rural phenomenon, considering India contributes 46 per cent of global open defecation in urban areas. Gender-related issues exist with 70 per cent of crimes against women occurring due to defecation in the open.

Major Milestones

- 1986—CRSP to improve the quality of life of the rural people and also to provide privacy and dignity to women
- 1999—Total Sanitation Campaign, demand-driven, including large IEC component
- 2003—Nirmal Gram Puraskar, award for 100 per cent sanitation
- 2012—Nirmal Bharat Abhiyan, community-led and people-centred approach; IEC; solid and liquid waste management
- 2014—The Swachh Bharat Abhiyan campaign
- 2015—49,01,277 household toilets constructed (FY 2014-15)
- 2016—The total number of households with toilets reached 8,33,44,188
- 2017—Out of total 679 districts in India, 150 districts declared ODF
- 2018—296 districts declared ODF[2]
- 2019—To achieve a Swachh Bharat, as a fitting tribute to Mahatma Gandhi on his 150th birth anniversary.

The CRSP was formulated in 1986 with the objective of providing 80 per cent subsidy for construction of individual sanitary latrines for BPL households on a demand basis. The CRSP was restructured in 1999, with a shift from a high subsidy to a low subsidy model. The supply-driven approach was altered to a demand-driven model with increased emphasis on public participation. In 2001 the CRSP was overhauled with the introduction of the Total Sanitation Campaign (TSC), which carried forward the demand-driven approach focusing on awareness building.

As a fillip to the TSC, the Nirmal Gram Puraskar (NGP) was launched to recognise the achievements and efforts of gram panchayats towards full sanitation coverage. In 2007 the TSC was renamed the Nirmal Bharat Abhiyan. The NBA envisages facilitating individual household toilets for BPL and identified APL households and providing school and community level sanitation. The NBA has now been converged with the Mahatma Gandhi National Rural Employment Guarantee Scheme (MGNREGS) to facilitate rural households with fund availability for creating their sanitation facilities. It was not until the inception of the National Urban Sanitation Policy (NUSP) in 2008 that urban sanitation was allotted focused attention at the national level. The NUSP instituted a framework for cities to prepare city sanitation plans under the scheme of a State Sanitation Strategy. Urban sanitation awards and ratings were also introduced based on the benchmarking of sanitation services.

3.8 SANITATION CRISIS

Aarti Kelkar-Khambete, in a post on India Water Portal (18-4-2012), points out that recent evidence indicates that India is heading towards a major sanitation crisis in the coming years. Efforts made at meeting the sanitation challenges have been found to have very limited results, with as high as 65 per cent of the population not having toilet facilities coupled with very low use of existing toilets in urban and rural areas. It is perhaps the right time to critically evaluate and move beyond the excessive focus we have on "provision" and pay attention to the underlying complexities of the mechanisms involved, that influence sanitation behaviour among people. If we don't do so, we stand the risk of "missing all the trees for the forest", i.e., missing the social and economic dimensions of the sanitation needs of the people, in the hurry to count the number of toilets provided.

According to the census of 2011, 53.1 per cent (63.6% in 2001) of households in India do not have a toilet, with the percentage being as high as 69.3 per cent (78.1% in 2001) in rural areas and 18.6 per cent (26.3% in 2001) in urban areas. Within India, among the different states, Jharkhand tops the list with as many as 77 per cent of homes having no toilet facilities, while the figure is 76.6 per cent for Odisha and 75.8 per cent for Bihar. All three are among India's poorest states with huge populations that live on less than ₹50 a day. In addition to more than half of Indian homes having no toilets within their premises, access to water supply and drainage facilities is another serious problem. For example, two-thirds of Indian homes have no drinking water facility from a treated tap source, and four-fifths are devoid of closed drainage connectivity for discharge of wastewater. Only 47 per cent have the source of water within the premises. A good 36 per cent of households still have to fetch water from a source located within 500 metres in rural areas and 100 metres in urban areas.

This has a significant impact on sanitation and hygiene practices and the health of women in terms of extra workload and evidence indicates that 17 per cent of women in rural areas have to walk more than half a km to get water for their families and for their cattle, and 55 per cent of them are forced to bathe in the open because they do not have any private bathing facilities. The situation is even worse in areas which are drought-prone or face perennial water shortage such as the Bundelkhand region in Uttar Pradesh and states like Rajasthan, Bihar, Jharkhand and Odisha.

Manual scavenging is still widespread in India. Over 1 per cent of all households in both urban as well as rural areas continue to rely even today on this practice. Evidence indicates that there are 7.94 lakh dry latrines in the country and excreta is regularly cleaned by scavengers. In over 13 lakh toilets, the waste is flushed into open drains and cleaned by humans. Around 25 crore households, nearly 12 crore in rural areas and 13 crore in urban areas, depend on manual scavengers to remove night soil from the toilets. In Jammu & Kashmir, 8.9 per cent of households still have their toilets emptied by manual scavengers.

The officials from the Ministry of Drinking Water and Sanitation, Government of India, have admitted that although a lot is being done by the government (like doubling the budget for this sector), to tackle the problem of sanitation, and although efforts are yielding positive results, a lot still remains to be done, looking at the needs of the population.

A lot of confusion exists in terms of the reliability of the information available. For example, the Ministry of Drinking Water and Sanitation claims 74 per cent sanitation coverage in the urban areas of the country while the Joint Monitoring Programme quotes 39 per cent and the census report puts sanitation coverage at 30.7 percent, which is less than half of the figure presented by the ministry.

Even in the case of rural sanitation, the ministry claims that the coverage is 53 per cent whereas the Joint Monitoring Programme and census data keep the figure at 33 per cent and 30 percent, respectively. The Ministry of Drinking Water and Sanitation claims that in states like Uttar Pradesh and Madhya Pradesh only 31.7 per cent and 34.8 per cent of the population respectively lacks sanitation facilities. However, according to the Census data, 78 per cent of the population in Uttar Pradesh and 86.9 per cent of the population in Madhya Pradesh does not have access to sanitation facilities. The ministry claims that only 23.4 per cent of people do not have sanitation coverage in Tamil Nadu, while the Census data reports that 76.8 per cent of people lack sanitation coverage in the state.

A number of factors have been found to play an important role in determining toilet use. Sticking to the toilet-using habit depends on construction aspects such as a good and well-maintained, user-friendly structure that protects privacy, has availability of water and where the owners are aware of the benefits of good sanitation.

Experience regarding the use of public toilets in urban areas of the country has also identified that a number of factors have been found to lead to poor use of toilets. These include:

- Absence of mechanisms to maintain the toilets
- Lack of plumbing and drainage facilities
- Lack of water, lack of adequate and systematically designed sewage systems
- Inadequate mechanisms to maintain these sewage pipelines
- Absence of grievance redressal mechanisms
- Poor consideration of gender-based factors such as security concerns, extra charges for women and lack of attention to accessibility factors such as a separate entrance for women have further led to reduced use of toilets among women

Just making laws for preventing manual scavenging might not help, unless they are coupled with efforts that eliminate the very need for the shameful practice of manual scavenging through use of modern and appropriate technologies for toilets, and sewage collection and processing systems, ensuring adequate water supply, and importantly, changing the sanitation behaviour of people based on building awareness and responsibility in the community. Evidence also suggests that there cannot be blanket centralised solutions for all parts of the country. There are significant differences among urban and rural populations in terms of the attitudes, perceptions, resources available, local needs as well as those of states and which need to be taken into consideration while meeting the sanitation needs of the people. It has now been realised that there is a need to focus on what can be called software or addressing a range of factors that affect demand generation of toilets among people, which is as important as the hardware or, in other words, social engineering as much as conventional construction.

The outlines of the new rural development policy that focuses on 2022 as the new target date for ODF India has been set and includes a much larger budget, more than double the hardware subsidy to individual households, removing positive discrimination towards poorer households, and decentralisation of funds at the gram panchayat level. The focus is on achieving ODF communities, rather than toilets constructed, which is a welcome step.

3.9 TOILET AS A TOOL OF CHANGE—SOCIAL AND TECHNOLOGICAL

"No power if you go in the open," sub-divisional officer tells villagers in Bhilwara district in Rajasthan, India (*The Hindu*, 21 August 2017).

Notwithstanding the fact that open defecation remains a critical health challenge in India, one has to be cautious about the disastrous psychological impact of incidents such as above, which are on the rise recently. Under the pressure of targets, many resort to the easy option of coercion, humiliation and threat. Behaviour Change Communication to address open defecation in India is half-cooked and needs deeper understanding of a contextual behavioural change ecosystem.

Until now, the dominant behaviour change models of open defecation inter alia hinge on "reflective drivers" such as pride, shame, rationality and social norms. Based on the framework popularised by Kahneman, these factors are "System 2" drivers of behaviour, which are relatively automatic cue drivers and motivational factors. In a recent paper titled "Nudging and habit change in the context of open defecation", Neal, et al. (2016) have brought together a set of "system 1" principles to augment open defecation behaviour change. These factors include people's hygiene habits, e.g., mindlessly repeated behaviour cued by context and "nudges", i.e., small changes to the environment that can channel decision-making and behaviour in new ways. Thus, the most challenging behavioural change problems will invariably require a set of targeted System 1 and System 2 variables working in unison.

Behavioural change involves both adoption of new behaviour and at the same time curbing a prior pattern. To override and alter dominant response tendencies, people must possess a sufficient degree of self-regulatory strength, which is a limited yet renewable cognitive resource. External force, coercion or regulation can severely undermine or drain that same self-regulatory strength, which is the primary cause of behavioural slippage and relapses. Creating a favourable behavioural change ecosystem where the behavioural traits have the DNA to self-assemble will augment self-regulatory strength.

Technology plays an important role in behavioural change.[3] In the case of sanitation from simple technology to the most modern, every single phase and every unit of sanitation device has contributed to sanitation habits and progress:

- Garderobes
- Sewerage Systems
- Public Water Supply
- Pit Toilets
- Squat Toilets
- Dry Toilets
- High-tech Toilets
- Bamboo Toilets
- Nano Membrane Toilets
- Eco Scan Toilets
- Chamber Pots
- Drainage Systems
- Urinals, Baths
- Flush Toilets
- Chemical Toilets
- Portable Toilets
- Floating Toilets
- Safi Choo (made of plastic) Toilets
- Bio-digester Toilets

Hence, achieving ODF and sustaining new habits requires priming of the self-regulatory strength at individual and societal levels, devoid of threat or coercion. Ending open defecation by disrupting sticky behaviour through leveraging self-assembly behavioural principles has enormous potential.

The Sulabh International Social Service Organisation (SISSO) has engineered an innovative, affordable and environment-friendly toilet that has helped over one million marginalised people in India. Understanding that traditions take time to evolve and require initiative from all members of society, Sulabh has implemented the concept of "social adoption." The non-profit organisation encourages citizens to formally and publicly adopt a Balmiki family. The pairs of families closely interact and visit each other's homes. At times, the adopting family helps the adopted family to overcome social adjustment problems. Adopters are typically persons of high social standing and prestige, and so their approach and interaction become an example for others to reinforce the integration of the Balmikis into mainstream society.

Along with adopters and non-adopters we must also take into consideration aggregators i.e., sanitation programmes. They must solve important customer problems and thereby increase demand for sanitation solutions. Programmes need to start differentiating between the existing market demand (customers that would anyway have invested in sanitation irrespective of the programme) and the new demand a programme creates by solving a customer problem.

Other actors include enablers (government bodies), supporters (financing institutions), implementers (sanitation micro-entrepreneurs) and customers (rural households). Understanding the roles, strengths and weaknesses of each stakeholder, how they interact and complement each other is and complement each other, was key to achieving India's ambitious goal of ending open defecation by 2019.

Sanitation programmes also need to look at the range of interdependent problems that affect adoption of sanitation solutions. For example, if water is a problem in a particular area, this needs to be addressed simultaneously with sanitation.

Today, 1.2 million Sulabh household toilets have been constructed and 54 million government toilets constructed, based on the Sulabh design. There are over 8,000 Sulabh community toilet blocks in the country and 10.5 million people use toilets based on the Sulabh design daily. As a result, Balmikis are not condemned to their traditional role in 640 towns.

Sulabh has also constructed 200 biogas plants all over the country. The simple production of biogas from public toilets and recycling and reuse of waste is a breakthrough in the field of sanitation and community health.

It is important to support social enterprises and encourage the business community to continue working to improve the health of society, which is why Women Deliver had organised a Social Enterprise Challenge in 2016 in Copenhagen.

3.9.1 Sulabh Toilets

Seven conditions of a sanitary latrine laid down by the WHO:

- The surface soil should not be contaminated.
- There should be no contamination of groundwater that may enter springs or wells.
- There should be no contamination of surface water.
- Excreta should not be accessible to flies or animals.
- There should be no handling of fresh excreta; or, when this is indispensable, it should be kept to a strict minimum.
- There should be freedom from odours or unsightly conditions.

Sulabh is popularising the two-pit pour-flush toilet and tent toilets. The Sulabh flush compost toilet is eco-friendly, technically appropriate, socio-culturally acceptable and economically affordable. It is an indigenous technology and the toilet can easily be constructed by local labour and materials. It provides health benefits by safe disposal of human excreta on-site. It consists of a pan with a steep slope of 25° to 28° and a specially designed trap with 20 mm water seal requiring only 1 to 1.5 litres of water for flushing, thus helping conserve water. It does not need scavengers to clean the pits. There are two pits of varying size and capacity, depending on the number of users. The capacity of each pit is normally designed for three years' usage. Both pits are used, alternately. When one pit is full, the incoming excreta is diverted into the second pit. In about two years, the sludge gets digested and is almost dry and pathogen-free, thus safe for handling as manure. Digested sludge is odourless and is a good manure and soil conditioner. It can be dug out easily and used for agricultural purposes. The cost of emptying the pit can be met partially from the cost of manure made available. The Sulabh toilet can also be constructed on the upper floors of buildings. It has a high potential for upgradation, and can later be easily connected to sewers when introduced in the area. Sulabh has so far constructed over a million individual household toilets in different parts of the country.

Tent toilets are an ingenious way to tackle the problem of open defecation. They are not only portable but also easy to set up. The waste is collected in a biodegradable bag that contains ChemiSan, a material that helps to deodorise and decompose the waste.

Advantages of Sulabh Toilets

- Hygienically and technically appropriate, and socio-culturally acceptable.
- Affordable and easy to construct with locally available materials.
- Design and specifications can be modified to suit the householder's needs and affordability.
- Eliminates mosquitos, insects and fly breeding.
- Can be constructed in different physical, geological and hydro-geological conditions.
- Free from health hazards and does not pollute surface or groundwater, if proper precautions and safeguards are taken during construction.
- Can be located within the premises as it is free from foul smell and fly/mosquito nuisance, etc.

- Can be constructed on upper floors of houses.
- Pits are generally designed for three-year desludging interval, but if desired, it can be designed for longer periods or can be reduced to two years.
- Maintenance is easy, simple and costs very little.
- Needs only 1 to 1.5 litres of water for flushing, while a conventional flush toilet needs 12 to 14 litres of water.
- Needs less space than a septic tank toilet system.
- Does not need scavengers for cleaning the pits or disposal of sludge. This can be done by the householder.
- Makes available rich fertiliser and soil conditioner.
- Can be easily connected to sewers when introduced in the area.
- A low-volume flushing cistern can be attached to avoid pour flushing.

The Sulabh flush compost toilet does not cause water pollution. When constructed in homogeneous soil, horizontally, bacteria do not travel more than three metres, and vertically the seepage is not more than one metre. To this is to be added the precaution that the toilet is built at a safe distance from the source of water, keeping the above points in mind. If there is a tubewell or hand pump sunk, the first joint should be lower than the limit of the vertical seepage. No vent pipe is needed since the gas gets absorbed in the soil facing the chamber, as the brick lining inside is in lattice formation. The parameters change depending upon the coarseness of the soil and the type of terrain where the toilet is being constructed. Depending on the availability of space, the shape of pits may be designed. It may be rectangular, circular or linear in shape. It fulfils all the seven conditions of a sanitary latrine laid down by the WHO.

3.10 PUBLIC-PRIVATE PARTNERSHIP

The PPP Knowledge Lab defines a public-private partnership (PPP) as "a long-term contract between a private party and a government entity, for providing a public asset or service, in which the private party bears significant risk and management responsibility, and remuneration is linked to performance".

For governments seeking to expand infrastructure, the PPP offers an option that lies somewhere between public procurement and privatisation. Ideally, it brings private sector competencies, efficiencies

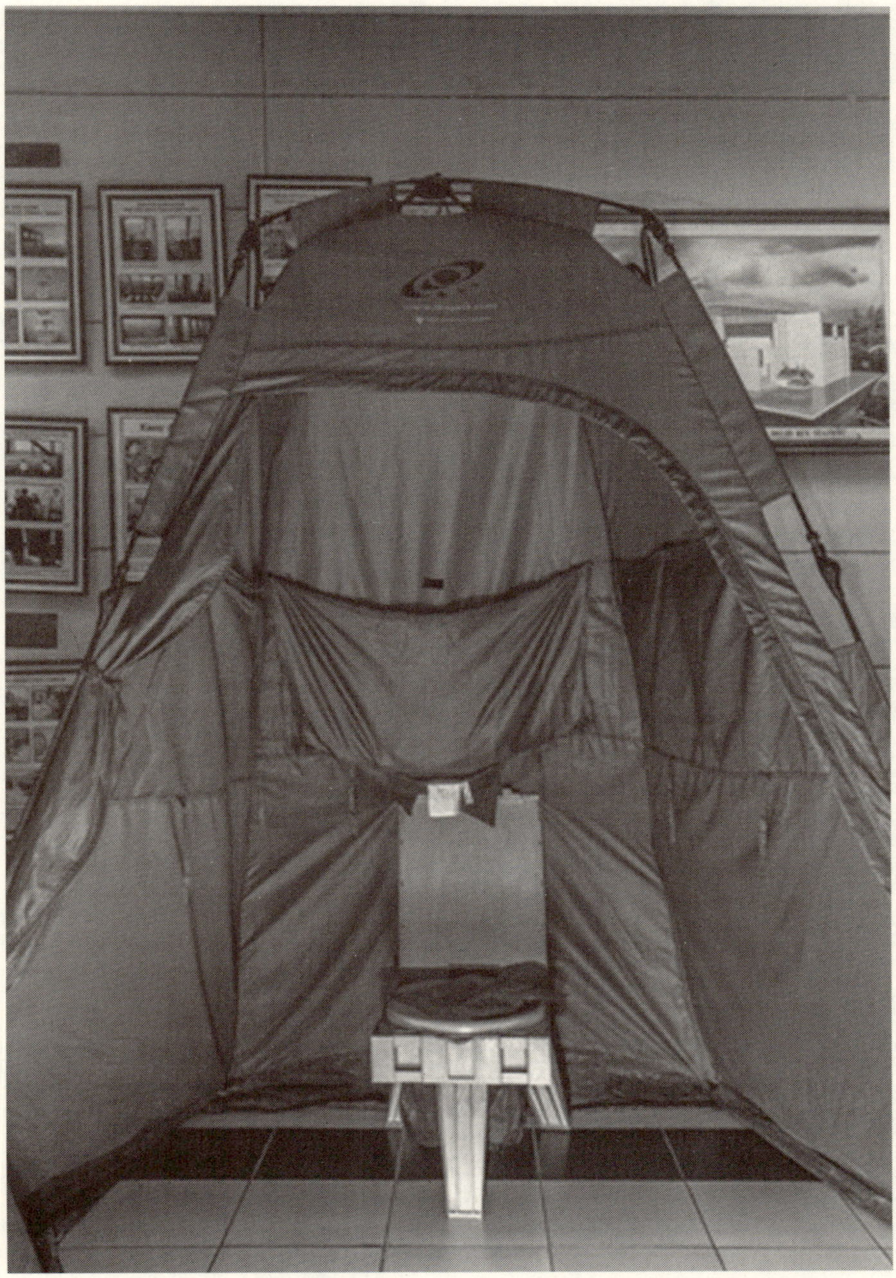

Sulabh Tent Toilet

Source: Sulabh International Toilet Museum

and capital to improving public assets or services when governments lack the upfront cash. Companies agree to take on risk and management responsibility in exchange for profits linked to performance.

PPPs are partnerships between the public sector and the private sector for the purposes of designing, planning, financing, constructing and/or operating projects which would be regarded traditionally as falling within the remit of the public sector. Infrastructure projects such as roads and bridges are prime examples.

A PPP can be viewed also as a means of delivering a service and not merely an asset enabling the service to be delivered. A key objective of a PPP is to allocate risk to the person best placed to manage and deal with the particular risk. Certain risks may be more effectively managed by the private sector rather than the public sector.

The private sector has always been involved in the water sector in some form or other, from tendering for construction contracts in large urban supplies to the informal provision of vended water in unserved areas. However, a new role is currently being negotiated globally. Three terms have been used (often interchangeably) to describe this new role:

- Privatisation: This term was commonly used towards the end of the 1980s to describe the increase in private involvement; in this chapter it refers to the full handover of assets (or divestiture) to the private sector.
- Private sector participation (PSP): PSP refers to the role that the private sector can play in the delivery of services. There are varying degrees of private sector involvement from service contracts to concessions.
- Public-private partnership: PPP acknowledges the key role that both the public and private sectors have in service provision. The term is becoming increasingly popular as it emphasises the need for partnerships to maximise the benefits which both sectors can contribute.

PPP is carried out by institutions which have elements of both public and private involvement. The two main methods of operation are:

1. Corporatisation: Public utilities are formed as autonomous commercial enterprises with a board of directors. It remains in public ownership. This is often the model put forward in opposition to full PPP.

2. Public-private joint ventures: This involves the formation of a separate corporate entity, with responsibility shared between public and private interests. Responsibilities, representation, finance and profits are all agreed beforehand. This is what is traditionally referred to when PPP is mentioned. These PPPs range from service contracts to full divestiture, with an increasing level of private involvement and control.

"Infrastructure is difficult for the public sector to get right," notes the World Bank. "Public-private partnerships can help; they can provide more efficient procurement, focus on consumer satisfaction and life cycle maintenance, and provide new sources of investment." At the same time, PPPs typically cost more than straightforward public procurement: they only attract investors if the public pays both for the project and a profit for the private partners.

Research on PPPs published in the journal *Sustainability* traces the model back to 15th-century Italian city-states. Today, researchers say, the model is effective for high-cost, high-visibility projects that involve social and technical complexities, with the potential to build in synergies, develop competencies, and create an effective framework for alliances and cooperation, especially when community stakeholders and experts are involved from the start.

PPPs are an important tool for developing infrastructure and therefore fostering economic development. They are used with infrastructure like roads, airports, ports, power, water and solid waste treatment and typically involve investment, and operation and maintenance. PPPs are also used in social infrastructure like health and education, e.g., construction and maintenance of a hospital or school facilities, but can also include total or partial clinical or education services.

In an infrastructure-intensive sector, improving access and service quality to meet the SDGs cannot be done without massive investment. Around the developing world, the water sector is chronically underfunded and inefficient. In this context, PPPs can be a mechanism (among others) to help governments fund much needed investment and bring technology and efficiency that can improve the performance and financial sustainability of the water sector.

Governments are using PPPs in the water and sanitation sector increasingly to finance and operate bulk water supply and wastewater treatment. Governments turn to PPPs to introduce new technology and innovation where traditional sources are being scarce, such as in desalination and water reuse. Utilities are drawing on specific expertise, such as non-revenue water reduction and pressure management, to bring efficiencies and service improvements. Private investors and providers are increasingly local and regional, increasing competition and bringing down prices. Since the 1990s, China has emerged as one of the world's most active markets for PPPs in water and sanitation, while in India the private sector has played a rather limited role in the water sector. From 2001 to 2012, there were 237 PPP projects in water and sanitation in China, accounting for 40 per cent of the total number of such projects globally, and the Chinese population served by private water companies increased from merely 8 per cent in 1989 to 38 per cent in 2008. Development of PPPs in the water sector in India during the same period was insignificant.

There is potential for PPPs in any sector. Interesting examples are agriculture and social housing. Regarding agriculture, in countries where government institutions have an important role in food security, such as India or Pakistan, PPPs can be introduced.

The Indian economy has been delivering strong economic growth across most sectors for the last few years. However, to achieve inclusive and sustainable growth, it is vital to develop the country's infrastructure, such as power, water, roads, ports, airports, urban bus and metro lines, health and education facilities. Infrastructure demand was expected to go up to US$1 trillion under India's twelfth Five-Year Plan (2012-17). The Government of India has therefore focused on developing several enabling tools and activities to spur private sector investments in the country through PPPs. These are vital for catalysing investments in new infrastructure, and for efficient operation and maintenance of assets, existing and new, over their lifetime and ensuring focus on service delivery. Civil society organisations also have a role in mobilising awareness among communities, building their capacity (through self-help groups), developing alternative models of service delivery, and strengthening local supply chains for water and sanitation services.

In India, virtually all water and wastewater systems are currently managed by the public sector, and most fail to meet the needs of citizens or businesses they serve. Enlisting the private sector in the water sector brings finance, reduces waste, and lowers costs when supported by effective governance and transparency. It is not public versus private but the public and private sectors and civil society that need to come together to ensure access to drinking water and sanitation for all, says a report on urban water. The report finds that successful PPP projects have benefitted from a combination of public funding, specialised project expertise and ownership, support from diverse stakeholders, strong demand for the project, reduced revenue risk and high degree of interest among private operators for the project. Meanwhile, the most important risk is associated with lack of specificity in contracts or of shifting targets once contracts had been awarded. Standardised provisions in contracts would help create common understanding among all parties about the technical, operational and financial risks to address in an urban water management PPP.

Mainstreaming PPPs in India is a joint programme of the Asian Development Bank (ADB) and the government, through India's Department of Economic Affairs. Since 2006, the ADB has been supporting the programme through seven technical assistance projects:

- 40243-012: Mainstreaming PPPs at state level
- 41575-012: Mainstreaming PPPs in ministries of the Government of India
- 42510-012: Supporting an initiative for mainstreaming PPPs for providing urban amenities in rural areas
- 41643-012: Preparing the PPPs Pilot Projects Initiative (mainstreaming PPPs)
- 43013-012: Assisting in framework development for mainstreaming PPPs
- 42271-012: Sustaining the Government of India-ADB initiative for mainstreaming PPPs
- 42272-012: Deepening capacity building for mainstreaming PPPs.

Examples:

- The Tirupur project (Tamil Nadu) is a great example of how private sector involvement in public service delivery can dramatically improve access to water and sanitation. Started in the 1990s, it is now providing water and sewerage services to thousands of Tirupur residents.
- Navi Mumbai near Mumbai has shown how to improve water and sanitation services by using performance-based contracts to

manage the water distribution and transmission system. The results are astonishing. Revenues increased by almost 45 per cent the year following the introduction of the new contracts! The city was also able to reduce unnecessary expenditure over a two-year period. The city reduced its annual energy consumption by ₹45 lakh on sewerage contracts alone. Significantly, customer complaints to the utility decreased to almost zero. Performance-based contracts allowed the utility not only to provide better service to its customers, but also at lower operational costs.

3.10.1 PPP Model of Sanitation

The public sector might not be able to cope with the challenges regarding sanitation and management and therefore cooperates with the private sector through a "partnership".

Building PPPs is one possible step when building an institutional framework for sanitation and water management in diverse ways (see Table 3.2). More information on building an institutional framework for sanitation and water management might help to get an overview of what else can be done. In general, sanitation and water management can be in public hands (say, nationalisation), or in private hands (say, privatisation) or a mix of both (i.e., PPPs).

Making water and sanitation services accessible for everyone was one of the main targets of the MDGs. It is also the core responsibility of both national and local governments to satisfy the legitimate (human) rights of all citizens and safeguard the interests of the poor. In this regard, governments are increasingly seeking professional expertise through various forms of PPPs, which are expected to significantly contribute to achieving local and national objectives in affordable ways. PPPs are thus one institutional option to cope with the challenges of water and sanitation services, and they take part in the process to enable the environment for sustainable sanitation and water management.

PPPs are applicable in urban areas (including slums and informal settlements), small towns and rural areas, as long as a serious private partner can be found. PPPs do not necessarily have to take over a big part of sanitation and water management. Contracts can also be made for small, specific sectors, so their applicability is good on a local level.

Table 3.2 : Types of PPP Contracts in the Water & Sanitation Sector

Contract Type	*Description*	*Examples*
Cooperatives	They can position themselves to be the service providers for certain (often poorer, informal) areas of a city and manage facilities in these areas. Often used in rural areas, in conjunction with NGOs.	Port-au-Prince, Haiti; Orangi, Pakistan
Service Contracts	Public authority retains overall responsibility for the operation and maintenance (O&M) of the system, and contracts out specific components. Service contracts last 1-3 years and include services such as meter reading, billing and maintenance.	Mexico City; Santiago, Chile; Chennai, India
Management Contracts	Public authority transfers responsibility for the management of a full range of activities within a specific field, such as O&M. Remuneration is based on key performance indicators. Public authority typically finances working and investment capital and determines cost recovery policy. Usually contracts last between three and five years.	Cartagena, Colombia; Gdansk, Poland; Mali; Johannesburg, South Africa
Lease contracts	Private operator rents the facilities from a public authority and is responsible for O&M of the complete system and tariff collection. Lessor effectively buys the right to the revenue stream and thus shares significant commercial risk. Usually 5-15 years.	Côte d'Ivoire; Guinea; Czech Republic
BOT (Build Operate, Transfer)	Usually used to procure large discrete items of infrastructure e.g., water treatment plants that require significant finance. The private operator is required to finance, construct, O&M the facility for a specific period of time (usually more than 20 years) before transferring the facility back to the public authority. Variations: BOOT (Build, Own, Operate, Transfer) and BOO (Build, Own, Operate).	Mendoza, Argentina; Izmit, Turkey
Concessions	Private operator takes responsibility for O&M and investment; ownership of assets still rests with the public authority. Concessions are substantial in scope (usually a whole city or region) and tenders are usually bid for on the tariff of 25 to 30 years.	Buenos Aires, Argentina; Manila, Philippines; Cancun, Mexico
Divestiture	Full private ownership and responsibility	England and Wales

Source: Water Page, http://www.africanwater.org/ppp_new_main.htm

3.10.2 Sulabh in PPP

Quality Service Delivery

The technologies developed by Sulabh have attracted various agencies towards management of human waste. These have been fully or partially supported by different departments of the Government of India. The "pay & use" concept in public toilets is saving local bodies considerable expenditure annually in the maintenance of the complexes. Now, it is only a one-time investment by the local government towards construction. The maintenance of the toilets is paid for from the users' contribution. Since Sulabh takes maintenance guarantee of the system, there is a continuous public participation in the projects.

Financial viability

As human excreta is generally considered repugnant by society, it was difficult for people with this mindset to even consider financial investment in projects relating to the disposal of human waste. Sulabh, however, has made it financially viable. The cost of construction of the toilet complex is met by the local body. The maintenance of toilets and day to day expenses are met from users' payments. Sulabh does not depend on external agencies for financing as it is generated through internal resources. All the toilet complexes in the slums and less developed areas are not self-sustaining. The maintenance of such toilets is cross-subsidised from the income generated from the busier toilet complexes in the urban and developed areas.

Elimination of Social Stigma and Psychological Taboo

Earlier, there was a social stigma and psychological taboo about human excreta and only people of the lowest economic strata were associated with these programmes. Through the efforts of Sulabh, by making the projects financially viable, people of higher social status are also competing to join this venture without undue psychological inhibitions.

Employment Opportunity and Security

Altogether there are over 50,000 associate members/voluntary associate members working with the Sulabh organisation who include technocrats, professional managers, scientists, engineers, social scientists, doctors, architects and planners along with other support staff. Since Sulabh takes a 30 years' maintenance guarantee for the toilet complexes it constructs, all workers associated with Sulabh get almost regular employment. Besides, workers associated with construction jobs are engaged on new sites throughout the year.

It is now accepted that improving sanitation has a direct impact on health and in turn, on overall productivity and quality of life of the common people. In India improvement in sanitation is directly related to social upgradation of scavengers. The on-site treatment of human waste and wastewater treatment is the best suited option available to tackle the problem effectively. Any economically viable technology having the least operational and maintenance costs is more applicable in the developing countries of Asia, Africa and South America.

3.11 E-SANITATION

Two recently developed solutions may find mention here.

The first, the DRDO Bio-Digestion toilet, a serendipitous innovation born of the need for sanitation for army personnel in the Himalayas, was not invented to address the civilian sanitation crisis. Soldiers stationed in high altitude regions of Siachen and elsewhere in Ladakh need toilets and sustainable disposal of human waste. Scientists at the Defence Research Development Organisation (DRDO) chanced upon a strain of bacteria, Psychrophile, on a scientific expedition in Antarctica in the 1990s. They brought home a strain of the bacteria and subsequently developed a microbial consortium comprising four clusters of bacteria from Antarctica and other low-temperature areas.

Following research, the consortium was introduced in their makeshift toilets in Siachen and elsewhere in Ladakh. As these bacteria thrive in extreme temperatures, the experiment succeeded and was emulated, but largely within the confines of the army establishment. It was not until 2012 that the technology gained ground elsewhere, including in Indian Railways.

Introduced into a chamber constructed below the water closet, the self-sustaining bacteria feed upon the faeces; the anaerobic process degrades the matter within 48 hours. These odour-free, water-sealed, off-grid toilets are a sustainable alternative to septic tanks and pit latrines, the mainstay of sanitation in the south. The small one-time price to procure the inoculum (₹6,000) possesses the potential to transform Indian urban space.

More than 50 developers have signed up to build these toilets in various parts of the country, and retrofit septic tanks and pit latrines sustainably.

The second, at about the same time the DRDO toilet was available for civilian use in 2012, a retired chief engineer from Andhra Pradesh, M. Dharma Rao, developed an affordable alternative. The inoculum is replaced by a handful of earthworms that generate compost from faeces. Dharma Rao has constructed a few hundred such toilets in Hyderabad. Six months of toilet use produces a bucket (10-litre capacity) of compost, thus rendering the toilet maintenance-free. Dharma Rao's innovation scores high on the sustainability index; importantly, the toilet is affordable and costs less than ₹12,000 to build.

There are probably more undocumented solutions. Exasperatingly, the sanitation crisis has not yet attracted the imagination of the global talent pool to develop lasting, affordable solutions. India may want to scale up manifold innovations like those discussed.

If the years 1974 and 1989 marked important contributions from South America for mobility (Mayor Jamie Lerner's design of the Bus Rapid Transit System for Curitiba) and municipal budgeting (Participatory Budgeting in Porto Alegre), the year 2016 was to see development of affordable, sustainable and scalable sanitation solution.

3.11.1 E-Toilets

Apart from a lack of toilets, their maintenance also poses a major challenge. A large majority of people do not use public toilets due to their unhygienic and unclean condition. This alarming situation calls for immediate action, and a brilliant solution is e-toilets. Kerala-based Eram provides a brilliant solution.

The e-toilet is India's first unmanned electronic public toilet and is portable, hygienically maintained and eco-friendly. E-toilets are unmanned toilets which work on sensor-based technology. The self-cleaning and water conservation mechanism in the toilet makes it unique. The user has to insert a coin to open the door and its sensor-based light system is automatically turned on once you enter the toilet. It also directs the user with audio commands. When a person leaves the unit,

Photo's courtesy: https://www.google.co.in

the toilet cleans itself.

To conserve water, the toilets are programmed to flush 1.5 litres of water after three minutes of usage and 4.5 litres if the usage is longer. This "smart" toilet also washes the platform by itself after every five or 10 persons use the toilet. An instructional note is pasted outside the toilet to make the user familiar with the functioning of this toilet. All the e-toilets are connected over a GPRS network. The web interface at the control centre keeps track of the performance of the e-toilets and collects data regarding usage, downtime, usage charges collected, etc. This provides accountability of the public infrastructure. The respective municipalities can check the usage pattern in real time.

Challenges Include

(i) Finding the right site—the toilet needs to be easily accessible but also not very close to crowded areas.

(ii) Maintenance and repair—though the e-toilet is self-cleaning and automatic, sometimes people throw litter or use it wrongly.

(iii) "It is difficult to make people understand the importance of an e-toilet. They are so used to the idea of a mop and a cleaning lady that they find it difficult to accept that this idea could actually work" says Bincy Baby, the brain behind the e-toilet.

(iv) To make the technology more accessible and approachable, Eram wants to launch a low-cost version of these toilets which would cost `1 lakh. It is a huge challenge to provide quality services at such a low cost.

(v) Challenge in scaling up and getting a foothold in the private market.

Eram's idea was interesting but it still required regular research and development to sustain itself in the market and Marico Innovation Foundation's Social Innovation Acceleration Programme (MIF-SIAP) came as a blessing. MIF, in collaboration with various B-schools, gets students to work in various social sector projects. They mobilised the students of XLRI Jamshedpur to prepare documentation for the sanitation project and brainstorm on how it could be approved.

The most important part played by MIF was to provide value engineering and to help Eram come up with better versions of the e-toilets. MIF's intervention in Eram's case has helped them to not only market the technology but also develop the product as per the needs of users. Eram Scientific Solutions has named this e-toilet "Delight".

In addition to this, their major contribution was in re-evaluating the targets—while Eram hoped to install 400 e-toilets before the MIF intervention, they reworked this target to instal 18,200 e-toilets in the next two years!

Till date, Eram Scientific Solutions has installed more than 600 e-toilets and around 200 STP units across 13 states in India. More than 150 e-toilets have been set up in various schools. They have managed to set up over 200 sewage treatment plants and have been recognised with over 30 awards globally. In 2016, in Bengaluru, the civic body, in association with Eram Scientific Solutions, installed 80 e-toilets in the city, including 12 in Electronic City Zall of which have been mapped under the new app.

In a city like Bengaluru, where everything from taxis to laundry can be ordered via a smartphone, the latest to go smart are toilets. Now citizens can find the nearest electronically controlled self-cleaning toilets or e-toilet through an app, available on Android and iOS. Users can locate an e-toilet and give feedback on its functioning. A voiceover in Kannada or English explains the toilet's functioning. After five uses, the toilet floor also cleans itself with the help of sensors.

As many as 11 service engineers and three service personnel will maintain the toilets in the city. The toilets commissioned by the Bruhat Bengaluru Mahanagara Palike (BBMP) are called "he toilets" by their manufacturers and for a good reason too. They have no special provisions for incinerators for disposing of sanitary napkins. At present, the BBMP has installed e-toilets common to men and women. Of the 75 installed, 62 are operating at present, says S. Somashekara, chief engineer (projects). "We are planning to instal toilets for women soon, with incinerators and napkin facilities. We will be floating tenders for the same," he says, adding that the existing services were well-maintained. Cost per unit (including taxes and maintenance for two years): ₹5.6 lakh.

On 27 January 2017, the Greater Hyderabad Municipal Corporation (GHMC) introduced unique and modern electronic toilets (e-toilets) for women. Made of prefabricated steel, the toilet is furnished with amenities like a chair, fan, and mirror along with baby feeding and diaper changing stations for the convenience of mothers amidst the visitors. Two units of "she toilets," each costing ₹7.3 lakh, were installed near the Charminar on that day, with an aim to instal 100 she toilets and e-toilets in the next six months around public spaces across the city. The toilet units were sponsored by the State Bank of Hyderabad as part of its corporate social responsibility (CSR) initiative.

On Women's Day in 2017, Thiruvananthapuram got a unique gift: The city zoo got a new attraction, an automated woman-friendly toilet.

Photo courtesy: https://www.google.co.in

In Kerala 58 she toilets have been established. The cost of installation of each she toilet is ₹5.37 lakh and maintenance will incur costs of ₹5,200 per month.

There is no dearth of e-toilet manufacturers. Altersoft Innovations India Pvt. Ltd., Kochi, Kerala, manufactures portable and public toilets which are automated intelligent public sanitation (IP toilets). Alfa Next Gen Tech India Private Limited, Noida, Uttar Pradesh, is another such company. Tata's IP toilet has luxurious interiors with hydrophobic coating to address Indian conditions and touch-free operation. Travellers prefer the comfort of the IP toilet because of its neatness, hygiene, convenience and safety. IP toilets are designed with the aim of giving a world-class experience in public toilets with IoT and robotics.

NOTES

1 This NGO named WaterAid is based in the UK and works in the domain of sanitation and safe water. Its report is named "Overflowing Cities: The State of the World's

Toilets 2016" and is the second such yearly report by the group that has been looking at the condition of toilets across the world. It studied the condition of at least 700 million people living in urban areas around the globe without any proper sanitation. The report was released a day before the World Toilet Day, which is celebrated on 19 November.

2 Udupi becomes the first such district of Karnataka.

3 There is an invention to replace the conventional toilet brush and bleach with a water-powered contraption (shifter). Similarly, four schoolboys of Kurumbapathy village (Karuru district, Tamil Nadu) have made urinals from water cans (Safe Mode Pissing System). Three students of IBS Hyderabad have developed an indigenous vending machine that absorbs plastic bottles and aluminium cans, and plan to develop it further for other disposables. These are but a few examples of young, innovative Indians dreaming to make India clean and pollution-free.

Chapter 4

Sanitation Policy and Programmes

Sanitation here refers mainly to the facilities and hygiene principles and practices related to the safe collection, reuse and/or disposal of human excreta and domestic wastewater. Sanitation, as per the National Urban Sanitation Policy (2008), is defined as safe management of human excreta, including its safe confinement, treatment, disposal and associated hygiene-related practices.

There must be a sound and effective policy for sanitation so as to provide guidelines and an action plan in the form of a national sanitation programme. An enabling environment can be created not just with financial and physical infrastructure, but also strong legal and regulatory mechanisms. Similarly, adequate and appropriate programmes are necessary to lay down pragmatic ways to make progress on the ground. Such a policy will link sanitation to health and hygiene, water and housing as well as city planning and rural development.

The demonstrable reality is that, despite the best efforts of the global water sector over several decades, a major part of the developing world continues to lack adequate sanitation. This failure, stems from shortcomings at the national policy level. Often, there has been no national sanitation policy and in other instances a declared policy has been unclear, or even contradictory, in its aims and objectives. Without a sound national policy there is no focus for the planning of sanitation programmes and no sure basis for developing the multi-layered organisational structures needed to devolve responsibility for sanitation to lower levels of government. When these essential support mechanisms are missing there is little hope of extending sanitation coverage on any meaningful scale. Conversely, when NGOs or other sub-national agencies implement a worthwhile local pilot sanitation project, the same missing links prevent a scaling up to state, regional or national level. One principal reason put forward for this is that, although many countries are now moving to water and sanitation sector reform, the national policy emphasis is on water supply. While that is no different from past practice in all countries it points to the need for separate sanitation policies with a clear line of responsibility to one or more specified institutions. Too often responsibilities have become blurred because of overlapping and sometimes conflicting interests in government departments or other institutions variously responsible for housing, rural development, environmental protection, or other aspects of national life.

4.1 MEANING AND TYPES OF POLICY

Policies should address the public health aspects of dealing with solid household waste and waste from animals even though separate policies might be planned to cover removal and reuse of these residues. Policy is the set of procedures, rules and allocation mechanisms that provide the basis for programmes and services. Policies set priorities and often allocate resources for their implementation. Policies are implemented through four types of policy instruments:

1. **Laws and regulations.** Laws generally provide the overall framework. Priorities and regulations provide the more detailed guidance. Regulations are rules or governmental orders designed to control or govern behaviour and often have the force of law. Regulations for sanitation can cover a wide range of topics, including the practices of service providers, design standards, tariffs and discharge standards.
2. **Economic measures.** Examples of economic measures are user charges, subsidies, incentives and fines. User charges, or tariffs are charges which households and enterprises pay in exchange for the removal of human excreta and wastewater. Subsidies are allocations in cash or kind to communities and households for establishing recommended types of sanitation facilities or services. Creating the right economic incentives is often the most efficient way to find appropriate solutions. Fines are monetary charges imposed on enterprises and people for unsafe disposal, emissions and/or risky hygiene behaviour and practices, which are a danger to people and to the environment.
3. **Information and education programmes.** These programmes

include public awareness campaigns and educational programmes designed to generate demand and public support for efforts to expand sanitation services.

4. **Assignment of rights and responsibilities for providing services.** National governments are responsible for determining the roles of national agencies and the appropriate roles of the public, private and non-profit sectors in programme development, implementation and service delivery.

Although the focus here is on national policies, sub-national policies must also be considered, especially in large countries.

4.2 IMPORTANCE OF POLICIES

A very important aspect to take care of in developing and implementing sanitation policies and programmes is the understanding that while toilets are individual assets, sanitation is a public good. With a few exceptions, national-level sanitation policy frameworks, within which national, state and municipal government agencies and the private and non-profit sectors operate have not been adequate. A growing body of practitioners and policymakers has come to recognise this as a key constraint to improving sanitation coverage and programme quality. How can sanitation policies help improve sanitation coverage and programme quality?

- Good sanitation policies help to create an enabling environment that encourages access to and use of sustainable sanitation services. In turn this greatly facilitates the tasks of those concerned with sanitation provision on a large scale; good policies are critical for the replication and scaling up of successful pilot programmes, improving access to services on a scale that matters.
- National sanitation policies can serve as a key stimulus to local action by including local initiatives in the overall strategy. By articulating needs and promoting the importance of sanitation, an effective national policy can promote the setting of priorities and provide the basis for translating needs into actions at different levels. In effect, sanitation policies help to create the conditions in which sanitation services can be improved.
- Sound policies set the scene for more sustainable and effective

programmes. When widely accepted, such policies are an expression of commitment and serve to articulate priorities and allocate resources for implementation. Without such policies in place, efforts to improve access to services will remain local in scope and will not have the support needed to expand efforts on a large scale.

- Policies help shape incentives. Policies and programmes are linked and each is linked to organisations. Policies often directly influence organisational actors. As programmes are implemented over lengthy periods they impact the incentives framework, challenging programme managers to maintain a fit between activities and policies. Thus, understanding the incentives at work and the interplay between policies and programming actors and interest groups, is essential to success.
- Good policies are ever dynamic. Old measures must be supplemented by recent efforts. One cannot be complacent about vital issues. Learning by doing and sharing by experience are gainful in innovative and best practices.

4.3 GLOBAL POLICY

The consumption of water and the generation of human waste are such commonplace aspects of human life that planning for their appropriate use or removal is often overlooked.

The WHO estimates that 2.5 million people died from diarrhoeal diseases in 2000, 80 per cent of them being children under the age of five. The number of people without adequate water and sanitation facilities could reach 5.5 billion in the next 20 years.

Access to safe water and sanitation is a human right as declared by the United Nations. In carrying out their humanitarian mandate in alleviating and improving the condition of the vulnerable populations of the world, both in ordinary times as well as in emergencies, the International Federation of Red Cross and Red Crescent Societies and individual National Red Cross and Red Crescent Societies are increasingly involved in the provision of water and sanitation services as part of overall health and care interventions.

When the United Nations General Assembly adopted the Universal Declaration of Human Rights (UDHR) back in December 1948, 58 member states voted for a historic document covering political, economic, social and cultural rights. Nearly 62 years later, a widely-expanded 192-member General Assembly adopted another memorable resolution: this time recognising access to clean drinking and sanitation as a basic human right. The resolution proved politically divisive, with 122 countries voting for it and 41 abstaining, but with no negative votes. Still, it fell short of a North-South divide: a rich-versus-poor split, as originally expected.

In 2010 the UN declared water and sanitation as a human right fundamental to human development and well-being. Twenty-five years of progress has brought clean, safe water to 91 per cent of the world's population exceeding the MDG target. By 2015, 68 per cent of the world's population was using an improved sanitation facility, missing the MDG target by almost 700 million people, still leaving 2.4 billion without improved sanitation facilities. The numbers, however, mask large differences between the least developed countries and the rest of the world and between the rich and the poor.

In the 48 least developed countries, most of which are in sub-Saharan Africa and southern and southeastern Asia, 69 per cent of the population gained access to improved drinking water since 1990 but just 12 per cent had piped water on their premises and just 27 per cent gained access to an improved sanitary facility.

Sustainable Development Goal 6 aims to ensure availability and sustainable management of water and sanitation for all by 2030. Four of the targets relate to urban WASH: (6.1) by 2030, achieving universal and equitable access to safe and affordable drinking water for all; (6.2) by 2030, achieving access to adequate and equitable sanitation and hygiene for all and ending open defecation, paying special attention to the needs of women and girls and those in vulnerable situations; (6.3) by 2030, improving water quality by reducing pollution, eliminating dumping and minimising release of hazardous chemicals and materials, halving the proportion of untreated wastewater and substantially increasing recycling and safe reuse globally; and (6.4) by 2030, substantially increasing water-use efficiency across all sectors and ensuring sustainable withdrawals and supply of freshwater to address water scarcity and substantially reducing the number of people suffering from water scarcity. In addition, Target 1 of SDG 11, "Make Cities and Human Settlements Inclusive, Safe, Resilient and Sustainable" aims by 2030 to ensure access for all to adequate, safe, and affordable housing and basic services and to upgrade slums.

While the aspirational goal is to provide on-plot water supply for every household and a toilet with safe management for faecal waste, for the poor in developing countries a more realistic goal is to provide basic services to all. Basic water supply means a water source within a 30-minute round trip, basic sanitation means an improved toilet and basic hygiene means having a washing station with soap and water for all households.

Financing the water and sanitation gap for the urban poor to achieve the SDG targets will require Herculean efforts from developing countries, the international donor community, the private sector, NGOs, and the residents themselves. Based on past experience with the MDGs, the picture is not encouraging. The WHO estimates the likely costs of achieving universal access to WASH by 2030 is close to $50 billion per year, accounting for increased population. The World Bank suggests this is three times the current investment levels. The 2014 GLAAS report found that 80 per cent of reporting countries fell short of meeting financial requirements to meet the SDG targets. "The Costs of Meeting the 2030 SDG Targets on Drinking Water Sanitation and Hygiene" (2016) report by WaterAid has suggested that African countries should spend 4.5 per cent of GDP on water and sanitation, yet, according to Development Finance International and Oxfam, in 2014 just 10 per cent of countries met WASH targets and spending averaged less than one per cent of GDP and a majority of countries have actually recently reduced spending on WASH as a percentage of GDP.

The international community has been stepping up its support for WASH, increasing its commitments by 30 per cent from 2010 to 2012 to over $15 billion (including official development assistance of $10 billion and non-concessional loans of $3.6 billion). This represents an increase in the proportion of development aid for WASH from 4.7 per cent to 6.1 per cent from 2010 to 2012 and almost a doubling of the proportion since 2002. International aid for WASH and national investments have tended to favour large-scale water and sanitation schemes in urban areas, usually excluding the urban poor and only upgrading existing conditions.

Despite recent increased attention to WASH, meeting SDG targets for WASH in low-income urban areas of the developing world will require an even stronger commitment from governments to bring together coalitions of the public, private (including philanthropic) and non-governmental sectors and the international community around a sound WASH plan that targets those most in need living in the burgeoning slums and informal peri-urban areas.

In March and May 2017, the UN member states gathered to discuss how to improve global governance of water and sanitation in the UN. The two dialogues were mandated by the UN General Assembly resolution 71/222 of 21 December 2016, titled "International Decade for Action: Water for Sustainable Development 2018-2028." Katalin Bogyay, Permanent Representative of Hungary, and Lukmon Isomatov, Ministry of Foreign Affairs, Tajikistan, served as co-moderators. The first dialogue included panel discussions on the implementation of the water-related SDGs and the role of the UN system and in the second dialogue the co-moderators' summary of the first dialogue was discussed.

4.4 SOME CASE EXAMPLES

Concern for national sanitation policies is evident in most countries despite wide variations between countries. It is widely accepted that without political will, sanitation policies will not be effective. The importance of clearly defined institutional roles and responsibilities is also widely accepted. Other aspects of sanitation policies are country-specific, for example, levels of service, the nature and level of subsidies, or views on what responsibilities should be assigned to different levels of government. Countries vary greatly in population, level of development, household income, availability of water resources, and in many other ways. In large countries such as China, Brazil, India, Indonesia or Nigeria, the role of sub-national government in policy formulation is much greater than in smaller countries. In some countries, state, provincial and local governments play an important policy role and have the resources to plan and implement sanitation programmes.

South Africa

South Africa is one country that has developed a strong national sanitation policy. The process began in 1994 with development of a White Paper on water supply and sanitation in which the importance of developing a national sanitation policy was highlighted. In 2001 the National Sanitation Task Team published a National Sanitation Policy.

This comprehensive statement defines sanitation, discusses the sanitation problem in South Africa, lists 12 clear policy principles, articulates the strategic interventions, clarifies the institutional arrangements at all levels of government, describes sources of financing and discusses the importance of monitoring and evaluating policy implementation.

The attention to a national policy has served to galvanise support for sanitation across a range of national agencies and local governments. It has also fostered wide agreement on the approaches and elements needed to improve access to sanitation services. Nevertheless implementation of the policies, especially at the local level, has been uneven. Local governments generally lack the technical, managerial and financial capacity to address sanitation needs. Programmes also tend to focus on facilities and give less attention to software such as health and hygiene promotion. South Africa does, however, provide an excellent example of national sanitation policies and how they can be used as a starting point for a national effort to improve access to sanitation services.

Uganda

Over the past 15 years Uganda has created a dynamic environment for the formulation of sanitation policies that address national needs while taking into account both the constraints and the resources of the national economy. New policies have been established for sanitation in terms of health, water, environment and local and national governments. However, although these policies were accompanied by considerable political and governmental support when they were first created, the original high levels of enthusiasm and political support have declined somewhat in the last few years. Moreover, implementation programmes have not matched the initial enthusiasm for policies, and sanitation services, especially in rural areas and small towns, have received little attention.

Overall, Uganda has a reasonably well-developed framework of national sanitation policies. Laws and regulations have been established or revised to support these policies, a process that is incomplete but currently continuing. The new constitution established in 1996 states that every Ugandan has the right to a clean and healthy environment. In 1997, the Kampala Declaration on Sanitation considered a major indication of political will and defined ten areas of action to improve sanitation. There have also been several efforts to develop an official national sanitation policy, the latest being the draft National Environmental Health Policy for Uganda. These policies take into account the needs of different population groups in urban centres, small towns, rural growth centres and rural communities and have led to the preparation of development approaches and technical guidelines appropriate to the social and economic conditions of the user communities. The approaches are based on sound methodologies (stakeholder participation, hygiene education, behaviour changes, low-cost technologies, etc.), reflecting the combined inputs of government, donor and NGOs in the policy formulation process. As statements of well-informed government intentions in Uganda, the national sanitation policies provide good guidance to all organisations concerned with sanitation, and a starting point for programme planning, budgeting and eventual field implementation. Responsibility for implementation, however, is found primarily at the local government level where sanitation rarely receives priority because of competing political, financial and resource issues. To some extent the essential follow-on activities are occurring primarily through donor-funded programmes for water supply and sanitation. The emphasis, however, tends to be on water supply projects, and funding allocations tend to favour urban over rural areas. Sanitation is not considered a separate programme area, either in funding or project development terms. Moreover, individual households, where sanitation needs are greatest, generally receive no material support for the construction or maintenance of latrines. Promotional and technical guidance for sanitation is available at the household level, but even these means of assistance are inadequate to meet the need.

India

Encouraged by its success in rapidly improving access to safe water through the introduction of the one-standard, quality-controlled hand pump (the India Mark II), the Indian government applied the same approach to sanitation. In 1986 a Technology Advisory Group (TAG) comprising representatives from the Indian government, UNDP, UNICEF and the World Bank, recommended one standard design for rural and urban on-site sanitation, the double-vault pour-flush latrine. The Central Sanitation Programme provided 100 per cent subsidy for this latrine for Scheduled Castes, Scheduled Tribes and landless labourers. Subsidies for other user groups were decided by the respective states. Achievements in coverage and use were low. The cost of the double vault permanent model was relatively high and the focus was on construction, with little attention given to demand creation, loan repayment where applicable, or to user participation in such matters as latrine sitting, superstructure design or future maintenance needs. Coverage in rural areas through government support hardly increased: from 0.5 per cent in 1980 to 2.7 per cent in 1992. The greater part of progress to 11 per cent in 1989 was achieved by households who preferred and could afford to use the private sector.

In 1992, following a National Seminar on Rural Sanitation, the government launched a new strategy. Subsidies for households below the poverty line were reduced to 80 per cent and the policy stressed participation of householders in the choice of four latrine options with different cost levels. It also directed implementing agencies, both government and nongovernmental organisations, to use 10 per cent of the government funds for promotion and hygiene education. Implementation remained driven by the implementing agencies. This changed in the policy guidelines of 2001 when the programme moved to a "Total Sanitation Campaign" with an emphasis on informing and educating rural households without sanitation about the importance of having and using sanitary latrines. Interested households can apply for a flat subsidy of ₹500-600, depending on the type of latrine. The implementing agencies can set up outlets where households can buy the required materials. State governments decide which agencies can implement the programme under a separate bank account, various government departments, NGOs and CBOs, district water and sanitation missions, etc. Community government (panchayats) can also carry out the programme in their communities, together with local committees. The latter approach is the state policy in Kerala (developed in cooperation with an NGO), while sanitation in West Bengal has been promoted among rural households directly through NGOs and CBOs.

The Total Sanitation Campaign is part of the Sector Reforms Project introduced in April 1999 to make rural water supply and sanitation more sustainable. It is piloted in 200 districts. Limitations on success arise from the absence of guidance and training opportunities and from a lack of appropriate expertise in some implementing organisations, particularly in knowledge of current gender and poverty-sensitive promotion and participation strategies. Similar deficiencies are seen in the organisations responsible for allocating funds and monitoring implementation. Without all preconditions in place it is likely that only part of the funds will be used effectively.

Nepal

Over the past 10 years Nepal has made a more concerted effort to raise awareness and formulate clearer sanitation policies. Considerable change has resulted. The importance of sanitation was noted in national planning documents, giving recognition to the health and environmental impacts of the lack of coverage for more than 60 per cent of the population. This focus was most evident in the development of the Eighth Five Year Plan (1992-97), and the commitment to improved sanitation coverage was further expanded in the Ninth Five Year Plan (1997-2002). The goals of the latter were ambitious to double the population coverage of sanitation by 2002.

International attention to Nepal's sanitation coverage is in part responsible for these advances. Meetings of the regional South Asian nations' forum (SAARC) in 1992 brought out the very low position of Nepal in relation to its neighbours. The 1992 Enhanced Eighth Five Year Plan increased the allocation for water and sanitation four-fold and called for organisational changes to support improved and expanding sanitation implementation. In 1994 Nepal adopted the National Sanitation Policy Guidelines for Planning and Implementation of Sanitation Programmes and, in 1995, formed national and district water supply and sanitation coordination committees. These new Nepalese government commitments in turn spurred increased international donor support for sanitation. These new national policies were accompanied by considerable political and governmental support when they were first created and this important high-level backing continued in 2002 with a renewed push to endorse a national sanitation policy agenda. Implementation programmes, however, have ebbed and flowed, largely because the enthusiasm for sanitation-specific policies and programmes has not been accompanied by continued budget allocations or attention to decentralised management.

The above examples of country experiences highlight three important factors:

1. They serve as models for understanding key components and levels of sanitation policy. The policy statements are quite comprehensive and thorough in coverage of the various dimensions to the sanitation issue. As governments and advisers look to support the development of sanitation policy, the developments in Uganda, Nepal, India and particularly South Africa stand out as key references for policy content.
2. Policies are seen to be an important motivating force for focused programme planning on sanitation. Policy sets the stage and provides incentives. Too often sanitation is not singled out, or is lost behind water supply programming initiatives. The sanitation policy statements as seen in South Africa, Uganda and Nepal are effective in placing a spotlight on sanitation and mobilising resources for addressing service shortfalls.
3. The presented country examples help to illustrate the complexity of policy implementation, and the many stages and facets of policy change. Enacting a sound policy, while an important step, is not sufficient. Results will be realised with full implementation. As part of decentralisation, sanitation is being devolved to local governments. This transition un-bundles the roles of policymakers by level of government, creating challenges to sustain national-level momentum by working through varying levels of capacity at the sub-national levels. Each country case reinforces the fact that success depends on implementation, and implementation is a slow and challenging process. In fact, the major difficulty in all cited cases is how to get the policy implemented at the lowest level of government. Therefore, large countries need to have general national policies with increasingly more specific policies for lower-level political sub-divisions such as provincial, county, municipal, village or community.

4.5 POLICIES AND ACHIEVEMENTS IN SOME STATES OF INDIA

West Bengal

While the Central Government formulates national policy for jointly financed programmes such as rural sanitation, Indian states formulate their own state policies and programmes. Two relatively successful approaches are those of West Bengal and Kerala. The approach in West Bengal emerged as the most successful of a series of pilot projects which the UNICEF undertook with the respective state governments. It has had a considerable impact on the change in national policy.

The Midnapore Intensive Sanitation Project in West Bengal was formally launched in 1990 after some five years of work with the local NGO, the Ramakrishna Mission. The policy was, from the outset, to offer no subsidy to any households. A network of trained local volunteers offers a variety of technical options in latrine construction, with different costs to suit different abilities to pay. The volunteers get a small incentive when a household decides to build a latrine. Credit is available for the poor. Associated policies generate local employment through training of masons, and demand for latrines through information and education. The gram panchayat is actively involved, and the "promotion" of latrines occasionally resorts to peer and local government pressure on community members. Important factors in the success are the extensive network and deep roots of the principal NGO, the high population density and consequent reduction of private places for defecation, high literacy rates and strong community organisation. With 100 per cent coverage, Midnapore has inspired other districts in the state so much that the overall sanitation coverage in the state is 65 percent, well above the national figure of 32 percent.

The number of households with a latrine on the premises grew by 15.1 per cent in West Bengal from 2001 to 2011. On 19 November 2013, World Toilet Day, the people of West Bengal took a pledge to achieve ODF in rural Bengal by 2017. In terms of physical coverage, the state reached World Toilet Day 2013 with a target IHHL (individual household latrines) of nearly 64 lakh. Between the two World Toilet Days, it could construct 5,13,736 individual household toilets, 5,411 school toilet blocks, 3,875 toilets in anganwadi centres and 118 community sanitary complexes. But even in terms of numbers this is far below the pace that is required to achieve complete coverage. The state government constructed 8.47 lakh toilets in 2014 which was the highest in the country. It has also been working to implement Nirmal Gram projects and to improve the sanitation infrastructure across the state.

Why the gap? There are various reasons, ascribable to the policy indecision at the central and state levels as well as to the lack of initiative at the district and sub-district levels.

Kerala

The policy and programme in Kerala emerged from a bilateral sanitation project supported by Denmark and the Netherlands since early 1980. As in West Bengal there are specific factors at play: high population density, reduction of private places for defecation, high literacy rates (including among women) and strong community organisations. Like West Bengal in Kerala also, the NGO linkage is strong in this case with two local NGOs, the literacy movement for public information and the Socio-Economic Unit Foundation which developed and tested the strategy and now provides training and backstopping to the national programme. Differences in the Kerala approach are the focus on community management with cooperation between the local government, specially elected neighbourhood sanitation committees and other civic groups, and a stronger gender element in participation.

The Twelfth Five Year Plan (2012-17) in Kerala addressed the issue of high development in the state alongside improving the material and quality of life of the people. The National Urban Sanitation Policy (NUSP) of the Government of India announced in 2008 entrusted state governments with preparing their state sanitation strategy (SSS) in line with constitutional provisions. The Kerala SSS recognises the primacy of integral solutions that cover sub-sectors of drinking water, wastewater (including septage), solid waste and stormwater drainage. The strategy has looked at the dimensions of capacity enhancement, finance, technology, inclusiveness, climate change responsiveness, institutional and governance strengthening.

Characteristic of the Kerala policy and programme is the formation of local ward committees, each representing some 500 families and with a balance between male and female members. These committees make an inventory of sanitation in their areas and identify the households that need a subsidy for building a latrine. Subsidies are provided by the local government from its local resources, supplemented by voluntary support from the neighbourhoods and/or local voluntary groups. The central and state governments only contribute funds for information and training. Fundamental to the local successes of policy and programme are low-cost technology, transparency in household selection and fund use, promotion among both male and female householders, construction by trained masons (many of them women) and monitoring of construction quality. Subsequently, sound operation and use are also crucial for success. In Kerala, many males work overseas so there was a shortage of male masons. Moreover, male and female households preferred to have female masons work in their house or compound since costs were the same and the quality of work was equally good or better.

In 1997 five districts launched a programme for 100 per cent sanitation coverage by 2000. "Clean Kerala" ("sanitation for all") became an all-state policy and programme soon after when sanitation had come out as the second priority of rural women and men in the People's Planning Campaign. This campaign set the priorities for decentralisation of development initiatives and funding from state to local government.

Kerala is known for a high level of literacy and women's empowerment and hence gender and inclusive sanitation are among the outcomes. NGOs like Kudumbashree have played major roles. Kerala is known for the "Area Sabha Sanitation Committee" led by the concerned ward councillor and a representative from the Urban Health, Nutrition and Sanitation Committee (set up under the Urban Health Mission), women's SHGs and ward/zone-level Kerala State Sanitation Strategy (under the NUSP 2008); 27 officials are responsible for provisioning of water and sanitation services.

Ensuring 100 per cent hygienically safe and sanitary treatment and disposal is one of the goals. About 97.43 per cent of the households in the urban areas of Kerala have a toilet within their residential premises. Almost 56.69 per cent of them are connected to septic tanks and 21.87 per cent to pit latrines while households having a connection to the centralised sewer system constitute about 14.32 percent. With the lessons learnt from about 20 cities' sanitation plans, now Kerala has the Smart Kerala Campaign as part of its sanitation strategy. Its "Suchitva Mission" is already in progress.

There are still problems. Wastewater disposal and treatment was a major problem in cities in Kerala. The wastewater from toilets is being disposed through septic tanks and soak pits and a grey form of wastewater from kitchens and bathrooms is directly discharged into the sludge drains without any treatment.

Karnataka

The efforts of the government of Karnataka and its partner agencies, urban local bodies in the state, the Karnataka Urban Water Supply and Drainage Board (KUWS&DB) and the Bangalore Water Supply and Sewerage Board (BWSSB) are to ensure universal coverage of water and sanitation services that people want and are willing to pay for.

High fluoride and nitrate levels in drinking water, dismal sanitation with rampant open defecation, high incidence of chikungunya, and a higher risk of fungal and other infections in women are some of the key findings of ASHWAS, a survey of household water and sanitation in rural Karnataka conducted by Arghyam, an Indian public charitable foundation. With the survey indicating that 94 per cent of women in rural areas use cloth for protection, there is a high risk of fungal and other infections among women. Increasing urbanisation has resulted in greater pressure on the existing urban water supply and sanitation systems leading to increasing demand on the one hand to augment the source and improve distribution and on the other to increase the coverage of underground drainage.

According to the most recent census, only 31 per cent of the urban population has safe sewerage while 53 per cent has clean drinking water. Half of the schools in Karnataka have no toilets. In every fourth high school, girls have to share toilets with boys! These shocking revelations are among the findings of a nationwide survey on the condition of schools and schoolchildren conducted by the NGO, Pratham.

Karnataka's is a "two sides of a coin swachh story": sanitation coverage of rural areas is double that of urban regions. Open defecation-free in Karnataka: 11,958 villages out of 29,406 villages, 22 districts out of 30 and seven cities only. Rural sanitation coverage rose from 39.8 per cent in 2014 to 73.94 in 2017 and urban sanitation coverage rose from 30 per cent to 40.59. As per the Swachh Survekshan, which assessed 434 cities across India on the basis of cleanliness parameters, Karnataka cities' performance was not up to the mark. Mysore was ranked fifth, down from its position of number one in the previous two years. Bengaluru ranked a poor 210, dropping from its previous year rank of 38. The drop is drastic, considering that Mysore in the previous two years was known as the cleanest city of India whereas Bengaluru was the seventh cleanest city in 2015.

The cities of Karnataka that have not been able to perform well both in sanitation and cleanliness are now taking adequate steps just like the rural areas of the state, to up their swachh game.

The Karnataka government has had prepared a city sanitation plan (CSP) for 26 urban centres in five of the lagging districts from the All India Institute for Local Self-Government, Pune. The State Institute of Urban Development (SIUD), a Mysore-based urban sector apex state training institute, has primarily developed these plans. It is to use capacity building and research to establish good governance.

Belgaum district of Karnataka is a successful example of the national district administration partnering with the local population to completely reverse the existing sanitation scenario. For a district which needs over five lakh toilets to be built to become ODF, building of two lakh toilets in a single year is an achievement worth celebrating. Koppal district is well-known for its Swachh activities. On 11 August, the district formed a spiral human chain of 10,000 people covering about 15 km to celebrate Freedom from Open Defecation Week in a creative and educative manner. Moreover, the district set a record by building 20,000 toilets in 200 hours.

Delhi

In a study conducted across three unauthorised colonies in the capital, it was found that the incidence of diarrhoea among children was closely related to the lack of safe excreta disposal systems. According to the Mission Convergence Survey conducted by the Delhi government in 2012, a staggering 56 per cent of children in the city's unauthorised colonies and slums defecate in the open, compounding the sanitation crisis.

At present, the sewage treatment capacity of all 17 treatment plants is 512 MGD. However, actual treatment capacity utilisation is around 300-320 MGD of sewage only.

4.6 NATURE OF SANITATION POLICY

A series of key elements has come to be recognised as defining in outline the essential ingredients of good sanitation policies.These elements cover a range of important issues:

1. Political will: Politicall will refers to the support given to policies by politicians, government officials and representatives of influential organisations. Political will may be influenced by human resource commitments, budget allocations, high-profile events, or voting.
2. Inclusiveness: We need to develop policies that include all stakeholders. To be effective in guiding changes in sanitation services, sanitation policies must be developed and formulated with the involvement and participation of the stakeholders. Policies have legitimacy to the extent that all stakeholders (including political leaders, government officials, donor representatives, the private sector and the general public) collaborate in their development and see them as a valid expression of current government action and future intention. There has to be belief in the policies and their purposes and this can only come when stakeholders have been included in formulating the policies and in participating in making informed decisions.
3. Legal framework: A major aspect of legitimacy for sanitation policies is the legality of the policy statements. A legal basis is important and may take the form of laws, legislative acts, decrees, regulations and official guidelines. To be comprehensive, this basis should encompass the full range of legal instruments, from the essential legal statutes to the practical technical guidance materials used to implement the policies. Without a legal framework to guide overall policy implementation, sanitation programmes and projects run the risk of violating societal norms and failing to address the objectives for which the policies were established.
4. Target-oriented and goal-specific: Population targeting with focused attention on goals are the hallmarks of an ideal sanitation policy. Sanitation services are usually designed to serve the needs of specific population groups. Three population groups generally need priority attention because of their inadequate sanitation services. These groups, which can be found in almost all developing countries, are the urban poor in large cities (especially in the poor and periurban areas of large cities), residents of small towns and most of the rural population. National sanitation

policies are more likely to be effective if they specifically target such groups when it can be shown that they are underserved in comparison to other groups, such as the urban elite and wealthy populations in general. Population targeting involves not only statements of priority but also meaningful action programmes and budgets.

5. Gender-sensitive: Recognition of dimensions of gender and poverty are also essential features. Among households poor families are generally the last to improve sanitation, not because of differences in hygiene perception but because of reduced access to relevant information and to means of, or preconditions for, installation such as land, or, for poor female heads of households, labour. Within households men and women have different interests in sanitation, different reasons for installing a disposal system and different roles in the installation process. In managing sanitation programmes it is also important that women and men of different social and economic groups are equitably represented and involved. Recognising and catering for differences in means and interests, and achieving equity for women and men in the various strata, contributes to the effectiveness and sustainability of programmes. In contrast, excluding individual groups from sanitation policies, or overburdening them, may result in negative effects.
6. Multi-layered: Levels of service are many. Sanitation services can range from indoor flush toilets connected to sewers to simple pit latrines located some distance from the house. In most cases the level of service is determined by costs, the economic status of communities and households, and the willingness of users to pay for or otherwise contribute to the installation. The availability of water as a transporting agent, a cleaning agent, or a personal hygiene agent also affects the level of service provision, as do several other factors such as convenience, status (in terms of attractiveness and modernity) and perceptions of health impacts. To be sustainable, the minimum adequate levels of service for any given community are determined by all of the above factors. Considering that these will change with time, people should be given the opportunity to start with modest (but safe) facilities and improve as their financial capacity grows.

7. Addressing key health Issues: Health issues serve as key rationale in a sanitation policy. The health impacts of sanitation and the associated economic implications for national and household economies are a primary reason for developing sanitation policies. Adverse health impacts can result from unsanitary handling, disposal or reuse of human excreta and domestic wastewater. Although decisions may be made on the basis of service levels, convenience, costs or regulatory factors, the health consequences of sanitation provision should be the key rationale for formulation of policies. These policies should guide the subsequent implementation of sanitation programmes so as to encourage the desired health outcomes. To accomplish this, policies should address identified sanitation-related health concerns, such as diarrhoeal rates, infant mortality, helminthic infections or cholera epidemics. It is essential that the general public is made aware of the problems that arise from poor sanitation and understands the role that proper sanitation services can play in addressing these problems.
8. Environmental considerations: Increasingly, sanitation is being seen as a major issue in environmental protection. Improper disposal of human wastes can pollute surface and groundwater bodies and the land surface, causing great risks to health and impacting the local economy; and such practices can adversely affect general aesthetics and the overall quality of life for those living in the vicinity. A growing problem in many countries is the economic impact of environmental degradation on tourism, fisheries and other industries sensitive to pollution. The most serious problems occur when large quantities of human excreta are concentrated in limited areas, such as at sewer outfalls, sludge beds or septic tank disposal sites.
9. Financial issues: The costs associated with implementing national sanitation policies include: (a) the capital costs required for sanitation infrastructure and facilities; (b) the recurrent costs required to operate and maintain the facilities and; (c) the programme costs for such aspects as training, institutional development, community organisation and hygiene improvement. Capital costs are those of the initial investment, provided either in the form of a loan or grant, and are much higher in the

beginning than over time. Recurrent costs are those needed for ongoing management of the facilities and are paid by individual households through user fees. In addition to operation and maintenance, recurrent costs for sewered systems should include depreciation, debt service and expansion of facilities. Programme costs include such activities as training, promotion and technical assistance. These costs are generally ongoing, but are higher in the early stages of a project when the facilities are constructed. These three categories of costs can be allocated to various parties or stakeholders. Sources of funds typically include national governments, local governments, external donors and users. The national budget process is an important factor in determining how these costs are allocated.

10. Institutional dimensions: To be effective, sanitation policies and associated programme development and implementation must be the responsibility of one or more institutions. In most countries responsibility for sanitation is divided among a number of ministries, based on their involvement in urban affairs, housing and public services, rural development, environmental protection and local government administration. This can lead to a confusing mix of institutional activities, sometimes resulting in overlapping authorities or in a situation where no organisation seems to have clearly defined responsibilities, thereby resulting in gaps in sanitation coverage, or even conflicting directives. To avoid such problems the sanitation needs of all population target groups should be the clear responsibility of specified institutions

The World Development Report 1994 focused on "economic infrastructure" and includes services from:

- Public utilities such as power, telecommunications, piped water supply, sanitation and sewerage, solid waste collection and disposal, and piped gas.
- Public works, roads and major dams and canal works for irrigation and drainage.
- Other transport sectors, urban and inter-urban railways, urban transport, ports and waterways, and airports.

Today infrastructure activities, such as power, transport,

telecommunications, provision of water, and sanitation and safe disposal of waste, are central to the activities of an average rural household and to economic production. Without them economic production as well as the quality of life will deteriorate. We, therefore, have viewed these activities as essential inputs to the rural economic system. But we found that the reporting of statistical data in India is inadequate and low in accessibility. This is problematic for researchers. Moreover, there is no official infrastructure index at the moment. Attempts to construct development indices based on infrastructural variables are few and far between. This makes direct measurement of impact of infrastructure on economic development that much more difficult.

Rural markets are virtually the growth centres of the rural economy. They constitute the focal points for economic and trading activities. At present, however, infrastructural bottlenecks like inadequacy of godowns, carriage facilities, platforms (elevations), and sheds, water supply and sanitary facilities, garbage pits, etc., are affecting off-take and marketable surplus of farm produce. Healthy links between input and output markets are conspicuously absent.

4.7 SOLID WASTE MANAGEMENT IN URBAN AREAS: A CASE STUDY

At the end of the 19th century the Industrial Revolution saw the rise of the world's consumers. Not only did the air get more and more polluted but the earth itself became more and more polluted with the generation of non-biodegradable solid waste. Rapid population growth and uncontrolled industrial development are seriously degrading the urban and semi-urban environment day by day. As the limits of urbanisation are extending to far-flung areas in India, the problem of solid waste management is causing great concern for our environment. Rising incomes, changing consumption patterns and modern lifestyles along with advanced science and technology are aggravating the solid waste management problem. While traditional cities have become modern and high-tech, with e-commerce and e-governance, the new menace of e-waste has also emerged.[1]

Levels of municipal waste production are directly proportional to levels of industrialisation and levels of income. With thrust on human development as well as local governance in recent times, local initiatives for local problems necessitate discussion on issues like waste creation and management in towns and cities too. Such issues and challenges need to be taken up also as part of overall plan/policy of "democratic decentralisation with citizen participation". While some efforts, both at central and the state levels, have been made to meet these challenges, through legislation (primarily the 74th Constitutional Amendment and its several Schedules, and, more recently, the Jawaharlal Nehru National Urban Renewal Mission (JNNURM), as well as administration), there is much that remains to be done.

4.7.1 Meaning of Solid Waste and Its Management

According to the World Bank Report 1994, municipal solid waste (MSW) includes refuse from institutions, market waste, yard waste and street sweeping. In other words, the term "municipal waste" applies to the waste generated by households and also waste of similar character derived from shops, offices and other commercial units. Any useless, unwanted discarded material that is not a liquid or gas is referred to as solid waste or refuse. It may be yesterday's newspaper, junk mail, today's meal scraps, pieces of bread, roti, leftover rice, racked sludge, industrial refuse or street sweepings, etc. The refuse materials such as newspapers, cotton pieces, foodstuff, skin, clothes, leather, old fish etc., anything solid produced by humans is going to turn into waste sometime somewhere and somehow. Waste is produced as a result of human activity. The quantity of this material is increasing readily due to the hike in human population and increase in the standards of living. For example, in Mumbai 7,000 tonnes of MSW are produced every day. This is contributed by kitchen refuse, markets and slaughterhouses. This waste has to be disposed of so that the environment remains clean and healthy for habitation.

As per the Municipal Solid Waste (Management & Handling) Rules, 2000, garbage is defined as municipal solid waste which includes commercial and residential waste generated in a municipal or notified area in either solid or semi-solid form excluding industrial hazardous wastes but including treated biomedical waste, household waste, construction debris, sanitation residue, and waste from streets.

According to WHO (1971), solid waste management includes the process of generation, collection, storage, transport and disposal or reuse and re-circulation or incineration or any relevant method of disposal.

4.7.2 MSW Composition and Trends in India

Municipal waste in developing countries tends to have a higher organic and ash/grit content, and also a higher moisture content. It has been estimated that recyclable content in solid waste varies from 13 to 20 per cent and compostable material is about 65 to 80 percent. In India the biodegradable portion dominates the bulk of municipal solid waste. Generally, the biodegradable portion is mainly food and yard waste. It is around 48 per cent biodegradable and 52 per cent non-biodegradable, out of which plastic is 9 percent, metals and glass 2 per cent (e-article: National Solid Waste Association of India, 2012). Typical composition of Indian MSW is given in Table 4.1.

In India, waste generation is expected to increase to a mammoth figure of 300 MT by 2047, that is, from the present 500 gm to 945 gm per capita. The estimated land requirement for disposal of such a huge quantum of waste would be 169.6 sq km as compared to 20.2 sq km in 1997. This escalation could be attributed to India's population explosion, change in consumption patterns among urban populations and relatively high rate of waste generation, which has a direct relationship with the amount of waste generated in a community. By 2021 it is expected that India will have 500 large towns and 4,430 medium and small towns with a total of approximately 550 million people living in urban areas.

Table 4.1: Municipal Solid Waste Composition

Description	*Percentage by Weight*
Vegetable Leaves	40.16
Grass	3.80
Paper	0.81
Plastic	0.62
Glass/Ceramics	0.44
Metal	0.64
Stones/Ashes	41.81
Miscellaneous	11.73

Source: Position paper on PPP in Solid Waste Management, November 2009

It is estimated that about 1,15,000 metric tonnes of MSW waste is generated daily in the country (annually about 62 million tonnes). Per capita waste generation in India's cities varies from 0.2 kg to 0.6 kg per day depending upon the size of population. An assessment has been made that per capita waste generation is increasing by about 1.3 per cent per year. With growth of urban population ranging between 3 to 3.5 per cent per annum, the annual increase in overall quantity of solid waste is assessed at about 5 percent. The solid waste generated by the million-plus cities varies from 1,200 metric tonnes per day in cities like Ahmedabad and Pune to a maximum of 5,000-5,500 metric tonnes per day in metropolitan cities like Delhi and Mumbai. The per capita solid waste generation varies from 300 gm in Bengaluru to 500-550 gm in Mumbai and Delhi. Indian cities are still struggling to achieve the collection of all MSW generated. Metros and other big cities in India collect between 79-90 per cent of MSW. Smaller cities and towns collect less than 50 percent. The benchmark for collection is 100 percent, which is the most important target for urban local bodies (ULBs) at present (sustainable solid waste management in India). Table 4.2 shows the generation of solid waste in various types of cities in India.

Table 4.2: Solid Waste Generated in Various Types of Cities in India

Type of cities (2005)	*MT/Day*	*Percentage of Total Waste*
The 7 Mega Cities	21,100	18.35
The 28 Metro Cities	19,643	17.08
The 388 Class I Towns	42,635	37.07
Total	83,378	72.50

Source: Position paper on PPP in Solid Waste Management, November 2009

As is clear, the large cities (Class I and above) account for nearly three-fourths of the waste generated in urban areas. The annual increase mentioned above translates to an estimated 260 million tonnes of waste generation annually by 2047. This enormous increase in MSW will have significant impacts in terms of land required for disposing of this waste as well as in methane emission. It is estimated that if the waste is not disposed of in a systematic manner, more than 1,400 sq km of land will be required in the country by the end of 2047 for its disposal.

The collection efficiency ranges between 70 to 90 per cent in major metro cities, whereas in several smaller cities it is below 50 percent. It has been estimated that the ULBs spend about ₹500 to ₹1500 per tonne on solid waste collection, transportation, treatment and disposal. About 60-70 per cent of this amount is spent on collection, 20-30 per cent on transportation, and hardly any funds are spent on treatment and disposal of waste.

On an average, 91 per cent of MSW is dumped in landfills (CPCB, 2000). However, a very minor portion is scientifically dumped in sanitary landfills according to standards prescribed by concerned agencies. An sanitary landfill is primarily a slow process which requires scientific treatment over long periods. Average of 5 to 6 per cent waste is disposed using various composting methods.

Landfill sites have not yet been identified by many municipalities and in several municipalities the landfill sites have been exhausted and the respective local bodies do not have resources to acquire new land. Due to lack of disposal sites, even collection efficiency is affected.

4.7.3 Regulatory Aspects in Solid Waste Management

In India, solid waste management services are provided by the municipal bodies as per the provisions of the respective Municipal Acts. Many of the Acts are quite old and the provisions need many amendments to reflect the changes in the waste management needs. An analysis of legal provisions brings to our notice that initially there was no explicit statute dealing with solid waste management. The issues relating to SWM were scattered in provisions of the Indian Penal Code, Criminal Procedure Code, and the Constitution of India. Under the Constitution of India, we can read about solid waste management in the directive principles of state policy and the fundamental rights. Article 47 of the Constitution makes it a paramount principle of governance that "steps are taken for the improvement of public health as among its primary duties". Further, Article 51 A (g) points out that it is the duty of the individual to protect and improve the natural environment including forests, lakes, rivers and wildlife, and to have compassion for living creatures.

The Municipal Solid Waste (Management and Handling) Rules, 2000 is the first direct attempt at tackling the solid waste problem. These rules consist of certain concrete guidelines aimed at making the handling of solid waste more suitable and efficient. The Municipal

Waste Rules of 1999 were complemented by a Manual on Municipal Solid Waste Management which was developed by the CPHEEO in 2000 under the aegis of the MOUD (Ministry of Urban Development). The manual was prepared by an expert group and lays down guidelines and procedures for ULBs to improve SWM in their cities. The MoEF (Ministry of Environment and Forests) has constituted an expert group for preparation of guidelines for SWM in religious towns/cities in India (2004). Under directions from the Supreme Court, a TAG was set up to improve SWM in the country and oversee implementation of innovative technologies of waste management in the country. The report of the TAG was submitted in 2005. Further, model municipal bylaws have been framed/circulated for ULBs. Income tax relief has also been provided to waste management agencies. Tax-free municipal bonds have been permitted by the Government of India.

Some of the Acts and Rules are:

- Hazardous Wastes (Management and Handling) Rules, 1989/2000/2002
- The Hazardous Wastes (Management, Handling and Transboundary Movement) Rules, 2009
- MoEF Guidelines for Management and Handling of Hazardous Wastes, 1991
- Guidelines for Safe Road Transport of Hazardous Chemicals, 1995
- The National Environmental Tribunal Act, 1995
- The National Environment Appellate Authority Act, 1997
- The Environment (Protection) act, 1986
- The Water (Prevention and Control of Pollution) Act, 1974
- The Plastic Waste (Management and Handling) Rules, 2011
- Bio-Medical Wastes (Management and Handling) Rules, 1998 (Amendment Rules, 2003)
- Batteries (Management and Handling), Amendment Rules, 2010
- The E-waste (Management and Handling) Rules, 2011, was notified in advance in May 2011 to give various stakeholders adequate time to prepare themselves and also to place the required infrastructure for its effective implementation.[2] "These rules shall apply to every producer, consumer or bulk consumer, collection centre, dismantler and recycler of e-waste involved in manufacture, sale, purchase and processing of electrical and electronic equipment",

the guidelines said. However, the rules will not apply to lead acid batteries as covered under the Batteries (Management and Handling) Rules, 2001.

4.7.4 Problems Associated with the Solid Waste Management System

The major deficiencies associated with the solid waste management system are as follows:

Rapidly Increasing Areas to be Served and Quantity of Waste

The solid waste generated in urban areas is increasing due to rise in population and increase in per capita waste generation. The increasing solid waste and the areas to be served strain the existing SWM system.

Inadequate Resources

While allocating resources, including finance, SWM is assigned a low priority, resulting in inadequate provision of funds. Often, there is a common budget for the collection and treatment of sewage and SWM. There is also the absence of suitably trained staff.

Inappropriate Technology

A few attempts have been made to borrow the technology developed in other countries like highly mechanised compost plants, incinerator-cum-power plants, compactor vehicles, etc. However, these attempts have met with little success, since the solid waste characteristics and local conditions in India are different from those for which technology is developed.

Disproportionately High Cost of Manpower

Mostly, out of the total expenditure, around 90 per cent is for manpower of which a major portion is utilised for collection. It is mainly due to lack of segregation of waste at primary level and improper way of waste disposal by households.

Societal and Management Apathy

The operational efficiency of SWM depends on the active participation of both the municipal agency and the citizens. Since the social status of SWM is low, there is strong apathy towards it, which can be seen from the uncollected waste in many areas and the deterioration of the aesthetic and environmental quality at the uncontrolled disposal sites.

Low Efficiency of the System

The SWM system is unplanned and is operated in an unscientific way. Neither are the work norms specified nor is the work of the collection staff appropriately supervised. The vehicles are poorly maintained and no schedule is observed for preventive maintenance. There is no co-ordination of activities between different components of the system.

4.7.5 MEASURES TO COMBAT THE PROBLEM OF SOLID WASTE

Managing solid waste is not a small thing—big plans and sustainable measures, series of steps, effective execution and periodic evaluation are required. Based on studies the following measures can be suggested:

1. There is a need for formulation of a state policy for SWM by each state.
2. Specific urban funds at state level need to be set up for project development, long-term loans at concessional rates and capacity building for PPP in the urban sector.
3. With a view to promoting PPP, there should be a provision for free supply of garbage to the WTE plant or compost plant if no tipping fee is demanded by the private operator for waste processing.
4. States and ULBs must encourage the concept of a tipping fee for private sector participation in SWM. The tipping fee must be linked to critical inputs like diesel, WPI, etc. This should be entered in the concession agreement. Further, there should be periodic payment of a tipping fee to the operator. Any delay beyond 20 days should invite the liability of interest payment. This should be mentioned in the concession agreement.
5. State governments should take responsibility for all permissions/ clearances, being a partner. The onus of getting clearances should not fall on the private sector. This should be mentioned in the concession agreement.
6. Capacity building programmes should be organised to ensure

that ownership and clarity of concession agreements exists on the part of the authority.

7. There is a need to develop contract management capacity in the public sector.
8. The state government policy should encourage a cluster approach for a group of municipalities to select a common operator for economies of scale and because it makes business sense for the private operator.
9. We need to create public awareness and foster civil society's participation. All good practices show that success of SWM has been possible in only those areas where the community was mobilised and willing to contribute to the cause of waste reduction. Creating public awareness thus becomes an important criterion for successful SWM. In every area, citizen forums should be formed. These forums should comprise citizens' representatives, social workers, and municipal officers. Various programmes should be conducted for increasing public awareness.
10. There is urgent need for source segregation. Segregation of waste is a catalyst for the success of alternative means of waste disposal. The quality of the end product (manure in case of compost, pellets in case of WTE or waste to energy) and the cost involved has a direct dependence on the quality of segregation. Many cities in India with compost and WTE facilities are facing problems simply because of poor quality of segregation, and therefore, poor quality of the end product which has no market demand. This is supported by the directive of the Supreme Court to residents of all metro cities to undertake segregation of waste at source.
11. Collection of waste: Properly designed collection bins and implements should be used for the collection and storage of waste at primary and secondary levels of collection. Waste should be collected frequently in order to avoid accumulation, which leads to degradation of an environmental and aesthetic kind. The spacing and location of the bins should be fixed on the basis of the waste load and public opinion.
12. Transportation of waste: Selection of properly designed vehicles is important. Various factors like the width of the road, transport volume, road conditions, etc., play an important role in the selection of vehicles. The vehicle route should be properly

planned for the effective utilisation of manpower, the saving of fuel and the reduction of time. Time and motion studies should be conducted to reduce the non-productive idle time of the vehicles and increase productivity.

13. Disposal of waste: Sanitary landfill techniques should be adopted for the disposal of waste. The compaction of waste should be carried out regularly, preferably with a bulldozer.
14. Littering on the streets should be prohibited by ensuring storage of waste at source in two bins: one for biodegradable waste and another for recyclable material.
15. Primary collection of biodegradable and non-biodegradable waste should be done from the doorsteps at pre-informed time on a day-to-day basis using containerised tricycles/handcart/pick-up vans.
16. Street sweeping should cover all residential and commercial areas on all days of the week irrespective of Sundays and holidays.
17. Abolition of open waste storage depots.
18. Transportation of waste in covered vehicles on a day-to-day basis.
19. Treatment of biodegradable waste using composting or waste to energy technologies meeting the standards laid down.
20. Minimising the waste going to the landfill and disposing of only rejects from the treatment plants and inert material at the landfills as per the standards laid down.

4.7.6 SWM BUSINESS AND IMPLEMENTATION

Today it pays to handle waste. Waste is recycled, waste is business. Marketing the waste is community development activity and a social enterprise, which even NGOs are into as, for instance, in southern Karnataka, the Shri Kshetra Dharmasthala Rural Development Project (SKDRDP) promoting public participation, PPPs, micro enterprises and scavenger cooperatives in innovative and revenue-yielding mechanisms of waste collection, transport, disposal and recycling. Civil society organisations like the Rotary Clubs, Lions Clubs, etc. have also not lagged in such a socio-economic enterprise.

The entire responsibility of implementation as well as development of required infrastructure lies with municipal authorities. They are directed to obtain authorisation from the state pollution control boards/

committees for setting up waste processing and disposal facilities and furnishing annual reports of compliance. However, there is a definite awareness among local bodies as well as policymakers about solid waste management systems. There has been some progress in the right direction during the last few years in India. Let us be conscious of the fact that scientific waste management is no longer moral or corporate social responsibility, it is a legal obligation on the waste generating establishment, both public and private. The legal obligation has motivated the private sector to see business in waste management.

SWM has become a major environmental issue in India. The quality of the urban environment is rapidly deteriorating with rising levels of solid waste. India is currently facing a municipal solid waste management (MSWM) dilemma, for which all elements of society are responsible. Community sensitisation and public awareness are low. There is no system of segregation of organic, inorganic and recyclable waste at household level. There is adequate legal framework in the country to address MSWM. What is lacking is serious and effective implementation and "solid" and healthy combat mechanisms and practices.

In spite of stringent legislation in place, open dumping is the most widespread form of waste disposal. The possible reasons for poor implementation could be a combination of social, technical, institutional and, more important, financial issues. Solid waste management is a challenge to urban local bodies in India. We need to develop simpler, low-cost technology, keeping in view maximum resource recovery in an environment-friendly manner. Although it may seem obvious that planning is needed to implement a successful programme, in practice the need to formulate and follow a well-devised and comprehensive plan is sometimes forgotten. A leaking landfill or other waste management problems may exert pressure on a community to act quickly; hasty actions cause mistakes, which in turn result in delays and wasted resources. While all possible situations cannot be anticipated, many good models based on successful programmes do exist, and programme developers are encouraged to use them when possible to formulate their own programmes. Planning is especially important because of the potentially large number of factors in the waste management process. Political bodies, waste generators, waste haulers, regulatory agencies, construction contractors, plan operators, energy and material buyers, landfill site owners and citizens must be included for a programme to be successful. Each group has the potential to contribute to or delay or derail a project. By formulating and continually reviewing a project plan, programme managers can handle solid waste management in a better way.

4.8 CSR IN SANITATION

Good governance and practices in sanitation require that sanitation policies and programmes be people-centric, legible, accessible and an effective means of distributive justice by strengthening coherence between the public, private sector and civil society.

Corporate social responsibility emerges through a social discourse that focuses attention on the fact that business enterprises, besides making profits for their investors, have commitments and responsibilities to society. It has come to the forefront of public discussion only after the Second World War especially since the decades of the 1950s and 1960s and has seen significant progress since then. The concept and practice of CSR has moved ahead from mere philanthropy to strategic social responsibility. It is more than a knee-jerk reaction to open market business today, i.e., to laissez faire. This transition opens the opportunity and the need to trace the evolution of the concept as well as the practice of CSR by corporates. There is now not only a wide spectrum of CSR systems, based on civil regulation, but also a rising trend of counter arguments regarding principles and performance in relation to firms.

4.8.1 What is CSR?

Corporate social responsibility, also called corporate conscience, corporate citizenship or sustainable responsible business/responsible business is a form of corporate self-regulation integrated into a business model. CSR policy functions as a self-regulatory mechanism whereby a business monitors and ensures its active compliance with the spirit of the law, ethical standards and international norms.

Early definitions of CSR, or CSR1 (1950-1960s) in Frederick's well-accepted classification, carried heavy philosophic overtones. The new theoretical approaches to CSR went beyond the previous somewhat narrower focus and, instead, aimed to develop more comprehensive frameworks that incorporate operational and behavioural aspects of corporate endeavour, relate the corporation to its external environment and ground CSR/CSP theory in one or more social sciences humanities disciplines.

CSR is generally understood as being the way through which a company achieves a balance of economic, environmental and social imperatives ("Triple Bottom Line Approach") while at the same time addressing the expectations of shareholders and stakeholders. Key CSR issues include environmental management, eco-efficiency, responsible sourcing, stakeholder engagement, labour standards and working conditions, employee and community relations, social equity, gender balance, human rights, good governance and anti-corruption measures.

Proponents argue that corporations increase long-term profits by operating with a CSR perspective, while critics argue that CSR distracts from business' economic role. A 2000 study compared existing econometric studies of the relationship between social and financial performance, concluding that the contradictory results of previous studies reporting positive, negative and neutral financial impact were due to flawed empirical analysis and claimed that when the study is properly specified, CSR has a neutral impact on financial outcomes.

CSR is not a new concept in India; however, the Ministry of Corporate Affairs, Government of India, has recently notified Section 135 of the Companies Act, 2013, along with Companies (Corporate Social Responsibility Policy) Rules, 2014, "hereinafter CSR Rules", and other notifications related thereto which make it mandatory (with effect from 1 April 2014) for certain companies who fulfil the criteria as mentioned under Sub Section 1 of Section 135 to comply with the provisions relevant to CSR.

4.8.2 Need

India has a massive problem of open defecation. The WHO and the UNICEF estimate that there are more than 620 million people practising open defecation in the country, which is nearly half the population of India. Open defecation is prevalent among all socio-economic groups in rural India though the bottom two wealth quintiles bear the heaviest burden. Children, already vulnerable and marginalised, pay the highest price in respect of their survival and development. This well-established traditional behaviour is deeply ingrained through a practice which is transferred from parents to children. As per the World Bank statistics, India's GDP stands at $1.3 trillion and we are currently ranked 11th in the world on the basis of nominal GDP. If we could cut down expenses incurred due to illnesses and lack of productivity due to illnesses, our economy would get further impetus.

The ministry is committed to having India ODF by 2022, but achieving this requires combined fresh action and efforts/initiatives from all quarters whether from government, corporate or non-government organisation sectors. In a country like India, where more than 26 per cent rural people live below the poverty line, assuring basic hygiene for one and all is a major task. Poor sanitation affects the health of the people of the country as also the development of the nation. Women are the most affected by lack of proper sanitation.

The Government of India has been targeting sanitation aspects through its Nirmal Bharat Abhiyan for decades but still the problem persists, which clearly indicates that government incentives alone are not enough and are required to be supplemented by private industry and by the CPSEs through CSR.

4.8.3 CSR Guidelines for Sanitation

Some of the reasons cited for the persistence of open defecation in India include poverty (the inability to afford toilets), landlessness and tenants in housing without toilets, and deep-rooted cultural and social norms that have established open defecation as an acceptable habit.

Poor sanitary measures set India back by crores of rupees every year due to illnesses, and the cost to rural families and to the economy, as a whole, in terms of productivity losses, and expenditure on medicines and public healthcare, are enormous.

The Ministry of Drinking Water and Sanitation administers the NBA in the rural areas of the country. The objective of NBA is to accelerate the sanitation coverage in rural areas so as to comprehensively cover the rural community through renewed strategies and saturation approach. The NBA envisages covering the entire community for saturated outcomes with a view to creating nirmal gram panchayats. As per the 2011 Census, the rural coverage of access to toilet facilities has reached 32.70 percent.

4.8.4 Implementation

The Indian government introduced in 2009 the National Voluntary Guidelines (NVGs), mandating public disclosure of CSR initiatives and expenditure. Businesses should conduct and govern themselves with ethics, transparency and accountability. They should focus on 2 per cent spending (in identified "need" areas) that may take away attention from the way in which the profits are earned. The company that operates a toxic business is likely to implement and more loudly showcase CSR projects to gain a halo that blinds, to drown out critics and to "green wash" its image.

The CSR law enables CSR contributions to incubators providing legs to for-profit ventures working with social objectives. A high-level committee has recommendaed conducting a review of the CSR provision of the Act after three years.

The latest amendment to the Companies Act, 2013, with respect to the CSR policy, which came into force from 19 January, will provide much needed fuel to CSR. The amendment will facilitate faster channelisation of the ₹20,000 crore CSR budget into a sector like clean water and sanitation.

- Non-banking finance company Mahindra & Mahindra Financial Services Ltd (MMFSL) used a portion of their 2014-15 CSR funds to invest in two social start-ups through Villgro, a Department of Science and Technology (DST) and Indian Institute of Management Ahmedabad technology venture:
- Sustain Earth Energy Solutions—a start-up working to provide affordable biogas technology for rural areas.
- Sickle Innovations—a start-up making handheld cotton picking machines using a patented technology that enhances labour productivity.

Companies spent over ₹42 crore towards the Swachh Bharat Kosh as part of their CSR activities in 2014-15, as Parliament was informed on 3 May 2016 (see Table 4.3).

The funds were used for achieving the objective of improving cleanliness levels in rural and urban areas including schools. As many as 460 companies spent a little over ₹6,337 crore for CSR activities last fiscal.

Table 4.3 : Private Corporates Involved in the Construction of Toilets and the Toilets Constructed by Them under Swachh Vidyalaya Initiative (as on 01.03.2016)

S. No.	*Corporate Name*	*Approved /Booked*	*Completed*
1	CII	138	138
2	Coca-Cola India Pvt Ltd	14	14
3	FICCI	38	38
4	IFIG	150	150
5	ITC Limited	60	60
6	Infosys Foundation	252	252
7	Mahindra Group	1,171	1,171
8	Mercedes-Benz	1	1
9	Microsoft India	22	22
10	Tata Consultancy Services	1509	1,509
11	Titan Company Limited	42	42
12	Toyota Kirloskar Motors Pvt Ltd	69	69
	Total	3466	3,466

Source: Swachhta Status Report 2016, http://www.sulabhenvis.nic.in/Database/TabularData_9712.aspx

This included 51 PSUs which spent ₹2,386.60 crore. In a written reply in the Rajya Sabha, former Corporate Affairs Minister Arun Jaitley said companies spent a total of ₹42.64 crore on the Swachh Bharat Kosh. Besides, firms spent ₹15.49 crore towards the Clean Ganga Fund during the period under review.

Former Union HRD Minister Smriti Irani addressed the conference on the use of CSR funds for construction of toilets in schools in New Delhi on 14 October 2014 as part of the Swachh Bharat Swachh Vidyalaya campaign. The minister indicated that the prime minister's Mission of a Clean India by 2019 can only be achieved if we provide a clean environment in schools including functional toilets to every child so that she becomes a change agent for a larger goal that we have set for ourselves. She reiterated the government's resolve to provide toilets in every school with a separate toilet for girls within one year and invited the corporate sector to participate in this national endeavour by constructing toilets and also maintaining them for some time.

NOTES

1 E-waste is a collective term used for end-of-life electronics and electrical equipment such as computers, mobile phones, television sets, florescent tubes. These aspects are covered under the E-waste Law.

2 The law came into force on 1 May 2012.

Chapter 5

Models of Sanitation from the Indus Valley Civilisation Onwards`

Sanitation has gone through phases in the development of human civilisation. Toilets have a history (see Table 5.1) and they are also influenced by development thinking or models of the times. Around 2800 BC early human settlements starting digging small holes in the ground but they dug them far away from their villages because of the smell. Then came toilets. The word "toilet" is derived from the French word "toilette", which means little cloth. In the 17th century it was a cloth cover for a dressing table, called a toilet table. If a woman was at her toilet it meant she was dressing and preparing her appearance. By the 19th century toilet room or toilet was a euphemism for a certain room. The word "lavatory" comes from the Latin "lavare" meaning to wash. In the 17th century a lavatory was a place for washing. Later it became a euphemism for a certain room.

5.1 HISTORY OF TOILETS

In the ancient world people were capable of designing quite sophisticated toilets. Stone Age farmers lived in a village at Skara Brae in the Orkney Islands. Some of their stone huts had drains built under them and some houses had cubicles over the drains. They may have been toilets.

In ancient Egypt rich people had proper bathrooms and toilets in their homes. Toilet seats were made of limestone. Poor people made do with a wooden stool with a hole in it. Underneath was a container filled with sand, which had to be emptied by hand. (If you were wealthy, slaves did that!) In the Indus Valley civilisation (ca. 2600-1900 BC) streets were built on a grid pattern and networks of sewers were dug under them. Toilets were flushed with water. On the island of Crete, the Minoan civilisation flourished from 2000 to 1600 BC. They too built drainage systems, which also covered sewage. Toilets were flushed with water.

The Romans mastered the art of the bath. As early as the third century BC, elaborate baths were being included in the villas and townhouses of wealthy Romans. With separate rooms for damp and dry heat, and warm and cold baths, the buildings were heated with hypocausts, furnaces with flues extending through the floors and walls of the building. The furnaces also heated boilers that supplied hot water. The public baths, or thermae, of imperial Rome expanded on the facilities of the smaller private baths and necessitated the construction of reservoirs and aqueducts to supply the enormous quantities of water needed. These baths were also heated by hypocausts and had dressing rooms, warm rooms, hot baths, steam rooms, recreation rooms and cold baths. Hot spring spas in far-flung locations of the Roman empire, such as Bath in England and Aix-les-Bains in France, are still in use today.

The Romans also built sewers to collect rainwater and sewage. (They even had a goddess of sewers called Cloacina!) Wealthy people had their own toilets but the Romans also built public lavatories. In them there was no privacy, just stone seats next to one another without partitions of any kind. Despite the public lavatories many people still went in the street. After using the toilet people wiped their behinds with a sponge on a stick.

In the Middle Ages toilets were simply pits in the ground with wooden seats over them. However, monks built stone or wooden lavatories over rivers. At Portchester Castle in the 12th century monks built stone chutes leading to the sea. When the tide went in and out it would flush away the sewage.

In medieval castles the toilet was called a garderobe and it was simply a vertical shaft with a stone seat at the top. Some garderobes emptied into the moat. Wealthy people would use rags to wipe their behinds. Ordinary people often used a plant called common mullein or woolly mullein.

In 1547 people were forbidden to go in the courtyards of royal palaces so presumably it must have been a real nuisance. The first modern flushable toilet was described in 1596 by Sir John Harington, an English courtier and the godson of Queen Elizabeth I. Harington's device called for a two-foot-deep oval bowl waterproofed with pitch, resin and wax and fed by water. In 1775 English inventor Alexander Cummings was granted the first patent for a flush toilet. His greatest innovation was the S-shaped pipe below the bowl that used water to create a seal, preventing sewer gas from entering through the toilet. In the late19th century, a London plumbing impresario named Thomas Crapper manufactured one of the first widely successful lines of flush toilets with an upstairs cistern.

The first modern toilet was invented in 1596 but didn't become widespread until 1851. Before that the toilet had chamber pots and holes in the ground. Chamber pots were like bed pots which were to be put under your bed. In the 19th century toilet pans were made of porcelain. They were usually decorated, embossed or painted with attractive colours. Seats were of wood and cisterns were often emptied by pulling a chain. At first toilet bowls were boxed in but the first pedestal toilet bowl was made in 1884. Meanwhile, the vacant/engaged bolt for public toilets was patented in 1883.

The first indoor bathrooms that were made possible by the refinement of the toilet were communal affairs shared by many people. Previously, water closets were portable, so a dedicated space for their use wasn't necessary. More elaborate residences might have had a dedicated dressing room that contained a water closet, a moveable tin or iron bath and a washstand, but this type of centralised "bathroom" didn't become widespread until indoor plumbing and permanent water closets gained acceptance towards the end of the 19th century.

Bathrooms evolved as a response to fundamental needs for personal hygiene, as well as an expression of available technology and cultural standards. And in the short half-century between 1875 and 1925 the period between when indoor plumbing began to be widely available and when it became almost universal, our attitudes towards privacy and modesty changed significantly. What were once communal and family activities became a private activity.

However, indoor toilets were a luxury in the 19th century. Working-class homes almost always had outside lavatories. About 1900, some houses were built for skilled workers with bathrooms. Interestingly, the modern toilet and its associated plumbing was as much a response to urban industrialisation as it was a result of the manufacturing technology that industrialisation made possible. In a rural society, an indoor toilet may be a convenience, but it isn't essential. In a crowded urban environment, however, the sanitary elimination of human waste becomes a real problem, and in the absence of sufficient soil to contain and break down human waste, water became the only other medium available to carry it away. The development of municipal sewage systems in London and Paris in the 18th and 19th centuries respectively was a direct response to the threat of disease that came from increasing population densities and inadequate waste disposal. The modern world needed the modern toilet not so much for convenience but for its own survival. However, it was decades before inside toilets became universal.

Unfortunately, while 19th century engineers refined the process of using water to flush away waste, in the 20th century people found that it wasn't possible to just flush their problems away. Widespread contamination of large parts of the world's freshwater supplies is one of the legacies of the modern flush toilet. So the evolution of the toilet continues, necessitated by the need to use less water and so place less of a demand on water resources. Perhaps the next revolution will occur in the development of waste treatment systems that minimise our reliance on water.

In 1970 Sulabh International was established by Dr Bindeshwar Pathak as a non-profit NGO in Bihar. Now its central office is in Delhi. By 1980 auto control public toilets were set up. The organisation could effectively deal with the sanitation crisis in India, with the vision and leadership of Dr Pathak, "million toilet man". He is responsible for the construction of more than 8,500 toilets in India which employ the pay and use system for their maintenance. Everyone knows how Sulabh made public toilets at bus stands, railway stations, etc, really usable. They also make toilets for Indian Railways.

With the astonishing speed at which technology is advancing, we find it difficult to predict what the next big step will be. But it's most likely there will be some artificial intelligence involved. The design itself might also change to further disconnect it from the current norm.

Table 5.1: Timeline of the Toilet

2300 BC	At Skara Brae in Scotland stone huts have drains with cubicles over them. They may have been toilets.
2000 BC	In northwest India and Pakistan towns are built with networks of sewers. Toilets are flushed with water.
1800 BC	On Crete some toilets are flushed with water.
1200 BC	In Egypt rich people use a container with sand, which is emptied by slaves.

AD 100	In Rome sewers collect rainwater and sewage. There are public lavatories. The Romans have a goddess of sewers called Cloacina.
476	The Roman empire falls and in Western Europe sophisticated plumbing vanishes for centuries.
12th century	At Portchester Castle monks built stone chutes leading to the sea. When the tide went in and out it flushed away the sewage.
1200	In castles the toilet is a vertical shaft cut into the thickness of the walls with a stone seat on top.
1500	Ordinary people often use the leaves of a plant called woolly mullein as toilet paper.
1547	People are forbidden to go in the courtyards of royal palaces.
1596	Sir John Harington invents a flushing toilet but the idea fails to catch on. People continue to use cess pits, which are cleaned by men called gong farmers.
1775	Alexander Cummings patents a flushing lavatory.
1778	Joseph Brahmah makes a better design.
1850	Earth closets are popular. When you pull a lever granulated clay from a box covers the contents of the pan.
1852	The first modern public lavatory opens.
1857	Toilet paper goes on sale in the USA. It is sold in sheets.
1883	The vacant/engaged bolt is invented.
1884	The first pedestal toilet pan is made.
1890	Toilet paper on rolls goes on sale in the US.
1892	John Nevil Maskelyne invents the coin-operated lock for toilets.
1900	For the first time some houses for skilled workers are built with inside lavatories.
1928	Toilet paper on rolls goes on sale in Europe.
1942	Soft toilet paper goes on sale.
2001	The World Toilet Organization is formed.
2015	Indian Railways instals vacuum toilets for the first time on a train. The trial run was with the First AC coach of the Dibrugarh Rajdhani.
2016	Dr Pathak is appointed Brand Ambassador for Swachh Rail Mission by the Government of India.
2017	World's biggest toilet pot model unveiled at Marora, popularly known as "Trump village", in Haryana on the World Toilet Day in a bid to create awareness about sanitation and use of toilets.
2019	The final flush on train toilets that empty their contents directly onto Britain's tracks were pulled in.

5.2 RURAL DEVELOPMENT MODELS IN INDIA

Rural development thinkers and planners have some models before them. We have a Gandhian theory, rather, a "model" of rural development that is worth analysing, particularly in a study of infrastructure. The emphasis is on village-centred development or "movement" based on the principle of voluntarism. For Mahatma Gandhi, development, like freedom, had to begin from the bottom. The chief features of Gandhian philosophy are: the ideal village or self-sufficient unit, decentralised rural administration, role of small and cottage industries trusteeship in resource management and the development of khadi are symbols of simplicity and indigenous production. Although there is a clear emphasis on the "small" machines, and scale of production to meet the few and simple needs of villagers, we also see that Gandhi stressed the progress and good management of rural infrastructure, whether sources of drinking water or health and sanitation.

Gandhi did not visualise static conditions in the village. He was aware that the wheel of development must move forward but also that the process of development must not create imbalances. His concept of the village was anchored on the postmodern perspective of "quality of life". However, several people, including Jawaharlal Nehru, expressed doubts over this model. Nehru wrote, "The whole question is how to achieve this society and what its content should be."

Another grassroots model of rural development is the Gadgil Model developed by D.R. Gadgil of Pune's Institute of Political Science and Economics. It advocated specific planned action for rural development "planning from below" or the "bottom-up approach" as against the "top-down approach" or "centre-down approach" or the "trickle down paradigm". Local governments and local citizens are to be involved actively in planning and utilising the infrastructural facilities.

Gadgil was of the view that a plan which attempts a coordinated development of all sectors must attain a high degree of specificity. This would not only help avoid wastage of resources but also ensure planned development of specific resources in the sector, properly dovetailed with use or consumption in the development plans of each sector. There is thus the need for a large degree of correspondence between targets and achievements in both production resources plans and area plans for smooth progress. It was for planning locally rather than through a breakdown of programmes and estimates framed at the national level. The general thrust of the top-down theory is that a relatively few, large investments can be made in specific sectors of the economy or geographical areas and the benefits will spread and help other areas. Decisions are made by the government without consultation with local people, e.g., projects related to petroleum, forestry, infrastructure, etc.

In a sense, the traditional "centre down" theories of the classical era state that if something is constructed or invested in, benefits will come. A significant problem with this style of rural development is the risk of the backwash effect, a result that is unintentional. Some writers are of the opinion that the bottom-up approach leaves things to chance which is politically risky. An alternative approach, therefore, is one which is self-directed, which makes way for self-reliance through self-generated development that includes region-specific infrastructural facilities.

V.K.R.V. Rao and his associates developed the cluster approach, moving away from the thinking of "self-sufficiency" of villages to "interdependence" of villages. This move was clearly supported by V.M. Dandekar.

5.3 RURAL AND URBAN DEVELOPMENT AND SANITATION

Rural development and empowerment cannot do without good sanitation. For health, hygiene and human development in our villages, good sanitation is a must. Long ago, the United States of America conducted a public health service survey in 15 countries to ascertain more definitely the sanitary conditions in the rural districts of the US. The results of the study were embodied in a progress report, "Rural Sanitation" by Surg L.L. Lumsden. He writes:

> Time and again students of public health have called attention to the backward state of sanitary conditions in rural districts and to the influence of this on the health of city dwellers. There is considerable evidence, moreover, to show that whereas in cities health conditions, as measured by the general death rate, are quite generally improving, conditions in the rural districts are almost stationary. When one considers the many natural advantages inherent in life in the country, it is probable that the insanitary conditions responsible for the almost stationary death rate are the results of ignorance.[1]

In regard to sanitation in urban areas, the scene is no different though rural and urban sanitation are mired in pitiable sanitation conditions. Invariably, the poor face the brunt as public toilet provisions are unable to meet the needs. If we take the example of Mumbai city, an average of 81 persons share a single toilet. In some places, this figure rises to 273. Even the lowest average is still 58, according to local municipal authority figures. In many urban and semi-urban pockets it is still a common sight to see people squatting by roads and railway tracks or along the coast, openly defecating in the city where some of the world's richest people live.

Mahatma Gandhi not only fought for independence but also took up cudgels against a host of social problems. Known for social engineering, he conducted social experiments for the development of Indian villages. Gandhi wrote,

> Village tanks are promiscuously used for bathing, washing clothes and drinking and cooking purposes. Cattle also use many village tanks. Buffaloes are often to be seen wallowing in them. The wonder is that, in spite of this sinful misuse of village tanks, villages have not been destroyed by epidemics. It is the universal medical evidence that this neglect to ensure purity of the water supply of villages is responsible for many of the diseases suffered by the villagers.

He also wrote,

> Any city that would attend to its sanitation in a proper spirit, will add to both its health and wealth....An ideal village will be so constructed as to lend itself to perfect sanitation.... The very first problem the village worker will solve is its sanitation.

The Central Rural Sanitation Programme was launched by the Government of India in 1986. The objective of this programme was to improve the quality of life of the rural people and to provide privacy and dignity to women. This was intended to supplement the efforts of the states. The programme provided for 100 per cent subsidy for construction of sanitary latrines for Scheduled Castes, Scheduled Tribes and landless labourers and subsidy as per the rate prevailing in the states for the general public. The guidelines of the programme were circulated to the states in 1986.

Two decades later, it was seen that only the Government of India had taken up rural sanitation with a strategic approach.

After implementing the rural sanitation programme, the government decided to modify some of its earlier approaches. After several consultations and exchange of views with experts, the programme was revised. The revised programme aimed at an integrated approach towards rural sanitation.

The concept of sanitary marts for supply of materials required for construction of sanitary latrines and involvement of voluntary organisations in publicity campaigns and execution of the programme are also new elements. At least 10 per cent of the total funds are to be channelled through voluntary organisations, apart from the funds earmarked for activities under the Council for Advancement of People Action for Appropriate Rural Technologies (CAPART). Another salient feature of the revised programme is to develop at least one model village covering facilities like sanitary latrines, conversion of dry latrines into sanitary latrines, garbage pits, soakage pits, drainage, paved lanes, sanitary latrines in institutions, cleanliness in ponds, tanks, and clean surroundings around hand pumps and other drinking water sources.

The CRSP was revised in March 1993. Guidelines were developed based on the revisions made, which were in the nature of general guidelines. The technical details and guidelines on various types of sanitary latrines were compiled and sent to the states and implementing agencies for their use and guidance. One such guideline on twin-pit pour-flush latrines brought out by the Ministry of Housing and Urban Affairs, Government of India, the UNDP and the World Bank were distributed. The Government of India designed various strategies to address rural sanitation issues in a holistic manner. Afterwards, rural sanitation became a key intervention area in rural development policies of the Central Government.

Low-cost latrines were introduced to attract people's participation in improving sanitary facilities in homes, habitations or villages. In rural sanitation, the CRSP ushered in a sea change and got focus on women, which was a very forward-looking step in the rural sanitation sector. Public latrines have not been successful in the past as rural women faced difficulties in some areas. In many cases individual household latrines were not feasible. Therefore, on a pilot basis, village sanitary complexes exclusively for women were built.

On coverage of rural sanitation, the latest census enumeration throws up some important findings, officially released on 1 May 2013. The total population of the country is 1.21 billion, which is an increase of 181.96 million persons during the decade 2001-11.Interestingly, the Planning Commission review puts Sikkim as the first Nirmal Rajya (cent per cent ODF) state with Kerala and Himachal Pradesh attaining similar status in 2012.

New strategies were designed to involve rural local governance institutions such as three-tier PRIs, wherein the sustainability and community ownership will be gauged based on participating PRIs. Keeping this in view, the Government of India made certain provisions, which are already laid down in the 73rd Constitutional Amendment Act (CAA).

Revised CRSP implementation matched the Government of India's plans in the rural water and sanitation sector. Rural sanitation pilot projects were initiated in various districts along with reforms in the rural sanitation sector that were implemented during the Ninth and Tenth Five Year Plans. The adoption of various reforms took place based on the experiences and practices of the developing and underdeveloped nations. Three pilot programmes were Sector Reforms Project, Swajaldhara I and Swajaldhara-II, developed with a special focus on reforms of rural sanitation programmes in India.

5.3.1 Urban Areas and Sanitation

Urban sanitation is a form of sanitation which focuses on maintaining sanitary conditions in urban environments. Many people think specifically of the collection, treatment and disposal of human waste when they hear the words "urban sanitation", but sanitation in urban environments is a much more complex system. Sanitation is an especially pressing issue in slums, where crowded conditions and poor sanitation contribute to frequent outbreaks of disease which threaten the inhabitants of slums in addition to exposing other city residents to health risks.

Historically, urban communities gave little thought to sanitation, which turned into a major problem in some areas. The edges of many urban streets were piled with garbage which could would dead animals along with untreated human waste. Walking in urban streets was an exercise in avoidance, as people freely threw garbage and human waste out into the street without a care for those passing by, and diseases were rampant as a result of waste materials on the streets and in urban waterways. A growing understanding of hygiene combined with social pressure from people tired of living in filth eventually led to the development of urban sanitation.

The purpose of urban sanitation is to reduce risks to human health by managing factors in the urban environment which can contribute to health problems. One of the major factors is human waste, which is generated in large volumes in urban areas. Sewers which collect such waste and route it to central processing facilities are, therefore, a key aspect of urban sanitation. So are facilities like public toilets, which discourage people from using the streets as a bathroom, along with portable toilets for major events which are designed to provide attendees with a location to safely eliminate waste.

The vision for urban sanitation in India is that all Indian cities and towns become totally sanitised, healthy and liveable and ensure and sustain good public health and environmental outcomes for all their citizens with a special focus on hygienic and affordable sanitation facilities for the urban poor and women.

The Ministry of Housing and Urban Poverty Alleviation is administering a centrally sponsored scheme for Integrated Low Cost Sanitation (ILCS). Under this scheme, central subsidy to the extent of 75 percent, state subsidy to the extent of 15 per cent and beneficiary contribution to the extent of 10 per cent are provided for.

Components of National Urban Sanitation Policy:

- Awareness Generation
- Knowledge Development
- Financing
- National Monitoring & Evaluation
- Reaching the Un-served and Poor Households
- Institutional Roles
- Capacity Building
- Coordination

Key Principles

The National Urban Sanitation Policy has identified the following core principles that need to be addressed. These must be used as a guide by the cities:

- Institutional Roles and Responsibilities
- Awareness Generation for Changing Mindsets
- City-wide Approach
- Technology Choice
- Reaching the Un-served and Poor
- Client focus and Generation of Demand
- Sustained Improvements

Some of the elected members of the ULB must be members of the task force. The task force should be headed by the mayor with the executive head (e.g., municipal commissioner) as the convenor. Cities can also choose to appoint, as a part of the task force, city sanitation ambassadors chosen from eminent people who enjoy outstanding credibility and influence among the city's leadership and population. The city sanitation task force will be responsible for:

- Launching the city's 100 per cent sanitation campaign
- Generating awareness amongst the city's citizens and stakeholders
- Approving materials and progress reports provided by the implementing agency, other public agencies, as well as NGOs and private parties contracted by the implementing agency, for different aspects of implementation (see below)
- Approving the City Sanitation Plan for the city prepared by the sanitation implementation agency after consultations with citizens
- Undertaking field visits from time to time to supervise progress
- Briefings to the press/media and state government about progress
- Providing overall guidance to the implementation agency
- Recommend to the ULB for fixing of responsibilities for city-wide sanitation on a permanent basis
- The implementing agency will examine the law and rules in this regard and make recommendations for the task force to make the rules explicit regarding:
- Safe sanitary arrangements at unit level (household, establishment)
- Designs and systems for safe collection
- Norms for transport/conveyance
- Treatment and final disposal

Some of the bigger cities may choose to prepare the plans on a regional/

district or ward basis. This may be a good way to mobilise stakeholders of the respective wards/regions and generate competition.

Technology choice poses a major problem in Indian cities not only because of lack of information on what exists at present, but also because of the constraints of land, tenure and low budgetary priority accorded to sanitation historically. Technologies need to be incremental, for instance, even if sewers are ideal for dense settlements, they may not be feasible to execute immediately. In such cases, interim (e.g., on-site, or community septic tanks or latrines if space is a constraint) systems may be planned with a view to later upgrade these to more sophisticated systems (e.g., sewerage).

Experiences from many Indian cities show that a differentiated approach is necessary to extend good quality sanitation services to the poor—the group that suffers the most in terms of adverse impacts on health and lost earnings. Participatory approaches are needed to consult the poor settlements and involve them in the process of planning and management of sanitation arrangements. As Pramod Madhwaraj, Minister for Fisheries, Youth Empowerment and Sports, Government of Karnataka, said recently, officers of all departments should respond immediately to the demands of the safai karmacharis and give them required facilities.

Cities can institute their own reward schemes to incentivise local stakeholders to participate in the process of improvement for reaching 100 per cent sanitation. Rewards could be given following the national guidelines on an area basis. For example, the following could be units for rewards: a) Municipal wards; b) Colonies or Residents' Associations; c) Schools, colleges and other educational institutions; d) Market and bazaar committees; e) City-based institutions or localities e.g., railway stations, bus depots, office bhawans, etc.; and f) Other locations and institutions that may be in the city.

It may be noted that the awards will not recognise mere inputs, hardware or expenditure incurred in urban sanitation but assess how these lead to achievements of intermediate milestones towards the final result of 100 per cent safe disposal of wastes from the city on a sustainable basis. Cities will need to raise the awareness of city stakeholders (households, establishments, industries, municipal functionaries, media, etc.) since improved sanitation can ensure improved public health and environmental outcomes only if considerable changes in behaviour and practice take place across the spectrum of society.

A totally sanitised city will be one that has achieved the outputs or milestones specified in the National Urban Sanitation policy, the salient features of which are as follows:

- Cities must be open defecation free
- Must eliminate the practice of manual scavenging and provide adequate personnel the protective equipment that addresses the safety of sanitation workers
- Municipal wastewater and stormwater drainage must be safely managed
- Recycling and reuse of treated wastewater for non-potable applications should be implemented wherever possible
- Solid waste collected and disposed of fully and safely
- Services to the poor and systems for sustaining results
- Improved public health outcomes and environmental standards

The rating of cities in regard to their performance in sanitation improvement will be based on a set of objective indicators of outputs, processes and outcomes. On the basis of the above rating scheme, cities will be placed in different categories as presented in Table 5.2. National rating survey data will utilise these categories for publication of results.

Table 5.2: City Colour Codes: Categories

No.	*Category*	*Description*	*Points*
1	Red Cities	On the brink of public health and environmental "emergency" and needing immediate remedial action	< 33
2	Black	Needing considerable improvement	< 34 < 66
3	Blue	Recovering but still diseased	< 67 < 90
4	Green	Healthy and clean city	< 91 < 100

Source: www.worldbank.org/gwsp, 2018

5.4 JOURNEY FROM INDUS VALLEY CIVILISATION TO 21ST CENTURY

In October 2003, elected local representatives of gram panchayats were involved to promote collective community action through sanitation.

The Nirmal Gram Puraskar (NGP) was instituted for this purpose. NGP awards were given to districts, blocks and gram panchayats that have achieved 100 per cent sanitation coverage of individual households, 100 per cent school sanitation coverage and are free from open defecation and have a clean environment. On 24 February 2005, former president of India Dr A.P.J. Abdul Kalam gave away 40 NGP awards to gram panchayats from six states for ODF status. In 2012, the Government of India launched the Nirmal Bharat Abhiyan. This programme emphasised a new approach on awareness by linking it with the current sponsored schemes of the Government of India. The Total Sanitation Campaign closed in 2012 after striving for 13 years to achieve universal rural sanitation coverage.

There is no doubt that not-for-profit civil society organisations have played an important role in the field of sanitation and hygiene. It can be recalled that even during pre-Independence times, NGOs were actively associated in the sanitation movement and in the last four decades there has been an increase in the number of organisations working on sanitation issues. In our country, the Sulabh International Social Service Organisation is the pioneer in the field of sanitation. It has created history by continuously working on sanitation and rehabilitation of scavengers in India since its inception in 1970. Today, decades later, the organisation is one of the best known NGOs working in the sanitation sector.

The history of toilets in India is as old as the Indus Valley civilisation, which had grown in and around Harappa and Mohenjo-daro. The archaeological remains of the Indus Valley civilisation bear evidence to the use of water-borne toilets by the Harappan people living in Lothal, which is only 62 km from Ahmedabad. Each house in Harappa had a private toilet linked to the covered drains outside. The architects of the Indus Valley knew sanitary engineering, which got buried in the grave of the Indus Valley civilisation, thereby leading to the practice of open defecation.

According to some historians, the invention of the sitting-type toilet dates back to the Minoan civilisation in Greece, which is older than the Indus Valley civilisation. The Minoans of Crete are credited for the first flushing human waste management system. Rome has its own history of public and private toilets in bygone times. In ancient Rome, the public toilets had side-by-side seats without any partition. Each seat had a hole, and water kept flowing to flush away excreta. Archaeologists have confirmed the existence of the same toilet system in the Egyptian civilisation too.

Legend says that the slaves in Rome used to hold urine pots made of silver whenever the members of the royal/aristocratic families felt like urinating while playing cards at dinner parties. Evidence of the use of stools with keyholes for urination and defecation have been unearthed in Thailand and Sri Lanka. The ruins of the Housesteads Roman Fort in Britain have the remains of public loos consisting of seats with holes and without partitions. The men used to gossip about everyday matters while using the loos and had sticks padded with sponge to clean their behinds.

England witnessed a major development of the toilet system in the late 1500s. The invention of the first modern indoor flushing system is credited to John Harington, who devised the toilet flushing mechanism and installed it for Queen Elizabeth 1. In the 1800s and 1900s, flushing toilets were no longer confined to royal households. They were gradually reaching the common man.

In India, there was a dark period of human hygiene from 500 to 1500. Protrusions were used for defecation in aristocratic households and forts across India. Excreta was dumped onto the ground and in rivers. The fort of Jaisalmer bears testimony. In the medieval period, toilets were simple pits with wooden seats on the ground. Besides, the primitive practice of covering human waste with earth was prevalent in some parts of the Mughal empire. In the medieval castles of Europe, toilets were vertical chutes with stone seats on the top. They were called "garderobe" (which became wardrobe in course of time). In Europe, the well-to-do people would wipe their behinds with rags.

The history of toilets for public use is full of twists in several countries. Poor maintenance of public toilets has always been a concern. Mughal Emperor Jahangir had commissioned the construction of a public loo to be used by as many as 100 families, 125 km from Delhi, in 1556. But poor maintenance drove the people to defecate in the open. In 1872, the French municipalities mandated private organisations fund maintenance of public toilets for 20 years.

Several countries implemented measures to improve sanitary conditions. Provision of toilets and construction of cesspools were made compulsory in 1519. The British issued the first sanitation law in 1848 in England. The first sanitation law came in effect into India in 1878. The municipalities were mandated to construct toilets in the slums of Calcutta, the capital of British India. Toilets got curtains in 1880. The trend was known as Belle Epoque in France and Edwardian in England. With the onset of 1900, a bathroom with loo became an institution all over Europe. In India, it was called gusalkhana by the Mughals.

The history of toilets has come a long way with the evolution of human living and hygiene. Though the developed countries of the world have put an end to open defecation, the developing countries, including India, Indonesia, China and Korea, are still grappling with the challenge of controlling open defecation. In 2001, the World Toilet Organization was formed to encourage construction of toilets for the sake of public wellbeing in the developing nations.

The capital of India got a museum of toilets in 1992. It exhibits different toilet models from 50 countries in three sections—Ancient, Medieval and Modern—from 3000 BC till the end of the 20th century. The Museum of Toilets in New Delhi is one of the most offbeat places to visit in India.

5.5 SOME TOILET STORIES

A Bride Asked for a Toilet as Her Wedding Gift

In a first, a bride asked for a readymade toilet as a wedding gift from her parents during her wedding in 2015. The daughter of a farmer in Maharashtra was unaware of the fact that there was no toilet in her in-laws' house when the marriage was fixed. Chaitali was the first Indian bride to demand a toilet set up instead of jewellery or kitchen appliances or household gadgets.

A Bride Left Her Husband for Lack of a Toilet

Priyanka Bharti's story is an inspirational one for all brides in the rural pockets of India. In 2012, the 19-year-old newly-wed, Priyanka reached her in-laws' house in Uttar Pradesh's Maharajganj district only to run away the next day because she had to defecate in the open like all other members of her husband's family due to the lack of basic sanitation in their home. Her brave act of defying the in-laws' family tradition of open defecation led to a widespread campaign which drew the attention of Sulabh International. Sulabh International got Priyanka a toilet in her in-laws' house and awarded her with ₹2 lakh for bringing a revolutionary change in the lives of other brides.

He Gave up his American Dream to Become Poop Guy of India

On return to India in 2007 after four years of his "American Dream" pursuit in the US, Swapnil Chaturvedi was taken aback by the sheer lack of sanitation and the sorry picture of open defecation in his home country. He left his cushy job and luxurious lifestyle in America to educate the locals on hygiene habits and improve the existing community restrooms which were previously not safe for women. In 2011, he launched a programme, Samagra Sanitation, which became a Gates Foundation trustee.

A Teenager Went on a Two-day Hunger Strike for a Toilet

A 15-year-old girl staged a hunger protest in demand of a toilet in Tumakuru district of Karnataka. A 10th grader with a do-or-die attitude, Lavanya staged a 48-hour hunger protest to convince her parents of the pressing need to have a toilet in the home, which further fuelled the Swachh Bharat Abhiyan in her village, Sira.

School Students Crowdfund Toilet for a Friend

Not only women and men but also young students are the agents of change in some toilet stories in India. In Nagapattinam district of Tamil Nadu, four young Indians, Class VIII students, raised money to build a toilet in a friend's house where there was no basic sanitation facility. They approached their classmates to crowdfund the construction.

A 105-year-old Lady Sells Her Goats to Build a Toilet

In Chhattisgarh, 105-year-old Kunwar Bai Yadav joined the brigade of change makers in response to Narendra Modi's mission to make the country open defecation free by the year 2019. She became the first resident to build a toilet in her village. She paid for the construction by selling some of her goats, her only source of livelihood. Inspired by her, every household in the village got a toilet within a year. Today, Dhamtari, with a population of eight lakh, is the first ODF district in Chhattisgarh.

A Woman Sells Her Mangalsutra to Get a Toilet

Rural women, who are daily wagers, are playing an instrumental role in the nationwide campaign for toilets and sanitation in India. The story of Phool Kumari's praiseworthy act of choosing her dignity over her mangalsutra is an inspiring one. A cook at a local primary school in Barahkhanna village, Bihar, Phool Kumari sold her mangalsutra to raise money for the construction of a toilet in her house when her personal savings fell short. She was made the brand ambassador of a sanitation awareness campaign in the district.

A Man Mortgages His Wife's Jewellery for a Toilet

Kanti Lal Rot, a daily wager in Dungarpur district of Rajasthan, proved to be a caring son, husband and father by building a toilet for his family. He sold his cattle and mortgaged his wife's jewellery to raise money for the construction. Later, he received a grant of ₹ 8,000 from the municipality to recover the mortgaged jewellery.

Mothers Take Loans to Get Toilets for Children

Mothers can do anything to ensure the health and safety of their children. This is what a group of women in rural Tamil Nadu did. Open defecation is a menace to the health of children in general and the safety of girls in particular. Being daily wagers, they could not manage to fund toilet construction with their daily earnings. Instead of giving in to despair, they were determined to build toilets by any means. With the help of micro-finance, they accomplished the mission to secure the health and safety of their children.

A Mother-in-law Gifts a Toilet to her Daughter-in-law

Generally, mothers-in-law and daughters-in-law are at loggerheads. But a toilet became a means of bonding between a mother-in-law and a daughter-in-law in Bollavaram village of Guntur district, Andhra Pradesh. In a rare instance, Shamsun got a toilet built in the house by the time her son's bride arrived. She welcomed her daughter-in-law with such a precious gift.

Brothers Gift Toilets to Sisters on Raksha Bandhan

Prime Minister Narendra Modi's Swachh Bharat Abhiyan has inspired many stories of toilets in India. Gifting of toilets to sisters on the occasion of Raksha Bandhan is a laudable act by some brothers against open defecation in rural Rajasthan. It emanated from Udaipur and Ajmer where some people, motivated by the Swachh Bharat Abhiyan, constructed toilets for their sisters and inspired others to build toilets in the houses of their married sisters. They also received a grant of ₹16,000 each from the government.

A 50-year-old Mason on a Mission to Build Toilets

The saga of the Swachh Bharat Abhiyan would remain incomplete without a mention of 50-year-old Kalabati Devi's contribution to the mission. A mason by profession in Uttar Pradesh, Kalabati Devi didn't hesitate to go door to door and collect funds for construction of toilets in slums and low-income areas across the city of Kanpur. With her mission spiralling out of Kanpur, she is not at rest. She holds meetings with community leaders to raise funds and educate slum dwellers on the health benefits of sanitation.

NOTE

1 "Rural Sanitation a Present Necessity" Source: Public Health Reports (1896-1970), Vol. 34, No. 2 (10 January 1919). Available at http://www.jstor.org/stable/4574986

Chapter 6

Sulabh Road to Sanitation

The Sulabh story is no less thrilling than a Bollywood blockbuster. It is an inspirational one. The Sulabh International Social Service Organisation is in general consultative status with the Economic and Social Council of the United Nations. Sulabh has been working for the removal of untouchability and social discrimination against scavengers, a section of Indian society condemned to clean and carry human excreta manually. Sulabh is noted for achieving success in the field of cost-effective sanitation, liberation of scavengers, social transformation of society, prevention of environmental pollution and development of non-conventional sources of energy.

Dr Bindeshwar Pathak started the Sulabh Svachchh Shauchalaya Prashikshan Sansthan (Sulabh Clean Toilet Training Institute) in 1970, which was later registered as Sulabh Shauchalaya Sansthan (Sulabh Toilet Institute). It was renamed Sulabh International in 1980 before adopting its present name, Sulabh International Social Service Organisation. Sulabh International Social Service Organisation is located in New Delhi, at Sulabh Bhawan, Mahavir Enclave, Palam-Dabri Road, New Delhi—110 045. Sulabh employs 60,000 people, of which 35,000 are paid workers while the rest are volunteers. This non-profitable organisation is also the world's biggest sanitation provider.

Sulabh is the sanitation movement that started with 10 dollars and is now doing work worth US$50 million dollars. From a humble beginning in the form of the environmentally friendly two-pit pour-flush compost toilet known as Sulabh Shauchalaya that is socially acceptable, to a nationwide movement of sanitation liberating millions of manual scavengers, restoring human rights and dignity to more than a million scavengers, Sulabh has come a long way.

6.1 VISION, MISSION AND OBJECTIVES

Sulabh was envisioned as an agent of social and cultural change. Inspired by the Gandhian philosophy of truthfulness, non-violence and altruism, Sulabh believes and practises the Gandhian principle of trusteeship. Sulabh seeks to develop an egalitarian society, based on equal opportunity for every human being irrespective of caste, race and natural endowments. Sulabh International is striving to fulfil the dream of Mahatma Gandhi and Prime Minister Modi by providing toilets in all schools, houses and public places in collaboration with different multinational companies/ national companies, etc., under CSR. For example, Sulabh International, in collaboration with Sanlam, has built toilets in African schools like the primary school in Soweto Chiawelo, South Africa.

Sulabh adopts a holistic development approach and promotes the concept of a happy home. Sulabh toilet complexes will turn into a Sulabh Happy Home which will not only provide toilet facilities but also a healthcare centre for slumdwellers at a nominal price, covering the cost of medical examination, medicines, etc. It will also provide free immunisation to children and pregnant women and "free family planning service" to couples.

Some of the key objectives of Sulabh are as follows:

- Social and economic liberation of the scavenging community from their unhealthy and subhuman occupation of handling others' excreta through motivating people to have a Sulabh Shauchalaya facility in houses where none exists; conversion of bucket privies into Sulabh Shauchalayas; rehabilitation by training and placement in other jobs; opening English-medium schools to offer modern school education to their children along with other assistance in building their houses away from slums so that they can be taken out from the stinking environment
- Preventing of environmental pollution and improving health, hygiene and ecology by providing appropriate and low-cost technologies for individual toilets, pay-and-use community toilet complexes, community toilets with biogas energy and effluent treatment
- Tree plantation around public shauchalayas
- Procuring manure from Sulabh Shauchalayas and Sulabh toilet complexes and using it to raise farm productivity

- Promoting consultancy, research and development in technical and social fields
- Disseminating innovations and creating awareness, particularly on sanitation and hygiene, through mass communication and education

6.2 THE CONCEPT OF SULABH MOVEMENT: TARGET GROUPS

The target groups of this project are impoverished residents of Delhi's slums and resettlement colonies, in particular those who have no access to sanitary latrines. Special attention is given to the needs of women in these groups, as well as the scavengers who must carry away human excreta from dry latrines. Geographically, the target sites include locations throughout Delhi. Only seven of the 44 resettlement colonies have civic amenities and running water lines provided. In most of them, especially in areas across the river Yamuna, no sewerage facility or proper drainage exists. Most of these colonies are located in low-lying areas about 10 to 12 feet lower than the Yamuna bed. These areas across the river are primary targets for Sulabh. Given the state of affairs, the only solution to the problem lies in low-cost sanitation techniques or the Sulabh movement and people's readiness to accept and use them. With Dr Pathak a philosopher, a Gandhian and a modern messiah of scavengers who can think both conventionally and technologically Sulabh could become a gigantic movement of our times.

6.3 SULABH MILESTONES

Today, engineers not only from India but also the World Bank have accepted that the on-site excreta disposal toilet system is an alternative to scavenging. From a few toilets to thousands and millions and even a toilet museum these are marvellous achievements by Sulabh. Sulabh grew into a massive people's movement in stages, beginning from a hut. No wonder, its journey was neither smooth nor regular. However, the following are the landmark years of the Sulabh sanitation movement which were also the turning points in a story that is at once amazing and true.

1968—Sulabh Technology

Dr Pathak joined the liberation of scavengers cell of the Bihar Gandhi Centenary Celebration Committee in 1968 when he was entrusted with the task of finding an alternative to scavenging. He modified and developed the technology of the two-pit pour-flush toilet (popularly known as Sulabh Shauchalaya). He also succeeded in demonstrating the effectiveness of the two-pit pour-flush toilet system.

1970—Sulabh Organisation Registered (Sulabh Founded in Patna, Bihar)

By the time Dr Pathak found the alternative to scavenging, the Bihar Gandhi Centenary Celebration Committee was dissolved by the government. That year, Dr Pathak founded a non-profit voluntary social organisation, The Sulabh Sauchalaya Sansthan (The Clean Toilet Institute), now known as the Sulabh International Social Service Organisation), to carry out the work of liberation of scavengers from the sub-human practice of manual excreta cleaning in India and other related jobs. Thus, the seeds of the Sulabh sanitation movement were sown in 1970.

1970–Expansion

The mass movement by Dr Pathak started spreading all over the country with a cadre of about 50,000 Sulabh volunteers, working from Vaishno Devi in the north to deep in the south and in the farthest corners in the east and west of the country, in 25 states and 987 towns. An organisational set-up like this has not been seen to spread so fast and be managed by any other social voluntary organisation so far. Sulabh does not receive any aid or subsidy from internal or external agencies; it raises its own resources to run its pan-India system and its campaign against social evils, and helps the weaker sections of society.

1972—Catalytic Agent

After developing the technology, Dr Pathak evolved a methodology which also spelt out how a non-profit social organisation could work as a catalytic agent between the government, local bodies and the beneficiaries. It was felt that the government alone could not liberate scavengers from this sub-human occupation. House-to-house contact and campaigns in local languages for their liberation were suggested as part of the methodology which was adopted by the Bihar government. Now it has been adopted by many state governments.

1973 –Scavengers' Liberation

During the past 30 years, Dr Pathak brought the scavengers' liberation programme from the micro level to the macro level. In 1973, he had put up just two Sulabh Shauchalayas for demonstration in the compound of the Ara municipality, a small town in Bihar. Since then Sulabh has converted about one million bucket latrines into Sulabh Shauchalayas throughout the country; and more than 60,000 scavengers have been liberated and more than 240 towns have been made scavenging-free (base year December 2002).

1974 –Pay-and-use System

In 1974, the Sulabh founder provided another concept of maintaining the community toilets and baths on a pay-and-use basis. Before 1974, public latrines in India were regarded as hell-holes. Nobody was able to find a solution to this problem. Dr Pathak found one and, on that basis, over 6,000 public toilet complexes are being maintained absolutely clean, in 25 states and four union territories, in 1075 towns, including the metropolitan cities of Delhi, Mumbai, Kolkata and Chennai. These Sulabh toilet complexes are used by over ten million people a day.

1978–Historic Seminar

In 1978, seeing the success of the scavengers' liberation movement in Bihar, the Ministry of Works and Housing, Government of India, in collaboration with the WHO and UNICEF, organised a national seminar in Patna on conversion of bucket latrines and liberation of scavengers. In this seminar, representatives from the Planning Commission, Ministry of Health, Ministry of Works and Housing, international agencies like the WHO, UNICEF, World Bank, and the secretaries and chief engineers of all the state governments participated. They all approved the Sulabh technology and methodology for adoption by individuals as well as institutions. And thus the work of liberating scavengers and the maintenance of public latrines and baths started to spread from Bihar throughout the country in due course.

1980-81—Legal Protection

Dr Pathak persuaded the Ministry of Home Affairs, Government of India, to include liberation of scavengers and their rehabilitation programme on a "whole town approach" basis. Under the scheme, implementation of the Protection of Civil Rights Act, 1980-81, was taken up in two towns of Bihar, Biharsharif and Purnia. In 1981-82, three more towns Daltonganj, Chaibasa and Madhubani, now in Jharkhand, were taken up. Later, the programme was moved to other states. The state governments agreed to provide alternative employment to liberated scavengers and, hence, all of them got jobs. The Ministry of Welfare, Government of India, later took charge of this programme.

1984–Biogas from Public Toilets

The first Sulabh public toilet-linked biogas plant was set up in Adalatganj, Patna. It produced electricity from biogas which was supplied to the three km-long Bailey Road, Patna.

1984–Sulabh International Institute of Technical Research and Training

Sulabh International Institute of Technical Research and Training (SIITRAT) is a technical wing of the Sulabh International Social Service Organisation, registered in 1993, and has been renamed the Sulabh International Academy of Environmental Sanitation and Public Health (SIAESPH) in 2005 for further expansion of sanitation technologies and their dissemination at national and international levels. The objective is to treat sanitation as a major field of education and study, revitalising it through training programmes and professional studies involving highly qualified sanitation experts, engineers, health professionals, social scientists, ecologists and scholars from all other related fields.

The academy aims at bringing sanitation into the sharp focus of

Production of biogas

academic activities and research nationally, regionally and globally. The academy is also dedicated to promoting 'peace' in the developing world environmental sanitation; awareness and motivation; having children as agents of change and providing education for all in environmental sanitation.

In the course of the last two decades, the academy has carried out several important studies on social issues of scavengers' rehabilitation, their skill development, etc. Significant research and consultancy have been undertaken on sustainable technologies like biogas plants, wastewater treatment through duckweed, materials and designs of the pan and trap toilet, wastewater disposal and treatment, solid waste management, biomedical waste management, etc. The academy has a well-equipped laboratory with testing facilities and also for undertaking research and development.

The outcome of the academy's research and designing capabilities are tested and validated on ground realities and propagated for community use through capacity building and training. Accordingly, the academy has a much larger mandate of acting as an international centre of holistic learning and education on all issues related to promotion of sanitation. It has signed a memorandum of understanding (MoU) with the International Rainwater Harvesting Alliance of Geneva.

1985—Training and Rehabilitation

With the help of the Ministry of Welfare, Government of India, the Welfare Department, government of Bihar, and the Bihar State Scheduled Castes Co-operative Development Corporation, Sulabh started training and rehabilitation programmes for the wards of scavengers in shorthand, typing, driving, mechanics, masonry work, carpentry, cane work, etc. A large number of children of scavengers have already been trained. This programme is being extended to cover the entire country. The programme was later expanded to include regular education and technical training.

1985–Technology Evaluation

The UNDP and the World Bank after evaluation of the Sulabh technology of the pour-flush toilet and the methodology of the maintenance of public toilets and baths on pay-and-use basis, passed it on to the countries of South-East Asia, Africa and Latin America for adoption.

1986–Protection of Civil Rights (PCR) Act

Dr Pathak persuaded the Ministry of Welfare to give stipends to the wards of Muslim and Christian scavengers also for training and rehabilitation. Earlier, these were available only to Hindu scavengers. Without this, the wards of Muslim and Christian scavengers would have been left out and the movement for their liberation and rehabilitation would have suffered a setback.

1988–Scavengers in Temples

Dr Pathak solved the problem of entry of Harijans into Nathdwara temple in Udaipur, Rajasthan, for prayers in 1988. The controversy over entering the temple had taken a serious turn and many attempts made by others had failed. The situation became so serious that the then President of India R. Venkataraman wanted to lead Harijans into the temple. Even political leaders and the state government officials had to go to the temple with police protection. This attracted Dr Pathak's attention. With 100 scavengers and orthodox Maithil Brahmins, he entered the Nathdwara temple, offered prayers, and recited bhajans and kirtans. The scavengers and the whole group took their meal together. This programme was performed without police protection. On return from the Nathdwara temple, Dr Pathak, along with the scavengers and the Brahmins was given an audience by President Venkataraman, Vice-President Dr Shankar Dayal Sharma and Prime Minister Rajiv Gandhi. This act of Dr Pathak was in line with Dr Ambedkar's leading a group of Harijans to draw water from a public tank, Chodor Talen, at Mahad in Kolaba district of Maharashtra in 1927. Dr Ambedkar had led another satyagraha to establish the right of the untouchables to enter the famous temple of Kalaran in Nasik in 1930.

1989—Casteless Puja

On his return from Nathdwara, Dr Pathak launched a campaign to help the Scheduled Castes offer prayers in temples and perform puja in their homes with Brahmins. Also, he started common puja and dining programmes where members of the Scheduled Castes would fast, sit at the puja and prepare prasad. They also prepared food for lunch or dinner. After the puja was over, the prasad and food were distributed by the Scheduled Caste members to all, including Vedic Brahmins, who also ate with them. This programme continued and has got wide acceptance.

1990–Social Upgradation of Scavengers

To improve the social status of scavengers in India, Dr Pathak launched a movement to socially upgrade them. This was a novel concept. There was a question mark as to whether after liberation, training and education, scavengers and their children would have upgraded status in society to be at par with the so-called upper caste people. To socially upgrade the scavengers' status in society, Sulabh started a social upgradation campaign—one high-status family in society has to "socially adopt" a scavenger family and treat them like relatives.

The association with these high-status people will raise the status of the scavengers. This programme has taken off very well. So far, 5,000 scavenger families have been "adopted" by high-status people, including judges, advocates, journalists, ministers and planners. Among them are former Union Deputy Commerce Minister, Salman Khurshid; Planning Commission member Chitra Naik; the late Times of India editor Dileep Padgaonkar; the late Prime Minister, I.K. Gujral and many others.

1992–Awareness Campaign

In February 1992, Sulabh organised a National Seminar on Liberation and Rehabilitation of Scavengers in New Delhi in which vice-chancellors, professors, planners and administrators passed a resolution to make it

Social Adoption

a people's movement. The seminar was inaugurated by then President Giani Zail Singh.

Dr Pathak regularly takes steps to create social awareness against unfounded beliefs and prejudices. He organises conferences, seminars, workshops, plays and folk dances on these themes. The attempt is to involve a large number of people from all walks of life in order to speed up the pace of the movement. In 1992, based on the "educate, organise and agitate" principle of B.R. Ambedkar, Sulabh set up an English-medium school in Delhi for the sons and daughters of scavengers wherein education is given in three principal areas: general theoretical education, compulsory vocational education (knowledge of office management, shorthand, typing and computer training) and optional vocational education (intensive training in specific vocations) so that they may not have to wait in long queues for employment. This will also enable them to be self-employed or get jobs. Fifty per cent of the school's enrolment is of scavengers' children and the rest from other families to visibly obliterate discrimination. This unique experiment is being extended to other states also. The idea is: Education alone can empower the weak and poor.

1992–Housing Facilities

Sulabh started an endeavour to provide housing facilities to scavengers to take them out of their unhealthy living conditions. A survey of 1,000 scavenger families has already been done in Patna and an attempt is being made to get land from the government at a nominal price and loans from Housing and Urban Development Corporation Limited (HUDCO) in order to build houses for them. A similar attempt is to be made in other states.

1993–Sulabh International Centre for Action Sociology

Sulabh International Centre for Action Sociology (SICAS) is a voluntary, not-for-profit organisation and is an integral part of the Sulabh Sanitation and Social Reform Movement. Its main objective is to initiate steps for providing better information as well as formal education for students of different sections of society, specially the weaker section, through the network of its institutions throughout the country. It aims to (i) make

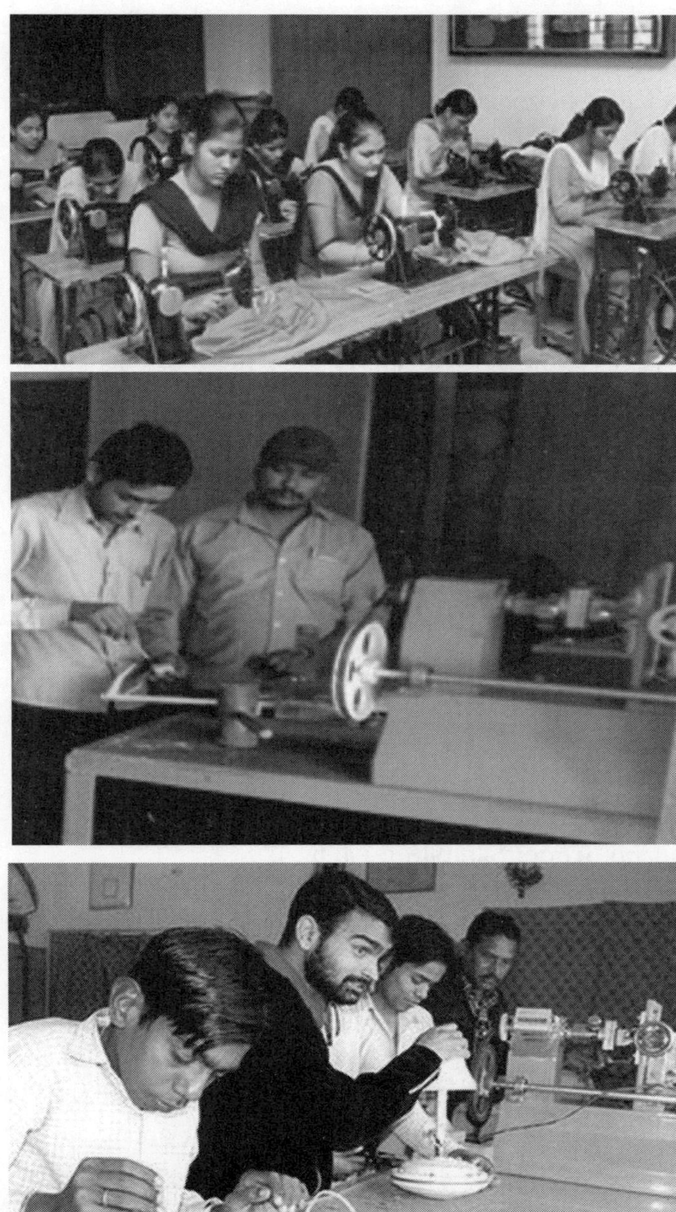

Programmes in Schools

Photo credit: Sulabh International.

children aware on the nexus between hygiene, sanitation and health and enable them to act as change agents in society, for this Sulabh School Sanitation Clubs have been initiated in different schools in various states of the country and (ii) promote social integration.

SICAS acts as a transmission belt and conduit for widespread effective dissemination of the Sulabh sanitation technologies for human excreta disposal, power generation and impact of steps for sponsoring motilities and status elevation launched for the benefit of deprived millions. It functions as an advance centre of research and training for students working on problems of sanitation, power generation, role of voluntary organisations, weaker sections and training and development. It runs:

- Sulabh Public School which aims to provide English-medium education to children from weaker and poor sections of society
- Sulabh Vocational Training Centre
- Courses in fashion designing, computers electrical, beauty, cutting and sewing, stenography (English), typing (Hindi and English), tailoring, embroidery

Programmes by SICAS include:

i. Sulabh Vocational Training Centre
ii. Children's Welfare Programme
iii. Sulabh Social International Programme
iv. Sulabh School Sanitation Club
v. Sanitation Programme, Community Health Programme
vi. Eco Club
vii. Sulabh School Sanitation Club

Surveys are conducted in urban slums and rural areas before medical check-up camps are organised in order to increase the efficiency of the medical check-up camps. Sulabh also conducts competitions like quizzes on sanitation from time to time for all school and college students, including foreign students.

SICAS–SA (South Africa) aims to provide and promote healthy, practical sanitation solutions through a range of innovative social programmes including the construction and maintenance of world class public toilet complexes, and the construction of toilets at rural schools and homes utilising Sulabh's innovative technologies and insights. Working with government, corporates and community groups, SICAS-

SA aims to make a meaningful and sustainable contribution to alleviating the sanitation challenge in South Africa.

1994–The Sulabh International Museum of Toilets

The first of its kind in the world, the Sulabh International Museum of Toilets was set up in Delhi. The museum, through artefacts, pictures, posters and other available materials, tells the story of the development of toilets through the ages. This is the star attraction at the Sulabh service centre, Palam. The museum is open 365 days a year. The museum website has so far been visited by about 27,50,000 people and over 1,00,000 have personally visited it. These visitors, hailing from different parts of the world, have found it unique and highly interesting. Most of the national and international media agencies, print and electronic, have done stories. Of late, it has been included in the list of the world's ten weirdest museums.

1996–Duckweed Project

Sulabh has demonstrated an eco-friendly low-cost technology for

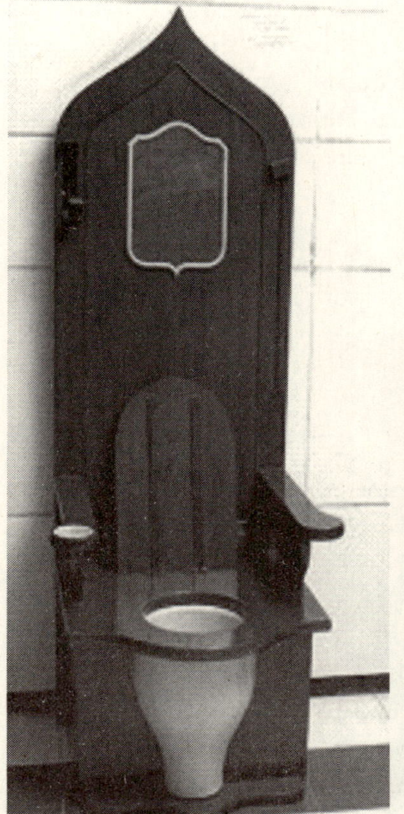

The International Museum of Toilets

Photo credit: Sulabh International.

wastewater treatment through duckweed. The technology, besides having low operational and maintenance costs, gives economic returns in terms of pisciculture.

1997–STAC

Sulabh developed new technology for composting of biodegradable wastes. The technology, known as Sulabh Thermophilic Aerobic Composting (STAC), requires only 8-10 days for degrading any biodegradable material without churning.

1998–People's Commission

Sulabh set up People's Commission on the Abolition of Scavenging. Prime Minister Atal Bihari Vajpayee inaugurated the commission at a function organised on 26 November 1998 to honour him with the Honest Man of the Year Award 1997. Justice M.N. Venkatachalliah, former chief justice of India, and chairperson of the National Human Rights Commission, is the chairman of the Advisory Board of the Commission.

2000–Sulabh Towards Villages

Sulabh started the programme, Sulabh Towards Villages, a national campaign to improve rural sanitation.

2001–Training of Women

Sulabh started a country-wide programme for involvement of women in sanitation, health and hygiene.

2002–SET Technology

Sulabh developed new and convenient technology to make biogas plant effluents free from colour, odour and pathogens. The technology, known as SET (Sulabh Effluent Treatment), lowers BOD (biological oxygen demand) of effluents to less than 10 mg/l, making it suitable for agriculture, aquaculture or safe discharge into a river or any water body or cleaning of floors of public toilets.

2003

- Steps taken to establish a Sulabh University of Sanitation.
- Compilation of an encyclopaedia on sanitation started.
- WASH campaign launched in collaboration with Water Supply and Sanitation Collaborative Council, Switzerland.
- Started another Sulabh Vocational Training Centre for liberated scavengers (Nai Disha) in Alwar, Rajasthan.
- The UNDP recognises Sulabh technologies in its Human Development Report 2003.
- Sulabh delegation visits Afghanistan to take up sanitation work.

Sulabh International Academy of Environmental Sanitation and Public Health

2004

Members of the UN Millennium Project Task Force on Water and Sanitation visit Sulabh Campus.

2005

- Sulabh International Academy of Environmental Sanitation registered under the Societies Registration Act, 1860, by the Registrar, government of Delhi.
- Twenty-three professionals from five countries attend the International Workshop on Sanitation Technologies organised by Sulabh International Academy of Environmental Sanitation in collaboration with the UN-Habitat.
- Sulabh activities find mention in President of India A.P.J. Abdul Kalam's book, *Mission India: A Vision for Indian Youth.*

2006

- The UNDP recognises Sulabh technologies in its Human Development Report.
- Twenty-four professionals including representatives of UN–HABITAT covering 10 African countries attend the International Capacity Building Workshop organised by the Sulabh International Academy of Environmental Sanitation in collaboration with UN–HABITAT.
- Stanford University includes article on Sulabh, "That Gandhi may not be born again" in its curriculum.
- Five public toilets with biogas plants set up in Kabul, Afghanistan, with the financial support of the Government of India.

2007

Sulabh organises the World Toilet Summit in collaboration with the WTO.

2013

Sulabh adopts widows of Varanasi and Vrindaran.

Sulabh adopts widows of Varanasi and Vrindaran

Source: http://www.sulabhinternational.org/widows-of-vrindavan/

2016

- UNICEF lauds Sulabh by stating that it has played a major role in reducing open defecation in India from 74 per cent in 1990 to 44 per cent in 2015.

- Sulabh starts a news weekly, *Sulabh Swachh Bharat*, a "good news" weekly for emerging India.
- The Ministry of Railways appoints Padma Bhushan Bindeshwar Pathak, founder of Sulabh International, as the brand ambassador for Indian Railways' Swachh Rail Mission.

Sulabh to help clean more than 82 stations across 20 states in India; 4,100+ Sulabh volunteers will be working with station masters and cleaning staff of Indian railways. Dr Pathak selected for the 2016 New York Global Leaders Dialogue Humanitarian Award. Making the announcement from New York, Scanlan said, "Dr Pathak is a great humanitarian who for decades has enhanced the quality of life for millions of fellow human beings. He embodies our philosophy that leadership is focused on creating collaborative new space in the service of others. We are especially attracted to leaders who transform lives for the better, and Dr Pathak stands tall in embodying these rarest of qualities."

2017

Marora in Haryana, rechristened Trump Village, gets the biggest toilet pot. It is a mega pot made of iron, fibre, wood and plaster of Paris—measuring 20×10 feet—and was unveiled in the hamlet to mark the World Toilet Day, which is observed on 19 November to inspire action to tackle the global sanitation crisis.

Action Sociology in India to get a facelift with Sulabh's plan to launch a journal to promote healthy sanitation and a healthy environment.

Sulabh International University of Sanitation is proposed. It will help the country propagate the message of Mahatma Gandhi and Sulabh. The university will be dedicated solely to training and increasing the capacity of our human resource to analyse, design and implement effective solutions that will help make not just India but the planet clean.

It will have a strong focus on the development of practical and policy skills and will address the critical future challenges of climate change, population growth and urbanisation. Emphasis will be laid on technical interventions in water supply, sanitation and solid waste management. The Sulabh International University of Sanitation will provide different courses for youth, consultants and professionals working in the international development and public health sectors.

Source: http://ww.sulabhinternational.org/pics-

These courses will train students in the essential skills and knowledge required to plan and implement along with communities, water supply and sanitation projects and programmes worldwide, particularly in less developed countries.

What will make it stand out will be its outreach to practitioners using its knowledge base and applied research to develop the capacity of individuals and organisations throughout the world, promoting the integration of social, technical, economic, institutional and environmental activities as a prerequisite for development.

Thus, Sulabh achievements in brief are as follows:

- 1.5 million Sulabh household toilets constructed
- 54 million government toilets constructed based on Sulabh design
- 8,500+ Sulabh community toilet blocks constructed and maintained
- 640+ towns made scavenging-free
- 15 million people using toilets based on Sulabh design on a daily basis

6.4 LIBERATION MOVEMENT

Sulabh in its 40+ years has been known for social reforms. Its founder, Dr Pathak, realised that the liberation and rehabilitation of scavengers or Balmikis was not an easy task. It was difficult for the worst victims of institutionalised discrimination over the centuries to break out of the vicious circle and join the mainstream of society. Hence, he devised a well-thought-out and multi-pronged strategy to rehabilitate the Balmikis by providing them alternative employment and integrating them into the mainstream. His strategy for liberation of Balmikis through the Sulabh movement consists of a mixed package of technology, rehabilitation, with alternative employment and social reform. This holistic approach is radically different from other social reform movements in that it combines technology with social idealism. His scientific and humane approach towards abolishing scavenging is inspired by a commitment to basic human rights and is based on years of research and study of the problem.

Traditionally, no attention was paid to occupational hazards of hygiene and health associated with scavenging. On the one hand, society required scavengers to remove night soil by hand and carry the buckets on the hip or head. On the other hand, they were socially looked down upon, and boycotted for their unclean work. Moreover, people don't realise how cruel and callous they have been towards this community and that Balmikis' civic disabilities are largely a result of the open and prolonged exploitation. There is need to sensitise people, particularly the new generation, about the nightmarish plight of this community.

Committed to stave off the historical and prolonged injustice against Balmikis, Dr Pathak strove hard and finally came up with a suitable technology to convert lakhs of bucket latrines into flush toilets. The two-pit pour-flush toilets developed by Sulabh caught the imagination of the nation and as a result Sulabh public and individual toilets came up all over India. At the same time, Sulabh took care to provide alternative jobs to the Balmikis, rendered jobless by large-scale conversion of privy latrines into Sulabh toilets.

The Sulabh approach to restore human dignity to Balmikis has five distinct stages:

a. Liberation;
b. Rehabilitation;
c. Vocational training;
d. Proper education of the next generation; and
e. Social elevation.

Skill development is important for all but it is crucial for the less educated. For the members of depressed classes, particularly Balmikis, it has a pointed relevance. Not only are they low in literacy and education, they also possess few skills that have market demand. Sulabh has paid special attention to skill development and vocational training of children from the Balmiki community. It has set up many centres and institutions across the country to equip children from this community with vocational training in many market-friendly trades.

Sulabh's determined and principled intervention has yielded good results. It has been able to liberate and rehabilitate more than a million Balmikis during its four-decade struggle.

6.5 SULABH INITIATIVES

Sulabh has developed and used technologies for human dignity, social well-being and innovative initiatives:

Eco-friendly Technology

The environment-friendly two-pit pour-flush compost toilet known as Sulabh Shauchalaya that is socially acceptable, economically affordable, technologically appropriate and does not require scavengers to clean the pits and implemented in more than 1.2 million houses all over India has helped liberate over a million scavengers.

Sulabh Public Toilet Complexes

Construction and maintenance of public toilets at public places and in slums on pay and use basis is a landmark of Sulabh in the field of sanitation. So far it has constructed and is maintaining over 8,000 such public toilets in India.

Provision of Sulabh public toilet complexes at public places and in slums on pay and use basis is an important activity of Sulabh in the field of community health and hygiene and environmental sanitation. It has constructed public toilet complexes in different parts of the country, where maintenance is provided round the clock. These complexes are located at public places like bus stands, hospitals, markets and in slums. For the construction, operation and maintenance of these complexes, the organisation plays the role of a catalyst and a partner between the official agencies and the users of the toilet complexes. When facility for bathing is also provided with the community toilets, and if they are kept clean, people have no hesitation in paying a nominal charge for use. For washing hands soap powder is provided to users. Children and indigent persons are exempted from such charge. The system of operation and maintenance of community toilets evolved by Sulabh has proved to be boon for local bodies in their endeavour to keep the towns clean and improve the environment. This is a unique example of partnership of local authorities, NGOs and the community.

Biogas from Public Toilets

Recycling and use of human excreta for biogas generation is an important way to get rid of health hazards from human excreta, besides promoting use of biogas for cooking, lighting and electricity generation. Biogas digesters, when attached to public toilet complexes, recycle human waste into biogas. The biogas from public toilets has multiple benefits—improving sanitation, community health and hygiene, the environment and providing dignity to women and girls in addition to using biogas for different purposes. To overcome the problems, Dr Pathak invented an efficient design of a biogas plant linked with public toilets. Under the system, only human excreta with flush water is allowed to flow into the biogas plant for anaerobic digestion. For biogas generation no manual handling of excreta at any stage is required. Sulabh installed 200 biogas plants in public toilets all over the country. Production of biogas from public toilets and recycling and reuse of effluent through simple and convenient methods is a major breakthrough in the field of sanitation and community health.

The biogas produced is used for cooking, lighting lamps and electricity generation. Cooking is the most convenient use of biogas. Recently, Sulabh has modified the genset which earlier required 20 per cent diesel and 80 per cent biogas. It does not require diesel now and runs on 100 per cent biogas. This has made electricity generation from biogas more sustainable.

Sulabh Effluent Treatment (SET) System

After a series of experiments, a simple and convenient technology named Sulabh Effluent Treatment (SET) was invented to further treat effluent from the biogas plant. The technology is based on sedimentation and filtration of effluent through sand, an aeration tank and activated charcoal followed by exposure to ultraviolet rays. The treated effluent is colourless, odourless and pathogen free, having biochemical oxygen demand less than 10 mg per litre and is safe for discharge into any water body without causing pollution. It can also be used for cleaning of floors of public toilets in water-scarce areas.

Environment-friendliness

In addition to conserving and reusing water, the system has an additional in-built advantage of reducing greenhouse gas effect arising out of carbon dioxide and methane production due to degradation of human waste. Due to the design of the leach pit of the Sulabh toilet in households, the carbon dioxide produced is diffused in the soil through honey combs and does not escape into the atmosphere. Because of anaerobic digestion of human waste during biogas production, methane is produced that is used for different purposes, it is not left to escape into the atmosphere. Thus, both these technologies help in reducing the greenhouse gas effect.

Duckweed-based Wastewater Treatment

Duckweed—a small, free-floating, fast-growing aquatic plant—has great ability to reduce the BOD, suspended solids, bacteria and other pathogens in wastewater. It is also a complete feed for fish, increasing yields by two to three times, and a highly nutritious feed for poultry and animals due to its high protein and vitamin content. Although duckweed is found in ponds and ditches, its potential in terms of wastewater treatment, nutrient value and economic benefits have not been fully exploited, due to almost complete absence of any know-how of relevant technologies. Sulabh has developed demonstration projects with cost-effective, duckweed-based wastewater treatment in rural and urban areas, which show direct economic returns from pisciculture. The Central Pollution Control Board has set guidelines—for the use of duckweed in wastewater treatment, based on the experimental results of Sulabh.

Financially Viable Projects

Since human excreta was considered the most repulsive object by society, it was difficult for anyone to conceive of financial viability of a project related to its disposal. However, Sulabh made it financially viable through cost-sharing by the local body. The maintenance of toilet blocks and day-to-day expenses is taken care by the user charge. However, all the toilet complexes are not self-sustaining, particularly those located in slums and less-developed areas. The maintenance of such toilet complexes gets cross-subsidised from the income generated from toilet complexes in busy and developed areas. The cost of Sulabh pour-flush composting toilets varies widely to suit people of every economic stratum. The cost ranges from US$10 to US$1,000 per unit, depending on the materials used.

Sulabh Social Integration Programme

It may be reiterated that the problems of the Dalits, particularly the

Valmikis, are both economic and socio-cultural. As a consequence, not only are Valmikis treated as "untouchables", they are also isolated, neglected and often economically deprived. This necessitates modification of group attitudes and behaviour implemented through a well-conceived programme called the Social Integration Programme. This programme is purely voluntary and does not involve any legal obligation on the part of anyone. All it costs is a "Will" to shed social prejudices, a sense of social responsibility and concern for the well-being of society at large. A conscientious citizen formally and publicly adopts a family of scavengers. Subsequently, the two interact closely and visit each other's homes and when required, the adopting person helps the adopted in overcoming his problems.

In order to enhance this process, field visits were made which covered almost the entire NCT of Delhi. Valmiki households within the radius of two kilometres or so from the residences of prospective adopters were identified.

Inclusive India

With a holistic approach, Sulabh helped the entire country. People of all walks of life have been touched. Earlier there was social stigma and psychological taboo attached to handling of human excreta. It could also be due to the fact that only people of the lowest economic and social strata were supposed to be associated with this job. Due to the efforts of Sulabh, and financial viability, people from higher social status now compete to take up sanitation projects without psychological reservations.

Altogether there are 60,000 volunteers working with Sulabh who include technocrats, managers, scientists, engineers, social scientists, doctors, architects, planners and other non-revenue staff. Sulabh undertakes 30 years' maintenance guarantee for the toilet complexes constructed by it.

Toilets at all places, of many sizes and structures, for all categories of people—Sulabh made it all possible. Many other organisations got inspired to take up sanitation reforms and projects. The corporate world too does big business in sanitaryware.

6.6 ADOPTERS AND NON-ADOPTERS

Traditions take time to change and require the will and support of all sections of society. Sulabh evolved the concept of "social adoption" with this end in view. It is purely voluntary and all it costs is the willingness to shed social prejudice and show some compassion for fellow humans.

A committed citizen publicly "adopts" a Balmiki family. Subsequently, the two families closely interact and visit each other's homes and occasionally, help is rendered towards social adjustment. As the adopters are usually persons of social standing and prestige, their action becomes something to emulate for others. Social adoption has helped significantly in the integration of the Balmikis in the mainstream of society.

So far 10,000 scavenger families have been adopted by well-known personalities including a former prime minister, the late I.K. Gujral. Dr Pathak also led 100 Harijans into the Nathdwara temple in Udaipur, Rajasthan, in 1988 to promote religious and social cohesion. This courageous act defied orthodoxy and helped evolve cultural integration, thus having a long-term impact on the cultural mindset of the people.

The efforts of Sulabh in the field of sanitation over the past four decades are a major reason why everyone today is openly talking about the need for toilets. Dr Pathak alone is responsible for removing the stigma attached to toilet activities.

Many adoption studies have been conducted to understand household consumers in the emerging sanitation philosophy and practice (including technology). There will be adopters and non-adopters. At present non-adopters travel to open defecation sites and public latrines, and in the latter case may join long queues in the morning or evening. Cultural beliefs push Indians away from using simple latrines and towards open defecation.

Sulabh has examined both motivational factors and constraint factors. Studies reveal the increase in the number of adopters: latrine/toilet issuers at household level. Linkage of low-cost sanitation technologies to community mobilisation campaigns led by the government, such as Community Led Total Sanitation has helped a lot in this regard. The non-adopters also know about the Sulabh Shauchalaya (the clean toilet) and that scavenging is a sub-human job and negates the principle of social justice. Making sanitation facilities accessible is the hallmark of Sulabh's achievements.

Sanitation comprises a very broad range of services and service delivery functions. Some focus on the safe containment, removal, treatment and disposal or reuse of human excreta, a process which we refer to as the sanitation "chain". Toilets come in as part of the supply chain. Applied to specific sanitation subtypes from an understanding of the wider context, the characteristics provide a broad analytical framework that can help governance and sector specialists go beyond technical design approaches to understand and unlock the underlying incentives for different actors. Households can indeed be motivated by private benefits to adopt the private good (the latrine). Toilet subsidy is not the answer to sanitation problems.[1] There must be participatory development and management. Economic logic and an understanding of social norms can help to understand the incentives for households to take action on sanitation.

Sulabh has gone offshore too; there are plans to construct toilets in more than 15 countries.

6.7 NEW MISSION

Sulabh adds vigour to a new programme in India, namely, the Swachh Bharat campaign (see Box 6.1) whereby Sulabh also gets rejuvenated and its tools sharpened. Dr Pathak says that his institution has set a model for clean India which can aid the dream of an "open defecation-free India" becoming a reality in 2019.

With this goal in mind, useful lessons can be learnt and implemented from the experiences of Sulabh International, which has vast experience building individual and public toilets, in developing appropriate sanitation technology and accordingly scaling them up nationwide.

According to Dr Pathak, nearly 12 crore toilets are required to be built in the country by 2019 to realise the vision of the mission and Sulabh is playing an important role in fulfilling the agenda.

Taking the population of the country into account, there are almost as many people without access to sanitation as there were 20 years ago. Against this backdrop, it is very difficult to achieve the vision of Swachh Bharat by 2019 but Sulabh has been working towards this goal since 1970. Sulabh is committed and dedicated in its task of achieving a Swachh Bharat by 2019 and has made significant contributions to achieve the vision. The contributions made by the organisation are:

- Conversion of bucket privies into water pour-flush latrines and construction of new ones where none existed. Sulabh has so far constructed 1.5 million toilets

- Liberating 1,25,000 scavengers from the inhuman practice of manual scavenging
- Rehabilitation of thousands of scavengers in various trades and occupations by giving them vocational training in market-oriented trades
- Making 640 towns scavenging-free
- Construction/operation and maintenance of 8,500 community/ public toilet complexes at important public places like markets/ cinemas/bus stops/railway stations/ hospitals.
- Construction of 200 biogas plants linked with public toilets for generating energy and organic manure
- Construction of 12,500 toilet blocks in schools in various states
- These sanitation facilities are being used by 10.5 million people every day
- Sulabh has also constructed a public toilet in Thimphu, Bhutan, and five toilet-cum-bath complexes linked with biogas plants in Kabul, Afghanistan.

BOX 6.1: SWACHH BHARAT MISSION

The Swachh Bharat Mission was launched by Prime Minister Narendra Modi on 2 October 2014 with the target of making the country clean and achieving 100% access to sanitation by 2 October 2019 as a fitting tribute to the 150th birth anniversary of Mahatma Gandhi. The main objectives of the Swachh Bharat Mission are as follows:

- To bring about an improvement in the general quality of life in the rural as well as urban areas of the country
- To eliminate the practice of open defecation
- To accelerate conversion of insanitary toilets into pour-flush toilets
- To eradicate manual scavenging
- To ensure 100 per cent collection and scientific processing/disposal/reuse/ recycling of municipal solid waste
- To bring about a behavioural change in people regarding healthy sanitation practices
- To generate awareness and motivate communities promoting sustainable sanitation facilities through health education and its linkages with public health
- To encourage cost-effective and appropriate technologies for ecologically safe and sustainable sanitation
- To create an enabling environment for private sector participation in capital

expenditure and operation, and maintenance expenditure

- To develop community-managed environmental sanitation systems focusing on solid and liquid waste management for overall cleanliness.
- To create significant impact on gender and promote social inclusion by improving sanitation especially in marginalised communities.

Source: www.swachhbharatamission.gov.in/

6.8 RECOGNITIONS

Sulabh's cost-effective and appropriate sanitation system has been recognised as a global urban best practice by the United Nations Centre for Human Settlements at the Habitat-II conference held in Istanbul, Turkey, in June 1996. It got Sulabh special consultative status by the Economic and Social Council of the United Nations in recognition of outstanding service to mankind.

The International St Francis Prize for the Environment Canticle of all Creatures was conferred on Dr Pathak in 1992 in recognition of his services to the cause of the environment and social upliftment of oppressed people. The national and international media have widely acknowledged the achievements of Sulabh. *The New York Times, The Washington Post, The Nation (Bangkok), The Times of India, Hindustan times, The Statesman, The Indian Express, India Today, Dinman, Water World, The Telegraph, Source* (UNDP monthly magazine) and others have published articles lauding the achievements of Sulabh in the fields of low-cost sanitation, liberation of scavengers, harnessing of energy from human excreta and environment improvement.

6.8.1 Sulabh Awards

Sulabh also recognises and honours meritorious service by an individual or organisation in the cause of community and humanity:

- Global Sanitation Award
- Sulabh Honest Man of the Year Award
- Rajiv Gandhi Memorial Sulabh Sanitation Award
- Sulabh Sahitya Academy Award
- Sulabh Save the Child Award

- Sulabh Fellowship Award
- Sulabh Habitat Award
- Sulabh International's Man of Letters' Award
- Excellency Award

6.9 EXTENDING THE HORIZON

Informing, educating and communicating are integral to any successful movement or campaign. In this regard, publishing books and other forms of literature will help the general public as well as researchers. As part of action sociology Sulabh has never held back from propagating knowledge and skills for readers.

Sulabh has prepared an Encyclopaedia of Sanitation. It gives a new dimension to public health and seeks to highlight the factors in the physical environment which exercise a deleterious effect on people's physical, mental or social capabilities. It is a unique academic exercise, spread over a decade, and compiled by a team of dedicated technical professionals with expertise in all areas of sanitation. The Encyclopaedia of Sanitation, a new reference work, is also designed to complement the existing literature available on health, hygiene and sanitation. One of the major objectives of this encyclopaedia is to encourage the rapid development of sanitation and hygiene throughout the world and to serve as a guide to public health professionals and administrators. The encyclopaedia aims at the standardisation of terminology and research procedures, largely through examples and articles that have been included expressly for this purpose. It will help all those who are working towards creating a pollution-free society. The encyclopaedia marks new openings for academics to prepare teaching modules for students and building the cadre for bringing about a social transformation in society. In the Third World, in particular, the major cause of environmental pollution is the absence of awareness of hygienic and safe human waste disposal systems. The encyclopaedia also creates awareness to shed conventional notions and develop a commitment to health and hygiene. As yet there is no single reference book on this topic. Indeed, knowledge about sanitation is scattered all over. The encyclopaedia seeks to consolidate such knowledge and make it a ready reference work for professionals and health workers alike.

Dr Pathak has written many useful books on sanitation, education, etc. He and his organisation have encouraged many others to write books such as:

1. *Social Exclusion Edited* by A.K. Lal (2003)
2. *Sociology of Sanitation* by Mohammed Akram (2015)
3. *Sociology of Sanitation* by B.K. Nagla (2015)
4. *Sociology of Sanitation* by Richard Pais (2015)
5. *Sociology of Sanitation Themes and Perspectives* by Ashish Saxena (2015)
6. *Sanitation in India: A Historico-Sociological Survey* by Hetukar

SULABH SWACHH BHARAT

RNI No. DELENG/2016/71561

Vol-1 | Issue-41 | September 25 - October 01, 2017 | Price ₹ 5/-

Good News Weekly for Rising India

04 NATIONAL

WASH CONCLAVE

The National WASH Champion Conclave was organised at Mavalankar Auditorium

08 MAURITIUS

HOMOGENEITY

Homogeneity of the women of Mauritius and India was discussed in an event

25 FESTIVAL

MAA DURGA'S HUES

With Pujas starting after Mahalaya, Devi Durga is getting a taste of London

PRIME MINISTER'S BIRTHDAY CELEBRATED AS SWACHHTA HI SEVA

HAPPY BIRTHDAY MODIJI

A unique celebration on the birthday of Prime Minister Modi by Sulabh International

Source: */sulabh-swachh-bharat-emagazine-english/Notes*

Jha (2016)

A few more books are in the pipeline. Sulabh has two important periodicals:

Sulabh India magazine in English and Hindi.

Sulabh also brings out a weekly newspaper, *Sulabh Swachh Bharat*, in print and online.

NOTES

1. Crores of rupees have gone into building toilets but they remain unused. Villages that were declared ODF are unable to sustain it, and sewage treatment continues to be a big challenge. In such a scenario, CLTS offers a different approach. It calls for the suspension of toilet subsidies and instead works towards securing collective behavioural change by instilling disgust or fear in the community.
   Himachal Pradesh was one of the early adopters of this concept, reaching about 67 per cent rural toilet coverage as per Census 2011 which was more than double the national average of 31 percent. Poverty and illiteracy are not the barriers; the only barrier, as Dr Kamal Kar, the pioneer of CLTS, says, is "intellectual constipation". It needs a change in perspective—that sanitation improves with collective behavioural change and not subsidy.

Chapter 7

Dr Bindeshwar Pathak's Mission and Movement

Dr Bindeshwar Pathak is a personality worth studying and his values are worth emulating. Dr Pathak is an Indian sociologist and social reformer who founded Sulabh International, a non-profit organisation that works to promote human rights, environmental sanitation, non-conventional sources of energy, waste management and social reforms. His pioneering work, especially in the field of sanitation and hygiene, has earned him various national and international awards. He is a philosopher, a visionary and a practitioner all at the same time.

Dr Bindeshwar Pathak's life has been greatly inspired by Mahatma Gandhi. Dr Pathak is the product of Sarvodaya Samaj. He started his journey with the Bihar Gandhi Centenary Celebration Committee in 1968. Based on his teachings, he took up sanitation and the human rights of manual scavengers as the mission of his life. He has dedicated almost five decades to fulfilling the dream of Mahatma Gandhi.

Dr Bindeshwar Pathak, PhD, DLitt sociologist, social reformer and founder, Sulabh Sanitation Movement

Pic courtesy: http://www.sulabhinternational.org

7.1 THE BEGINNING

Bindeshwar Pathak was born on 2 April 1943 to Ramakant Pathak and Yogmaya Devi in a traditional upper-class Brahmin family in Rampur Baghel village in Vaishali district, Bihar. Bindeshwar was the second of six siblings.

During his childhood he witnessed a lot of injustice and discrimination around him due to the caste system. He had his education in Patna. He received a traditional upbringing, typical for boys of his social stature.

He graduated in sociology in 1964. He did MA in sociology and MA in English and a PhD (1985) on "Liberation of Scavengers through Low-Cost Sanitation" from Patna University, and a DLitt on "Eradication of Scavenging and Environmental Sanitation in India: A Sociological Study" also from Patna University.

As a student he aspired to be a lecturer but failed to score enough marks in his university exams to achieve this dream. Over the ensuing years he worked at odd jobs and was unable to settle successfully in any profession.

As a young college student in the late 1960s he bagged a temporary writer's assignment with the Mahatma Gandhi Centenary Celebration Committee in Patna and joined the Bhangi-Mukti (scavengers' liberation) Cell of the committee. It was during this time that he gained a deeper understanding of the indignity and plight faced by millions of manual scavengers in India. Disturbed by the experience, he resolved to do something to change the situation and proceeded to ultimately found the Sulabh International Social Service Organisation. It was a social initiative to eliminate the dehumanising practice of manual scavenging while providing hygienic toilet facilities and sustainable waste management to citizens. He developed a technology of a two-pit pour-flush toilet, popularly known as the Sulabh Shauchalaya system which has been declared as one of the global best practices by UN-HABITAT/UNCHS (United Nations Centre for Human Settlements). In addition, he has also made vital contributions in the areas of bio-energy and bio-fertiliser, liquid and solid waste management, and poverty alleviation.

7.1.1 Purified to be a Messiah of the Dalits

Much has been written about Dr Pathak, who has dedicated his life to the fight against open defecation and manual scavenging, but few know how tough his struggle has been. The world-acclaimed social reformer was once on the brink of committing suicide.

Success, however, was in his destiny. "When I was just two years old, my grandfather had prophesied that I would earn a lot of name and fame in life," says the soft-spoken reformer. His grandfather, Shiv Sharan Pathak, was a renowned astrologer.

His prophecy came true. Starting in 1973, Pathak's non-profit, Sulabh International, has constructed over 1.5 million household Sulabh Shauchalayas (pour-flush toilets) across the country, with 20 million people using the facilities every day.

In August 1974, he built his first public toilet in Patna, with 20 bathrooms, urinals, washbasins, which had soap and clean water. Around 500 people used the toilet on the first day itself at 10 paise per user.

The social entrepreneur initially suffered so many setbacks that he seriously considered ending his life, but his vision and commitment saw him through the rough patch.

His father, Dr Ramakant Pathak, was an Ayurvedic doctor and the family was quite well-off but he recollects an incident from his childhood that left an indelible impression on his mind.

"I was around five or six," Pathak recalls. "A woman, who happened to be a Dalit, used to come to sell some household items to our village. One day, I touched her to say something...." All hell broke loose. He was punished by his grandmother for touching a scavenger woman—then considered untouchable. The untouchables are the lowest in the social order and are made to collect and dispose of human waste, since they will not be accepted for other jobs due to their caste status. Young Bindeshwar was made to swallow cow dung and urine and was then doused in holy Ganges water. This incident saw his transformation into a visionary striving to improve the country's sanitation for decades to come. Over the years he witnessed other cases where the scavenger community was discriminated against and humiliated. "This issue has bothered me since," says Dr Pathak, 75, who describes himself as a humanist and social reformer. "If they continue to clean human excreta, they will not be accepted into society."

7.1.2 Motivation for the Idea and the Way Forward...

Discrimination against scavengers was only part of the problem. There were various issues such as:

- A majority of the population in India lacks access to basic sanitation facilities
- Open defecation toilets which contaminate public places

- Spread of diseases such as diarrhoea, cholera and hepatitis
- Other environmental and social issues.

This motivated Pathak to write a doctoral dissertation on scavenging and ways to deal with it. After a certain time Pathak realised that academia alone cannot solve social problems due to its limitations.

On 5 March 1970, he took a personal loan of ₹50,000 and founded Sulabh Svachchh Shauchalaya Sansthan (Clean Toilet Institute), his non-profit organisation, and came up with his now famous innovative concept of the two-pit ecological compost toilet.

In this technology, there are two pits. One is used at a time and the other is kept as a standby. When the first pit gets filled up, the human excreta gets converted into bio-fertiliser with the help of bacteria present in the soil. It requires only one litre of water per use to flush.

He hired 7 to 8 people and the office was set up in an area of 200 sq ft in Patna. Later, he started getting support from corporates like State Bank of India, ONGC, Maruti, HDFC, Bharti Foundation and others. The non-profit organisation became Sulabh International in 1980, to have a more simplified name for the international network.

His work, predictably, attracted anger and protest from his community. "My parents and in-laws, along with society, were angry with me because they found it derogatory for a Brahmin to work for the lower caste," he says. "But I was out to achieve the dreams of Gandhiji."

To take his idea further he built Sulabh, an organisation focused on building sanitation facilities with state-of-the-art systems to collect, process and dispose of waste. However, this system is more than a mere toilet, because it also converts some of the waste into gas, fertiliser, etc., for utilisation in farms, for energy generation and so on.

7.1.3 Later Years

Deeply moved by the dehumanising practice of manual scavenging, Dr Pathak established the Sulabh International Social Service Organisation in 1970. By this time he had also developed the technology of a two-pit pour-flush toilet (Sulabh Shauchalaya) which could be conveniently built in Indian villages.

The idea caught over the years and in 1973 he had a chance meeting with a municipal officer in earlier Ara town, who sanctioned him, ₹500 to build two public toilets. This proved to be a catalyst and soon several other toilets were built all over Bihar. The toilet system spread to neighbouring states as well, freeing numerous manual scavengers from their revolting jobs.

Pathak introduced the pay-and-use system for maintaining the community toilets and baths in 1974. Within a few years, the Sulabh toilets were so popular for liberating the scavengers that the Ministry of Works and Housing, Government of India, in collaboration with the WHO and the UNICEF, organised a national seminar in Patna in 1978 on conversion of bucket latrines and liberation of scavengers.

In 1985, he started a training and rehabilitation programme for the wards of scavengers in different skills like shorthand, typing, driving, mechanics, masonry work, carpentry, etc., with the support of the Government of India and the Bihar State Scheduled Castes Development Corporation.

In the 1990s he focused on improving the social status of the scavenging community. In 1992, Sulabh organised a National Seminar on Liberation and Rehabilitation of Scavengers and encouraged steps to create social awareness against unfounded beliefs and prejudices. The Sulabh International Museum of Toilets was set up in 1994 to educate the general public about the development of toilets through the ages.

In 2001, Sulabh expanded its activities to include women's empowerment and started a country-wide programme for involvement of women in sanitation, health and hygiene. A vocational centre in Alwar, Rajasthan, was set up in 2003 to train women in tailoring, embroidery, food processing and beauty treatments.

Sulabh came up with a new and convenient technology in 2002 to make biogas plant effluents free from colour, odour and pathogens. The technology known as Sulabh Effluent Treatment (SET), makes the effluents safe and suitable for agriculture, aquaculture or safe discharge into a river or water body.

In collaboration with the World Toilet Organization, Sulabh organised the World Toilet Summit 2007 in which representatives of 44 countries participated. A Delhi Declaration for a cleaner world was issued following the deliberations.

A Padma Bhushan awardee, Dr Pathak is an early riser and wakes up at 5 am. He starts his day with a 45-minute exercise session and prays for an hour before leaving for office. One can sense his religious bent of mind by taking a good look at his office. A placard there reads:

"True men don't look for directions." Well he did not, indeed, writes Sunita Mishra Intelligent Entrepreneur (Magazine)–Touch of Success by Sunita Mishra (Volume 3, Issue-4). December, 2011.

7.2 MAN ON THE MOVE, MAN FOR THE MOMENT

Dr Pathak took the road less travelled but within a short span of time, the cleanliness crusader has paved the way for the biggest sanitation wave in the world. He has been moving like a restless saintly person, often visiting cities and towns all over the country where removal of human excreta and carrying it away as head load is a daily occurrence. As soon as he spots people engaged in this degrading occupation, he feels almost impatient to liberate them from this social curse (see Box 7.1). The Times News Network has said that he is a man on a mission to fight for the rights of "untouchables".

BOX 7.1: A NEW PARADIGM

During a visit to Alwar, a town in Rajasthan, some years ago Bindeshwar saw a group of young women carrying night soil to a dumping ground. When he stopped his car, got down and approached them, they were all stunned. Normally, what conversation could they have with any well-dressed person coming towards them, as the very sight repels people lest they should spoil their day with the stink from the excreta-loaded container on their head? To their great astonishment, the question he asked them was: "Would you like to change your profession?" Nobody had ever made such a query. Scavenging is the practice of manual cleaning of human excreta from service/dry latrines. The scavengers crawl into the dry latrines and collect the human excreta with their bare hands, carry it as head-load in a container to dispose it off.

More than 500 women had gathered to listen to Dr Pathak when he arrived there in the afternoon. They all wanted to know what would make their lives better. And when he asked about the rehabilitation programme for their better livelihood they all agreed with one voice. However, some of them asserted, "Sir, we would not like to touch or use handmade brooms for cleaning dry buckets." "No, of course you will not. Now you will live with dignity," replied Dr Pathak. And then he asked if they would come to Delhi and everyone agreed with one voice. In Delhi, when many of them arrived, they were told what they would be required to do at the training centre, which is to be named as "Nai Disha" (a new paradigm).

Source: Star Magazine Sunday News, Society, 6 November 2011

Night soil scavenging is slowly becoming obsolete in some areas, thanks to a sanitation revolution launched by Dr Pathak. He developed an eco-friendly, underground toilet system which he calls Sulabh, meaning "simple." It converts waste into dry fertiliser and biofuel inexpensively and with no daily maintenance.

Dr Pathak's passion for decades has been to eradicate societal discrimination against so-called "untouchables" like women. He recalls a defining moment in his life when he saw an entire community ignore an untouchable boy who had been attacked by a bull. "We took him to hospital, and the boy died. There, I took a vow to fulfil the dreams of Mahatma Gandhi," he says. Thus, a new "culture" of sanitation in India was born.

With and through Sulabh, Dr Pathak is slowly changing even attitudes, as some of the conditions that fostered untouchability are replaced by better hygiene and sanitation. But volunteers say plenty of work lies ahead, because attitudes 5,000 years old are not easy to wash away.

7.2.1 Lessons from Pathak

There are a few lessons we can draw from Dr Pathak and his organisation:

Strong Vision

One needs to have a vision or a mission to work towards a course in order to get a direction of what you intend to achieve. This has to be further broken into smaller goals and objectives.

Making a Difference at the Bottom of the Pyramid

Most of the successful businesses are those that made a difference at the bottom of the pyramid. The people at the bottom could be customers, employees, suppliers, business partners, the general public, etc. Today corporates also have a CSR wing to work in this direction.

Being Unique With Conviction

India is not short of talent for innovation and genius, but some people lack conviction. Generally, our culture sometimes holds us back from experimenting or innovating, because we are told to avoid mistakes, not take risks, and so on.

However, for entrepreneurs the rules are different, and they need to take risks, do experiments and come up with unique models. For example, if Captain G.R. Gopinath had not started and experimented with the low-cost airline, Deccan Air, most airlines in India would not have implemented the low-cost model.

Hesitation (or the Dignity Factor)

Most of us shy away from doing certain things (although legal and morally correct) because we think, "What will my family think?", "Will my image in society come down?", etc.

If Dr Pathak had been hesitant to start an initiative in sanitation, being a highly educated man, India would have just had another PhD but not the man who made a difference for millions. We have all heard of tech entrepreneurs and first-generation entrepreneurs in India in the last decade. In addition, we also have a large community of Indian entrepreneurs and experts abroad.

India has developed in many ways technologically, lifestyle-wise, and so on, but some of the fundamental problems remain unresolved, affecting millions of people.

His vision and mission are thus an inspiration, nay, a call to all entrepreneurs and experts to get into initiatives that can provide basic facilities to the lowest rung of the population in terms of education, healthcare, housing, sanitation, water, affordable energy, etc. Through such initiatives we can put India in the next league of developed nations in the years to come.

7.3 CHALLENGES AND OPPORTUNITIES

An estimated 650 million of India's poorest citizens lack access to basic hygienic toilets; open defecation toilets are still common. We might live in an information age with superior technologies, but lack of basic facilities and infrastructure always seems to take a back seat. This is where Dr Pathak sensed an opportunity to provide adequate public sanitation facilities so that waste can be properly collected, utilised and disposed without harming the environment and social ecosystems.

Although Dr Pathak started Sulabh International as a small outfit, it has grown by leaps and bounds in India as well as internationally. The organisation brings together design, resources and financing to produce low-cost and basic technologies to provide cost-effective sanitation solutions.

Its pour-flush compost toilet (Sulabh Shauchalaya or clean toilet) is outfitted with biogas converters to generate energy and reduce toxins. Since most operations are mechanised and have latest technologies, the old practice of removing human waste manually is done away with.

People who used to do scavenging are now able to lead a better life and have a steady source of earning through other livelihoods. Sulabh International has a presence in 26 states and 4 union territories and various nations.

Along with its initiatives in sanitation, Sulabh International runs rehabilitation programmes for out-of-work scavengers to train them in new skills, thereby enabling them to find new jobs, like vocational centre in Alwar, Rajasthan, where women are trained in tailoring, embroidery, etc.

Recently, some three dozen of the trainees were flown to New York city to participate in a fashion show held at the UN headquarters to mark the International Year of Sanitation.

Dr Pathak came up with an excreta-based biogas plant which generates biogas to be used for heating, cooking and electricity. His toilets, the design of which he's made available to NGOs around the country, are used by 10 million people daily, helping push the number of people in rural India with access to a toilet from 27 per cent years to 59 per cent in September 2009.

Sanitation is not a silly trade, but a serious billion-dollar opportunity with promising potential and stable returns. However, it also requires one to make investments, research and commitment to society in addition to running the commercial operations, which organisations like Sulabh have achieved.

7.3.1 Vision—Change the Situation

Sulabh International has become a household name and has become synonymous with public toilets. The word "Sulabh" means simple in Hindi, but today the word has become synonymous with the public toilet, almost the same way that Xerox has become synonymous with photocopying. Today, it is not merely the name of an NGO; it is a movement. Working with a workforce of over 50,000 volunteers in 26 states and four union territories, in 551 districts and 1,733 towns of India, Sulabh has also been invited to help out in neighbouring countries like Nepal, Bhutan, Afghanistan and Bangladesh. It has also taken up many programmes in collaboration with the United Nations Centre for Human Settlements, Nairobi, and the International Water and Sanitation Centre, Loughborough University of Technology, UK, through the Water Engineering and Development Centre.

It's easy to build a toilet, but to shift people's heart and soul towards its use is the real hard work. Sanitation in a country like India is a serious issue. According to a study, if 774 million people living without a household toilet in India stood in a queue, it would stretch from the earth to the moon and beyond. Clearing this line would take at least 5,892 years if each person took a minimum of four minutes to use the toilet. Sanitation is the major problem we are facing today. So this problem needs to be eliminated as soon as possible.

Dr Pathak has led a movement to overcome this problem. Due to his efforts and decisions, he is now known as "The Toilet Man of India".

7.4 MAJOR WORKS

Dr Pathak is the founder of Sulabh International which is today the largest non-profit organisation in India. The organisation promotes hygienic and sustainable sanitation and is committed to the causes of human rights, non-conventional sources of energy, waste management and social reforms through education. Besides contributing articles to newspapers and magazines, Dr Pathak has written many books such as *Sulabh Shauchalaya—A Simple Idea that Worked (1980); Road to Freedom: A Sociological Study on the Abolition of Scavenging in India (1991); Action Sociology and Development (1992); Rural Violence in Bihar (1993); Continuity and Change in Indian Society: Essays in Memory of Late Prof. Narmadeshwar Prasad (edited) 1998; Constitutional Safeguards for Weaker Sections and the Minorities in India (1999) [co-author: B.N. Srivastava]; New Princesses of Alwar—Shame to Pride—Concept & Vision (2000); Mukti Ke Marg Par: (Bharat Mein Gandagi Dhone ki Pratha ke Unmoolan ka - Samajshastriya Adhyayan 2001 [Hindi]; Preventing Wars & Terrorism (2004); Angels of Ghost Street (2005) [co-author: Xavier Zimbardo]; Gandhi: Sanitation and Untouchability (2009);*

Serfdom to Freedom (2009); Environmental Sanitation and Eradication of Scavenging in India (2010); Glimpses of Europe (2010) [co-author: S.P. Singh]; Dr Ambedkar: The Messiah of The Downtrodden (2010); Sociology of Sanitation: Environmental Sanitation, Public Health and Social Deprivation (2015); Caste Indian: End of Untouchability (2015); Widows in India: Study of Varanasi and Vrindavan (2016) [co-author Satyendra Tripathi]; Supreme Court of India & Widows of Vrindavan: Judicial Intervention and Efforts by Sulabh International Transformed the Lives of Widows of Vrindavan, Varanasi and Uttarakhand (2016); Untouchability No More (2016); Mahatma Gandhi's Life in Colour (2016) [Co-author: Gandhi Serve India]; Swachchhata Ka Darshan (2017) [Hindi]; Narendra Damodardas Modi: The Making of a Legend (2017).

Dr Pathak writes poems too. He loves children and always finds some time to chat and play with them. His new poem: "Son of India: A Song on Hon'ble Prime Minister Shri Narendra Modi" in 24 regional languages has also been set to music by Dr Pathak himself. The song vividly describes various welfare works and activities being carried out by Prime Minister Modi.

7.5 AWARDS AND HONOURS

Dr Pathak is called the messiah of sanitation. Those who have seen Dr Bindeshwar Pathak or his works or have in one way or another been impacted by the Sulabh initiatives feel that Dr Pathak is a great humanist and social reformer of contemporary India. To the weaker sections of society especially, his is the compassionate face of a paternal redeemer. He has the vision of a philosopher and the undying zeal of a missionary. He is an icon of sanitation and social reform who has made a difference in the lives of millions of people. Dr Pathak will be remembered in history for his innovative strides in the field of sanitation as well as social reform. With his efforts erstwhile untouchables have been allowed by society to intermingle with it and live on a par with it, dining with others and being allowed to offer prayers in the temples. He has created a new culture which embraces the poor and extols the dignity of labour.

Dr Pathak has received more than 70 awards so far given by organisations across the length and breadth of India and also abroad. He got the Limca Book of Records' Man of the Year Award in 1995. He is a recipient of the Padma Bhushan, awarded by the Government of India (1991), the St Francis Prize for the Environment "Canticle of all Creatures (1992), the Babu Jagjivan Ram Award for Abolishing Scavenging (1997), the Indira Gandhi Priyadarshini Paryavaran Puraskar (1994), the Stockholm Water Prize (2009), the Indian Affairs Social Reformer of the Year 2017 award and so on (see Table 7.1).

Table 7.1: List of Awards and Honours Conferred on Dr Pathak

1	The Weekend Leader–VIT Person of the Year 2018 by Vellore Institute of Technology (VIT), Tamil Nadu, on 20th March	2019
2	Gandhi Peace Prize recognizes the contribution of Sulabh International Social Service Organisation in improving the condition of sanitation in India and emancipation of manual	2019
	scavengers. The award was given by the Hon'ble President of India Shri Ram Nath Kovind in the presence of Hon'ble Prime of India Shri Narendra Modi on 26th February at Darbar Hall, Rashtrapati Bhavan, New Delhi	
3	Sewa Ratna Award by His Holiness Swami Avdheshanand Giriji, Founder, Prabhu Premi Sangh on the occasion of Ardh Kumbh Mela at Prayagraj on 24th January in the field of Women Empowerment	2019
4	Inspire Award 2018-19 in the field of Health and Wellness by Parivartan at New Delhi on 12th January	2019
5	Lifetime Achievement Award by SABERA (Social and Business Enterprise Responsible Awards) at Nehru Memorial Museum Library Auditorium, Teen Murti, New Delhi on 6th December	2018
6	The Legend Award, efforts to improve the sanitation infrastructure and accessibility in the country, recognised by Fiinovation on the occasion of 10th Foundation Day at New Delhi on 29th September	2018
7	Lifetime Achievement Award for improvement of sanitation and production of biogas is changing health and wealth outcomes for the poorest people by the PHD Chamber at New Delhi on 28th September	2018
8	Jeewangaurav Puraskar 2018 for social contribution by Dr Babasaheb Ambedkar Marathwada University Aurangabad in Maharashtra on 23rd August	2018
9	23rd Nikkei Asia Prize for Culture and Community at Tokyo, Japan on 13th June	2018
10	Member of National Committee for 150th Birth Anniversary of Mahatma Gandhi, Government of India on 31st October	2017

11	Lal Bahadur Shastri National Award for Excellence in Public Administration, Academics and Management: 2017 by Lal Bahadur Shastri Institute of Management on 10th October in Delhi	2017
12	Indian Affairs Social Reformer of the Year 2017 Award by Network 7 Media Group on 4th August at Mumbai.	2017
13	Bharat Gaurav Lifetime Achievement Award by Sanskriti Yuva Sanstha on 9th June at the United Nations headquarters, New York	2017
14	World Book of Records an exclusive honour for his contribution in creating "exponential awareness in cleanliness and mass hygiene" on 22nd May in the House of Loards, British Parliament, London	2017
15	Lifetime Achievement Award by ISC-FICCI Sanitation Awards and India Sanitation Conclave on 27th April in New Delhi	2017
16	Vishwa Vageshwari Samman 2017 by Vishwa Hindi Sahitya Parishad, New Delhi, on 19th April in Pune, Maharashtra	2017
17	Rashtriya Krantiveer Award for contribution for the national cause in the memory of Shri Ram Chandra Raghuvanshi (KAKAJI) on 4th April in Ujjain, Madhya Pradesh	2017
18	Sewadham Rashtra Vibhuti Samman for his lifetime work of leading a nationwide movement of sanitation and social reform given by Sewadham Ashram on 4th April in Ujjain, Madhya Pradesh	2017
19	Poorva Post Award for outstanding contribution towards society on 26th March in New Delhi	2017
20	"Swadeshi Vigyan Puraskar 2017" organised by CSIR-National Physical Laboratory in New Delhi	2017
21	Public Service Excellence Award by All India Management Award (AIMA) in New Delhi	2017
22	Indian Social Science Association's Award at its Golden Jubilee Conference at BHU for his immense contribution to Action Sociology and commendable support for social sciences	2017
23	Golden Peacock Lifetime Achievement Award for Leadership of Social Service-2016 by Institute of Directors (IOD) in Bengaluru	2017
24	Distinguished Engineer honour by Rocheston Accreditation Institute, New York in New Delhi	2017
25	Member of National Legal Services Authority (NALSA)	2016
26	Honorary Citizen of the French City of Montier honour from Mayor of Montier-en-Der	2016

27	Hon'ble Railway Minister Shri Suresh Prabhakar Prabhu, declares to Dr Pathak as Brand Ambassador of Swachh Rail Mission	2016
28	Member of Deen Dayal Upadhyaya National Committee	2016
29	CNN-News18 Indian of the Year, 2015—Outstanding Achievement award by CNN-News18 in New Delhi	2016
30	Mayor of the City of New York declares 14 April 2016 "Dr Bindeshwar Pathak Day" in New York	2016
31	2016 Humanitarian Award by New York Global Leaders Dialogue in New York	2016
32	WHO Public Health Champion Award by WHO in New Delhi	2016
33	Goyal Peace Prize by Kurukshetra University in Kurukshetra, Haryana	2015
34	Amity Lifetime Achievement Award by Amity University at Amity University Campus, Noida	2015
35	Lord Baden Powell National Award at Ghalib Auditorium, New Delhi	2015
36	Sardar Patel Award-2014 by Sardar Vallabhbhai Patel Foundation in New Delhi	2015
37	Lifetime Achievement Award for Sanitation for All: Toilet First by India CSR Group at PHD House, New Delhi	2015
38	Vivekanand Seva Samman by Shree Burrabazar Kumarsabha Pustakalaya in Kolkata	2015
39	Power Thinkers Award for Services to Humanity by Personality Plus International in Raipur, Chhattisgarh	2015
40	Lifetime Achievement Shaan-e-Lucknow Award for contribution in the field of Sanitation by Lucknow Book Fair at Lucknow, Uttar Pradesh	2015
41	Mother Teresa Memorial Award by Indian Development Foundation (IDF) in Chennai	2014
42	The NGO Leadership and Excellence Award by the World CSR Congress at Taj Lands End Hotel, Mumbai	2014
43	**The International Banga Moni Award by the Micheal Madhusudan Academy at Calcutta University, West Bengal**	2014
44	**The Late Madan Mohan Verma Smriti Samman from the Journalist Association of Electronic and Print, Dehradun**	2014
45	National Health Care Promotion Award by Heart Care Foundation of India in New Delhi	2013

46	Lifetime Achievement Award by ABP News in Mumbai	2013
47	Lifetime Achievement Award by Rotary Club of Madras in Chennai	2013
48	LEGENDE DE LA PLANETE Congres Fondateur Jeux Ecologiques at UNESCO, Paris	2013
49	Lifetime Achievement Award by 5th World Aqua Congress 2011 in New Delhi	2011
50	Bhagirath Alankaran by Ganga Seva Nidhi, Varanasi, Uttar Pradesh	2011
51	National Award for Innovations in the Services for the Urban Poor by the India Urban Space Foundation	2010
52	Bihar Ratna Award in Patna	2010
53	Sanitation Visionary Award by World Toilet Organization in Singapore	2009
54	FACE Award 2008 by FACE magazine, New Delhi	2009
55	Sat Paul Mittal Award in Ludhiana	2009
56	Vishwa Bhojpuri and Indian Diaspora Sammaan	2009
57	2009 Stockholm Water Prize, Sweden	2009
58	Intergovernmental Renewable Energy Organisation Award (IREO), New York, USA	2009
59	Hall of Fame Award by World Toilet Organization at World Toilet Summit, Macau, China	2008
60	Rashtriya Gaurav Award by Citizen Forum of Human Rights, New Delhi	2008
61	National Energy Globe Award, by Energy Globe in Brussels, Belgium	2008
62	Hindi Vachaspati Award by Rashtriya Hindi Parisad	2008
63	Aryavart Shikhar Samman by the Indian Nation Publication	2007
64	Bharat Gaurav Award by Citizen Forum of Human Rights, New Delhi	2007
65	Lifetime Achievement Award for Leadership in the Social Sector by Dr P. N. Singh Foundation	2007
66	Maharana Udai Singh Award	2006
67	One India One People Foundation Award	2006
68	International Human Rights' Award	2006
69	Sakshi Bharat Award	2006
70	AIWEFA Platinum Jubilee Award 2005	2005
71	Good Corporate Citizen Award	2005

72	Indira Gandhi Paryavaran Puraskar by Government of India	2003
73	Scroll of Honour by UN-Habitat in Rio-de-Janeiro (Brazil)	2003
74	Global 500 Roll of Honour Award by UNEP in Beirut (Lebanon)	2003
75	Dubai International Award for Best Practices for Improving the Living Environment by UNCHS at Dubai	2000
76	Samaj Ratna Award in Lucknow	1999
77	Distinguished Leadership Award	1997
78	Michael Madhusudan Dutt Award	1997
79	Babu Jagjivan Ram Award for Abolishing Scavenging	1997
80	Global Urban Best Practice by United Nations Centre for Human Settlements (UNCHS) in Istanbul	1996
81	Limca Book of Records' Man of the Year Award	1995
82	Vikas Ratna Award	1995
83	Manav Seva Puraskar	1995
84	NRI Gold Award	1994
85	Indira Gandhi Priyadarshini Award	1994
86	Ratna Shiromani Award by India International Society for Unity	1993
87	Rotary International Spectra-93, Par Excellence Award for Protection of Environment	1993
88	Anne Mukhopadhya Award for Social Work	1992
89	Shahid Bhup Singh Award for Social Work	1992
90	Bombay Citizen's Award	1992
91	Dr Pinnamaneni and Smt Seethadevi Foundation Award	1992
92	The International Saint Francis Prize for the Environment "Canticle of All Creatures" at Assisi, Italy	1992
93	National Citizens' Award	1991
94	Padma Bhushan on 23rd March	1991
95	Civic Betterment Award, Bombay	1990-91
96	Builders' Information Bureau Award	1990
97	Prabandhak Mahan Muzaffarpur	1990
98	K.P. Goenka Memorial Award	1984

Compiled from various sources

Dr Pathak received the Indira Gandhi Priyadarshini Award in 1994, New Delhi

Dr Pathak receiving National Citizen's Award from the then President, Dr Shankar Dayal Sharma

His Holiness Pope John Paul II gave an audience to Dr Pathak before conferring on him the St Francis Prize for the Environment "Canticle of All Creatures" in 1992

Note: All three pictures accessed from http://www.sulabhinternational.org/awards-and-honours/

Dr Bindeshwar Pathak was named alongside Pakistani teenager Malala Yousafzai and the then US President Barack Obama on an inaugural Global Diversity List. He was ranked by *The Economist* among the World's Top 50 diversity figures in public life along with US President Barack Obama, Angelina Jolie and Bill Gates (November 2015). Dr Pathak is among 50 global personalities "who have used their position in public life to make an impact on diversity", *The Economist* magazine, said. "Humanist, social reformer and diversity champion, Pathak works as an advocate for the so-called 'untouchable' caste, so that they may work, live and pray as a fully integrated part of Indian life," it said.

Dr Pathak was selected for the 2016 New York Global Leaders Dialogue Humanitarian Award. In making the announcement from New York, Scanlan said, "Dr Pathak is a great humanitarian who for decades has enhanced the quality of life for millions of fellow human beings.

He embodies our philosophy that leadership is focused on creating collaborative new space in the service of others. We are especially attracted to leaders who transform lives for the better, and Dr Pathak stands tall in embodying these rarest of qualities." In April 2016, Bill de Blasio, Mayor of New York City, declared 14 April 2016 as Bindeshwar Pathak Day.

A proposal is on the drawing board to establish a Dr Bindeshwar Pathak Chair at Banaras Hindu University (BHU) in recognition of his historic contribution in environmental sanitation and social reforms in contemporary India. Filmmaker Neetu Chandra is keen to make a biopic on Dr Pathak.

7.6 QUOTES OF DR PATHAK

1. "I announce to name one village in India as Trump Village."
2. "The toilet is a part of the history of human hygiene and constitutes a critical chapter in the history of human civilisation."
3. "Have a Sulabh toilet in your home at the earliest with or without government assistance. This will make you and your family healthy, happy and prosperous....It will also fulfil the dream of Mahatma Gandhi and Prime Minister of India."
4. "Cleanliness is Godliness."
5. "I believe that Sulabh is not an event but an idea...."

7.7 REMARKS BY CELEBRITIES/STALWARTS ON DR PATHAK

What Abraham Lincoln did for Blacks in America, Dr Pathak has done for scavengers in India. Both are great redeemers.

—Dr Mulk Raj Anand, writer

I read with great sympathy your account of the situation of the scavengers' community, and I congratulate you on the work which you are doing on its behalf. I am sure your International Saint Francis Prize for the Environment was richly deserved.

–Boutros Boutros-Ghali, former Secretary-General of the United Nations.

The Sulabh movement is indeed a reminder and jolt to conscience. It is performing the double task of socially rehabilitating the suffering segment of our society and providing healthy and clean municipal life. It deserves all support.

—Late I.K. Gujral, former prime minister of India.

Dr Pathak's work is very seminal. It is humane and educative.

—Dr Wally N' Dow, Secretary-General, Habitat

For his social reform movement, Dr Pathak can be compared to Dayanand Saraswati and Raja Ram Mohan Roy.

—Dr Karan Singh, former Union minister, diplomat, scholar and Member of Parliament (Rajya Sabha).

The centre of Sulabh is everything I imagined and much more. A centre of inspiration, liberation and human vitality. I will remember forever this visit and remain a disciple and willing promotee of their wonderful ideas and activities in an area most people are too shy even to talk about. Nearly everything which works began with an idea and a small group of people committed to work to realise it. Thank you, **Dr Pathak and your co-workers, for your inspiration and achievements.**

—Sir Richard Jolly, Special Advisor to the Administrator, UNDP, and Chairman, Collaboration Council for Drinking Water and Sanitation.

I am the grandson of Mahatma Gandhi but Dr Bindeshwar Pathak is the son of his soul. If we were to go to meet Mohandas Karamchand Gandhi he would first greet Dr Pathak for the noble work that he is doing and then greet me. Dr Pathak has restored human rights and dignity to people engaged in the manual cleaning of human excreta which they carried as head-load.

—Prof. Rajmohan Gandhi.

Dr Bindeshwar Pathak's genius lies not in his solution to the problem of open defecation which clearly remains an overwhelming issue for India but in his direct assault on social hierarchies that perpetuate the problem.

—Prof Tanvi Nagpal, Director of Water and Sanitation Initiatives, Global Water Challenge.

God has sent very few angels on earth and Dr Pathak is one of them.

—Neetu Chandra, filmmaker.

Truly, Dr Pathak is a humanist par excellence. For millions of the marginalised he is a paternal redeemer. He is a living example of how a modern Indian can still be a Gandhian with many conventional ideas. He is rightly called the "guru of toilets". We have much to learn from him.

Chapter 8

Environmental Sanitation

Environmental sanitation and public health have been closely interrelated for long. Provision of safe water and sanitation are part of the most basic first generation public health interventions. This central issue was highlighted by the Bhore Committee Report of 1946, and by the second and third Five Year Plans of India. The WHO in 1952 estimated that 50 million people in India were affected every year by water-borne diseases and two million died annually from this cause.

Problems of environmental sanitation in India include:

1. Disposal of human excreta
2. Disposal of waste
3. Water supply
4. Housing1
5. Public toilets

8.1 ENVIRONMENT AS A PUBLIC GOOD

Public goods are called social wants by Musgrave, to be satisfied by the government (not necessarily produced by it). They can be merit wants. For example, clean air is not only a social want but a merit want. The market fails to provide these goods to all in an unbiased manner. So, some collective action is justified for access and maintenance. Collective ownership and collective protection (i.e., prevention of damages like contamination, spoilage) are the principles here. Thinking beyond increased consumption and production to reduced toxicity, increased recyclability (down cycling), extended life span and cleaner production will be ideal eco-efficient corrective steps.

Now, environmental conservation and protection are more important and relevant than ever before and we must get together to save our one and only habitat, says Mihir Paul. Protecting includes aspects of preserving all that is good and useful and preventing the negative externalities.

The protection of public goods is not just to safeguard pecuniary interests but also to ensure a healthy and liveable environment. The right type of conservation policies and measures must therefore be in place on-site and off-site. Resource auditing, public participation, and implementation, and monitoring of policies and programmes must have its impact on human well-being and sustainable development for the people and the planet.

In this regard the roles played by the Ministry of Environment and Forests, Government of India, as well as the United Nations Environment Programme, South Asia Cooperative Environment Programme, International Centre for Integrated Mountain Development, etc., are significant.

8.2 ENVIRONMENT AND ECONOMIC DEVELOPMENT

The words "ecology" and "economics" stem from the same root word "oikos", meaning house. Man and other creatures live in this house called Planet Earth. But man is not living in harmony with nature.[2] If all were well there would be a healthy environment and healthy life for man and other organisms. Development is happening but at what cost? Our country has a historical philosophy of "unity in diversity". We are also suffering from loss of biodiversity. Environmental sensitivity calls for an interdisciplinary approach. The close relationship between society, economy and environment is seen in Figure 8.1.

We see that:

- The purpose of inter-linkages between society (meaning people), economy and environment is to make life bearable, equitable, sustainable and viable.
- Three circles enclosed within one another show how both economy and society are subsets of our planetary ecological system.
- We must know the relationship, and live in harmony or balance.

The relationship between environment and economic development is not only very close but complex too. Economic growth is becoming a source of ecological crisis. There is ecological imbalance. It is unhealthy growth. Normative economics should also be considered. The utilitarian model

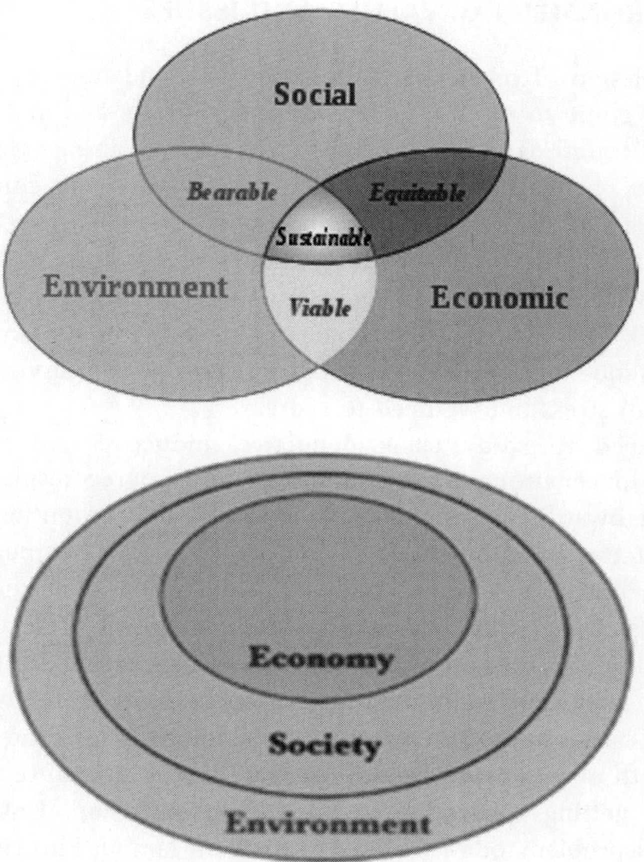

Figure 8.1: Society, Economy and Environment

should serve as the guideline for economics of environment. Economic approach to environment includes economic concepts, tools and methods of analysing ecological issues, economic causes and consequences of ecological crisis.

There are increasing threats to ecology from rapid population growth, severe pollution, neglect of community participation in environmental protection, ignoring the results of cost-benefit analysis, slowing down of environmentalism and so on. The fine balance between man and environment is lost.

8.3 ENVIRONMENTAL VALUES AND ISSUES

From depletion of resources to pollution and endangered species we have now come to discuss global warming, locally and globally. Both developed countries as well as developing countries discuss global issues like climate change and local issues like solid waste management. Ideas, institutions and policies are all becoming important to save the planet and keep it liveable for all species. As Lester Brown opines, "We need a vision of what an environmentally sustainable economy, an eco-economy, would look like—one that offers not only a vision of an eco-economy, but also frequent assessments of progress in realising that vision." There are signs of stress but we need to redress.

We need to study using deductive, inductive and intellectual methods for environmental issues beyond resource availability and utilisation towards environmental management and accounting. It means looking at the environment from both science and arts perspectives. Environmental economics as we know it is the science and art of utilising natural resources without forsaking the principles of preservation and conservation. It is the coming together of ecology, i.e., study of the oikos or house (earth) and economics i.e. management of the house.

Many causes harm the environment, including population explosion. Fast growth of population is bad for man as well as nature. Biological capital is getting spoilt due to population explosion. Unsustainable growth is a problem today. We need to apply the famous Ehrlich equation:

$$I = P x A x T$$

Where I stands for impact on environment, P for population, A for affluence (consumption) and T refers to technology.

The world population is expected to touch 10 billion by 2070. The obvious impact is on fragile natural resources' depletion and degradation. Effective use of resources, cleaner technologies, less population should go hand in hand with a slower rate of growth of population.

There are definite limits to growth. Barry Commoner suggests a path of "no growth" in the capital and productive system. Dean Meadows supports this view through his "Limits to Growth" (LTG) model which states that infinite growth is impossible on a finite planet. Quantity criterion alone will not help. We cannot ignore quality of life, resources and work. More food without good nutrition and health is of no use.

It does not mean that we must prevent the expansion of the economy, but synchronise it with positive culture and values. We must build a powerful set of checks against degradation of the environment.

A report by the WHO reveals that 24 per cent of global diseases and 23 per cent of all deaths are caused by environmental exposure or pollution. Creating public awareness and action should be the topmost agenda in this regard. The three Rs—reduce, reuse and recycle—should be followed judiciously.

As Gandhi said, "The world has enough for everyone's need, but not enough for everyone's greed." Environmentalism has now to defend against consumerism. This is the modern tragedy of the commons. Environmental equilibrium (EE) needs environmental renewal, not degradation:

$$EE = ES + E1 + E2 + S$$

Where ES refers to energy system, E1 is equity, E2 is efficiency and S stands for sustainability.

The interrelationship between the environment and socio-economic development combines the micro approach and the macro approach for the sake of growth with stability, security and sustainability, and not merely productivity.

We must look at nature not only with an aesthetic sense but also from the point of view of value creation and value addition. Environmental assets not only have beauty but also tangible benefits such as food for consumers (e.g., fruits, fish), raw materials for producers (e.g., medicinal plants). All these benefits are relevant in environmental valuation and restoration economics. Therefore, as individuals and eco-citizens we must be willing to pay for environmental gains and to accept compensation for environmental losses.

Environmental value refers to the worth that a community or society places on environmental goods and services. According to John A. Dixon, environmental valuation is "the process of putting monetary value on environmental goods and services".

Environmental valuation is important today and tomorrow, even if today some resources are unknown or less used. It reflects society's value and culture, even if expressed in the market, or even if there is a market failure.

According to J. Spurgeon, there are different types of environmental values:

1. Direct Use Value or Structural Value: Direct use value of the environment refers to the values of environmental goods and services consumed by the users. These values include (i) products edible, ornamental, recreational, etc.; (ii) recreation beaches, hill stations, etc.; (iii) waste elimination; and (iv) education.
2. Indirect Use Value or Functional Value: Indirect use values are the indirect benefits derived from the ecological systems. They include (i) biological support links to other species and habitats; (ii) physical protection coastal defence function; (iii) climate regulation; and (iv) global life support functions that aid in supporting life on earth.
3. Non-Use Value: Non-use values refer to values for those who anticipate using/visiting the resource. They include (i) option values; and (ii) existence values.
4. Intrinsic Value: This refers to valuing a resource like an organism regardless of its usefulness to humans.
5. Bequest Value: What and how much we leave to our children is bequest value.

An environmental issue refers to any issue that concerns the ecological and human environment. A variety of environmental problems are affecting us globally and locally. As globalisation continues and the earth's natural processes transform local problems into international issues, few societies are being left untouched by major environmental problems. Consumerism, global warming and climate change, loss of biodiversity, ozone depletion and such other things are by and large global environmental problems. They need international agreements to combat. Common pool resources, waste management, community participation, etc., come under local issues.

8.3.1 Local Issues

Local issues are faced both by rural people and the urban populace. Some local problems are:

- Abandoned parked vehicles
- Air pollution
- Dog nuisance
- Flooding

- Litter
- Mobile phone masts
- Noise
- Pest control
- Raves
- Common property resources
- Streets and pavements
- Traffic management and parking
- Waste disposal
- Open defecation, poor sanitation, etc.

Most environmental problems are essentially local in nature and require local solutions. Yet protecting the environment has too often meant more power for the Central Government, and less local responsibility. Policymakers need to do the precise opposite. There needs to be greater scope for local decision-taking and less top-down control. Even students and teachers work for (i) clean water by joining with local organisations to monitor water quality, restore habitat, build rain gardens, plant trees, or clean up debris; (ii) fighting global warming to save energy, and working with community organisations to educate and drive others to take the "pledge", and (iii) do school's waste management campaign, even help a local school avoid chemical mismanagement.

8.4 ENORMITY OF THE SANITATION SITUATION

Water and sanitation related diseases are widespread. An estimated 12.6 million deaths each year are attributable to unhealthy environments– nearly one in four of total global deaths. Environmental risk factors, such as air, water and soil pollution, chemical exposure, climate change and ultraviolet radiation contribute to more than 100 diseases and injuries.

Diarrhoeal diseases impact children most severely, killing more than two million young children a year in the developing world. Many more are left underweight, stunted mentally and physically, vulnerable to other deadly diseases, and too debilitated to go to school.

This situation in today's world is humiliating, morally wrong and oppressive. The global community has made advances in many fields but it has failed to ensure these most basic needs of deprived people. Worse still, if unprecedented global action is not taken, the lot of the poor is expected to worsen in the foreseeable future.

Water supply, sanitation and health are closely related. Poor hygiene, inadequate quantities and quality of drinking water, and lack of sanitation facilities cause millions of the world's poorest people to die from preventable diseases each year. Women and children are the main victims. Water, sanitation and health are linked in many ways:

Contaminated water that is consumed may result in water-borne diseases including viral hepatitis, typhoid, cholera, dysentery and other diseases that cause diarrhoea.

- Without adequate quantities of water for personal hygiene, skin and eye infections (trachoma) spread easily.
- Water-based diseases and water-related vector-borne diseases can result from water supply projects (including dams and irrigation structures) that inadvertently provide habitats for mosquitoes and snails that are intermediate hosts of parasites that cause malaria, schistosomiasis, lymphatic filariasis, onchocerciasis and Japanese encephalitis.
- Drinking water supplies that contain high amounts of certain chemicals (like arsenic and nitrates) can cause serious disease.
- Inadequate water, sanitation and hygiene account for a large part of the burden of illness and death in developing countries.
- Lack of clean water and sanitation is the second most important risk factor in terms of the global burden of disease, after malnutrition.
- Approximately four billion cases of diarrhoea per year cause 1.5 million deaths, mostly among children under five.
- Intestinal worms infect about 10 per cent of the population of the developing world, and can lead to malnutrition, anaemia and retarded growth.
- Six million people are blind from trachoma and the population at risk is about 500 million.
- 300 million people suffer from malaria.
- 200 million people are infected with schistosomiasis, 20 million of whom suffer severe consequences.

8.4 DETERMINANTS OF POOR HEALTH AND SANITATION

Determinants are the factors that contribute to the start and spread of disease. With increased awareness of environmental factors influencing the quality of life, epidemiologists now approach disease from a more holistic perspective, considering the role of environmental determinants.

Factors like living and environmental conditions, pollution, water contamination, climate change and global warming are affecting the health of an individual. To a large extent factors like social determinants, economic determinants, political interference and policy changes, cultural aspects within the community and ecological factors greatly influence the sanitation situation of individuals and of the community. Even wrong orientation of technology causes environmental degradation.

There are three levels of determinants—domestic, local and global. Domestic is used to denote the home environment. Local refers to the wider location of the region, and global to the worldwide context. Domestic determinants deal with such issues as water and sanitation, domestic pests, food contamination and common pollutants that have influenced health conditions. The direct link between poor living conditions and the prevalence of disease is to be noted. Residential factors are part of the domestic environment.

Local determinants deal with air pollution, water pollution and the influence of hazardous wastes on health. Modern lifestyles contribute to polluting the environment and thereby causing increasing risks to health. Global factors deal with ozone depletion, global warming, acid rain and the health hazards that have resulted from these major disruptions to the environment. Escalating human activities is resulting in new forms of pollution, threatening human survival.

One thing that has been confirmed in recent studies is the intricate link between health conditions and the state of the environment. In its conceptual framework, the development of an integrated approach linking environment and health will address three global objectives:

(i) to control and promote compatible lifestyles and consumption patterns in rich groups and developed countries;

(ii) to provide an environment with ability to promote health, through reducing physical, chemical and biological hazards and assuring the necessary resources for adequate health status for all; and

(iii) to achieve for all individuals and organisations the consciousness of their own responsibility for health and of the environmental.

8.5 SUSTAINABLE DEVELOPMENT AND SANITATION

Sustainable development was defined by the Brundtland Commission as "development that meets the needs of the present without compromising the ability of future generations to meet their own needs". It recognises that growth must be both inclusive and environmentally sound to reduce poverty and build shared prosperity for today's population and for future generations. It must be efficient with resources and carefully planned/managed to deliver immediate and long-term benefits for people, the planet and prosperity (see Figures 8.2 A and B). The Sustainable Sanitation Alliance (SuSanA) is an informal network of organisations with a common vision on sustainable sanitation, to provide a platform for knowledge exchange, networking and discussion on all sustainable sanitation topics.

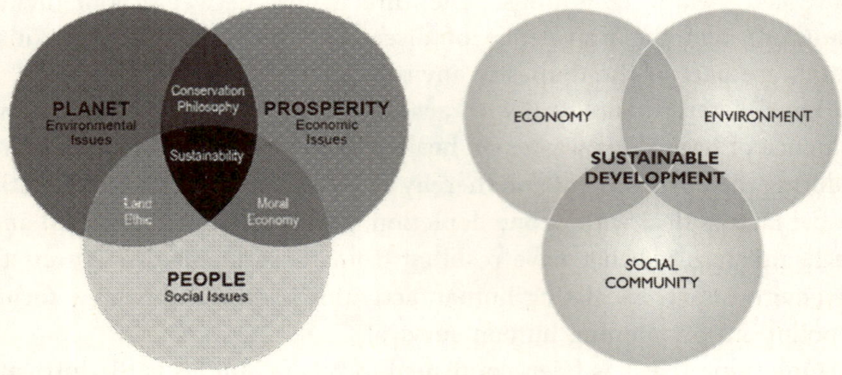

Figure 8.2 A and B : Dimensions of Sustainable Development

Source: https://www.google.co.in

The umbrella term 'sustainable development' even jells well with the new philosophy of inclusive growth and with women's empowerment, climate change, agrarian crisis, water problems, the clean Ganga and clean India campaigns, smart cities/villages, eco sensitisation, etc.

The Supreme Court in *Vellore Citizens' Welfare Forum vs Union of India and others* held that sustainable development is the balancing concept between ecology and development. In *Indian Council for Enviro-legal Action vs Union of India and others*, the court had emphasised on sustainable development and held that development and environment must go hand in hand.

Sustainable sanitation recognises that in order to be sustainable, a sanitation approach must be socially acceptable and economically viable. In this way, sustainable sanitation is a loop-based approach that differs fundamentally from the current linear concepts of wastewater management, and that does not only recognise technology, but also social, environmental and economic aspects. Sustainable sanitation is an approach that considers sanitation holistically. It recognises that human excreta and wastewater are not waste products, but valuable resources. This view is based on the fact that waste water and excreta contain significant amounts of energy, plant nutrients and also water that can be recycled and reused, thus protecting natural resources.

The main objective of a sanitation system is to protect and promote human health by providing a clean environment and breaking the cycle of disease. In order to be sustainable, a sanitation system has to be not only economically viable, socially acceptable, and technically and institutionally appropriate, it should also protect the environment and the natural resources.

Today, the need for sustainability means that resource saving and protection of the environment are vital and there is a need for innovation and rethinking. This cannot be achieved by conventional methods. Also, in our emerging consumer and chemical societies it will not be enough that residents pay for sanitation and water services–they have to be partners to make sanitation sustainable.

Sustainable sanitation is a simple approach: the most basic principle is that it considers wastewater and excreta not as waste but as resources, that sanitation has to be socially acceptable and should be as economically viable as possible. There is no one-size-fits-all approach; rather, the most adequate solution has to be found from case to case, considering climate and water availability, agricultural practices, socio-cultural preferences, affordability, safety and technical prerequisites, to name a few (see Figure 8.3).

CSR plays a vital role in attaining sustainable development. The company has a social and moral responsibility towards protecting the environment. Recently, this social and moral responsibility is being backed

What is Sustainable Sanitation?

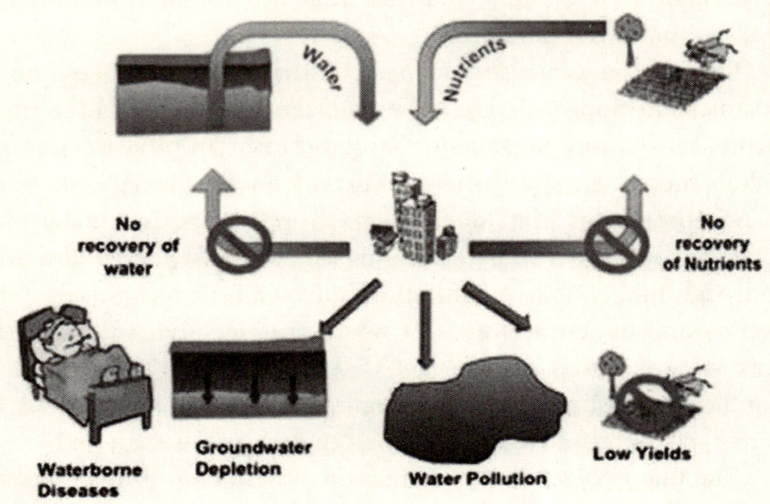

Conventional approaches to wastewater management that regard wastewater as a waste, and often are dysfunctional, have serious drawbacks. Source: CONRADIN (2010)

Figure 8.3:

Source: http://www.sulabhenvis.nic.in/Database/san_sustainable_2372.aspx

by rules and regulations. Many companies are focusing on environmental issues for their CSR activities. Sony, Panasonic and Orchard Hotels are focusing on issues related to environment such as toxic gases, waste production and water contamination.

When improving an existing and/or designing a new sanitation system, sustainability criteria related to the following aspects should be considered:

- **Health and hygiene:** Includes the risk of exposure to pathogens and hazardous substances that could affect public health at all points of the sanitation system from the toilet via the collection and treatment system to the point of reuse or disposal, and downstream populations. This topic also covers aspects such as hygiene, nutrition and improvement of livelihood achieved by the application of a certain sanitation system, as well as downstream effects.

- **Environment and natural resources:** Involves the required energy, water and other natural resources for construction, operation and maintenance of the system, as well as potential emissions in the environment resulting from its use. It also includes the degree of recycling and reuse practised and the effects of these (e.g., reusing wastewater, returning nutrients and organic material to agriculture), and the protection of other non-renewable resources, e.g., through the production of renewable energies (such as biogas).
- **Technology and operation**: Incorporates the functionality and the ease with which the entire system including the collection, transport, treatment and reuse and/or final disposal can be constructed, operated and monitored by the local community and/or the technical teams of the local utilities. Furthermore, the robustness of the system, its vulnerability towards power cuts, water shortages, floods, earthquakes, etc., and the flexibility and adaptability of its technical elements to the existing infrastructure and to demographic and socio-economic developments are important aspects.
- **Financial and economic issues**: Relate to the capacity of households and communities to pay for sanitation, including the construction, operation, maintenance and necessary reinvestments in the system. Besides the evaluation of these direct costs, direct benefits e.g., from recycled products (soil conditioner, fertiliser, energy and reclaimed water) and external costs and benefits have also to be taken into account. Some such external costs are e.g., environmental pollution and health hazards, while benefits include increased agricultural productivity and subsistence economy, employment creation, improved health and reduced environmental risks.
- **Socio-cultural and institutional aspects**: The criteria in this category refer to the socio-cultural acceptance and appropriateness of the system, convenience, system perceptions, gender issues and impacts on human dignity, the contribution to food security, compliance with the legal framework and stable and efficient institutional settings.

8.5.1 Measures to be Taken

In the rural economy land is the site of production. Our villagers live and work in close relationship with nature. Intensification of resource use and diversification of occupation (even if we call it technological advancement) pose serious challenges to balanced economic development in India. Villagers are facing the growing needs for food, fodder and fuel on the one hand, and fast encroaching urbanisation on the other. Both have disastrous consequences on nature's fragile fabric. Modern development in urban areas has resulted in stress and strain, and in rural distress and drain of resources. Hence, we need a thorough analysis of the strengths, weaknesses, threats and opportunities for economic development now and in the future. This will create the much needed awareness for prioritisation of economic activities in the country to make the best use of relatively limited available natural resources and be in harmony with nature. Sustainable development is not a choice but a need; good for us, good for our environment. As eco-conscious citizens we must practise the principles of eco-economy. For instance, for many people recycling is not just "economics" but also a "habit".

Keeping in mind the above factors, the environment and sanitation studies should try to draw the attention of academicians, policymakers, rural people and their urban brethren towards: (i) sustainable methods of environmental management; (ii) a holistic approach with multi-disciplinary, multi-locational and multi-institutional involvement; and (iii) making the practice of SWOT analysis an inbuilt mechanism in resource management for sustainable development.

Some of the few solid waste landfills India has, near its major cities, are overflowing and poorly managed. They have become significant sources of greenhouse emissions and breeding sites for disease vectors such as flies, mosquitoes, cockroaches, rats and other pests. In 2011, several Indian cities embarked on waste-to-energy projects of the type in use in Germany, Switzerland and Japan. For example, New Delhi is implementing two incinerator projects aimed at turning the city's trash problem into an electricity resource. These plants are being welcomed for addressing the city's chronic problems of excess untreated waste and shortage of power. They are also being welcomed by those who seek to prevent water pollution, hygiene problems and eliminate rotting trash that produces the potent greenhouse gas, methane. The projects are being opposed by waste collection workers and local unions who fear changing technology may deprive them of their livelihood and way of life. Along with waste-to-energy projects, some cities and towns such as Pune are introducing competition and the privatisation of solid waste collection, street cleaning operations and bio-mining to dispose of waste. A scientific study suggests public-private partnership is, in the Indian context, more useful in solid waste management.

8.6 ENVIRONMENTAL AWARENESS AND EDUCATION

Creating awareness and attitudinal change are possible through education and skill development. "Environmental education (EE) refers to organised efforts to teach about how natural environments function and, particularly, how human beings can manage their behaviour and ecosystems in order to live sustainably (Wikipedia)."

According to UNESCO, "Environmental education is a learning process that increases people's knowledge and awareness about the environment and associated challenges, develops the necessary skills and expertise to address the challenges, and fosters attitudes, motivations, and commitments to make informed decisions and take responsible action."

Environmental education should become a part of the growth of an individual. Right from childhood one must be given the knowledge and skill for dealing with environmental issues and the values of living in harmony with nature. Dr Martin Luther King said, "We must rapidly begin the shift from a thing-oriented society to a person-oriented society. When machines and computers, profit motives and property rights are considered more important than people, the giant triplets of racism, militarism and economic exploitation are incapable of being conquered." Practising simplicity and giving up cruelty will save mankind and natural resources. Such an education encompasses multi-disciplines and ideally promotes lifelong learning.

AWARENESS, ACCEPTANCE and ACTION are the watchwords of holistic environmental education. Schools, colleges, universities, training institutes should impart eco-education. There must be proactive teaching-learning not only in classrooms, but also in open spaces using groups like eco-clubs, adventure associations and so on.

Education for capacity building and resource conservation, better health and sanitation, and effective management should be promoted.

Pictures courtesy: https://www.google.co.in

Legal instruments, mass media and civil society have important roles to play in this direction. Quality education that is a healthy amalgamation of theory and practice is the need of the hour. Even non-science students and laymen should become participants in this process as facilitators. Awareness programmes should include tests, quizzes, demonstrations, exhibitions, training, etc., specially through the use of media. Organisations like Sulabh International, Energy and Resources Institute (TERI), etc., are strong on this point.

8.6.1 The 3 Rs Principle

We must practise the 3 Rs principle in our life—Reduce, Reuse and Recycle. This will help lessen the damage caused to the environment by consumerism. One must not forget that "too much is too bad". We can follow this principle in this way:

Reduce consumption and wastes by reducing

- fancy items
- consumption of soft/hard drinks
- tobacco consumption
- polythene bags
- the frequency of use of personal or private vehicles
- the usage of electricity
- the attendance to social functions and parties
- packaging by buying products in bulk
- demand for virgin wood products, and anything that causes disproportionately large or toxic pollution

Reuse the goods by:

- using second-hand goods which are still functional
- donating used clothes, stationery, etc., to the needy
- reusing water for gardening
- reusing gift wrappers

Recycle materials by

- Converting kitchen waste into compost as organic fertiliser
- Using sewage for fuel (biogas)
- Using cloth waste as raw materials in industries
- Using molasses as raw material in the spirits industry
- Converting used glass, paper, etc., into new products

Besides recycling, we must also give importance to treatment of wastes scientifically. There are several treatment techniques for waste, including hazardous waste. They include biological treatment, carbon adsorption, reverse osmosis, chemical treatment, distillation, electro-dialysis, etc. By using various technologies (e.g. electrochemical cells for water and odour treatment system) we can clean up wastewater and the whole environment. Waste treatment techniques seek to transform waste into a form that is more manageable, and reduce the volume or reduce the toxicity of the waste, thus making the waste easier to dispose of. Treatment methods are selected based on the composition, quantity and form of the waste material. In Sao Paulo, Brazil, wastewater is treated and reused to help solve dwindling water supply. In Oman golf courses are big consumers of treated effluent. Indian water consumers are also getting the benefits of many point-of-use (PU) treatment devices like ultraviolet technology, ultra filtration, nanotechnology, etc. It is good to note that several organisations (e.g., Water and Wastewater International) and individuals (e.g., Robert F. Kennedy Jr.) are contributing their mite for clean water, clean environment and growth with a future. Besides Acts, we need public-private participation supported by the media and civil society for the purpose.

While cutting down thoughtless consumption, we must increase thoughtful investment in sustainable businesses and infrastructure. This will keep everyone employed and fed as we transit from an unsustainable to a sustainable world.

Thoughtful investments for society include:

- Better schools and community infrastructure, including bio toilets
- Energy-efficient smart buildings
- Solar, wind and other alternative energy sources
- Urban and intercity mass transit, high-speed rail and cycling programmes
- Basic research to turn waste products into valuable commodities
- Production equipment to manufacture 100% recycled products
- Community-based organic agriculture
- Brown fields, reforestation, river clean-ups and land reclamation
- Preventative healthcare.

Thoughtful investments for the individual include:

- Very high-quality, long-life goods
- Locally made goods
- Locally available or recycled building materials
- Low toxicity goods and furnishings
- Locally grown, organic food
- Self-sufficient lifestyle products
- Low-emission or no-emissions vehicles
- Co-housing and innovative housing with eco-friendly ideas.

8.7 MANAGEMENT OF COMMON PROPERTY RESOURCES

Even though environmental resources are largely and generally open access resources, they need to be managed for the sake of conservation, promotion and effective use of the resources. They are common pool resources or community property resources (CPRs) at the local level. CPRs are an integral part of the social and institutional arrangements for meeting everyday requirements of local communities. They deeply affect the lives of farmers, landless labourers, artisans, etc. The dependence of these people on CPRs to fulfil subsistence needs is pronounced. They give rise to several issues.

Meaning

Generally, CPRs may be identified by access, common use and communal purpose.

- N.S. Jodha defines CPRs as "a community's natural resources, where every member has access and usage facility with specified obligations, without anybody having exclusive property rights over them".

CPRs are basic support systems of life on earth. All over the world these resources are depleting. They need to be properly managed by individuals and institutions in society.

There are different models of CPR management:

- Capitalist Model
- Socialist Model
- Anthropological Model
- Co-operative Model

The capitalist model of CPR management argues for "privatisation" of CPRs because resources commonly held are subject to degradation. We have the case of "Tragedy of the Commons". Fast population growth is always a threat to CPRs. Therefore, they need to be brought under supply-demand forces. This model scores on efficiency. The limitations of this model are (i) inequity and (ii) threat to sustainability.

The socialist model of CPR management favours "collectivisation" or nationalisation of CPRs as a solution to poverty caused by unequal distribution of resources. It tries to avoid over-exploitation of CPRs in the name of trade and to provide livelihood security to tribal people. The limitation of this model is that it does not give a holistic view of the ecosystem and its practical management.

The anthropological model supports "communal" management of CPRs because the local stakeholders' relationship with nature has a cultural core. The merit of this model is tapping of local knowledge/ local participation. The limitations are (i) it works well only in small/ homogeneous communities and (ii) all institutions cannot manage all resources equally well.

The cooperative model incorporates "voluntary" effort and "direct" participation of locals in CPR management. We have examples of fish farmers' societies, joint forest management, salt miners' cooperatives, etc. Advantages of cooperative management are that it (i) synchronises ownership right and user right, and (ii) ensures compatibility of efficiency, utility, security, equity, sustainability and responsibility. But as we all know, cooperatives have their own weaknesses—financial inadequacy, politicisation, etc.

Thus, we cannot recommend one model for CPR management. The best features of all models should be adopted in order to be eco-effective ("doing the right things in and for the environment") and eco-efficient ("doing the right things, the right way"). Managing CPRs is quite challenging. As noted environmentalist Vandana Shiva in her book, *Earth Democracy*, writes, "Enclosures create exclusions, and these exclusions are the hidden cost of corporate globalization." However, as Harwick, Olewiler, Fischer and Krutila feel, a CPR is neither exclusive nor discriminative, it is to be differentiated from private property.

What is important is genuine participation by people based on concern, knowledge, skill and responsibility. Community participation at a higher plane of culture, awareness and involvement can raise the state of CPR management. This will help make us green ambassadors and eco-citizens.

8.7.1 Role of Government and NGOs

Government

It is a known fact that when the number of people needed to produce a public good increases, the feasibility of market provision declines and welfare gains are accordingly difficult to produce through private exchange. This is a problem in welfare economics, called popularly "market failure". Therefore many have argued that government can potentially improve the situation by directly supplying or indirectly encouraging the provision of public goods. Indeed, Adam Smith argued that governments should be tasked with three main roles, all of which can be aptly described as the provision of public goods. Welfare economist A.C. Pigou justified government provision of such goods if there is a condition that social marginal net product (SMNP) is greater than private marginal net product (PMNP). Again, it is not the size or quantity alone that matters but the quality of the public goods that need to be produced, consumed and conserved.

Russell Madden feels that when the subject is the environment, the public perception is that a resource of such importance can only be adequately safeguarded by the benevolent, all-encompassing hands of the government. Governments at the federal, state and local levels must do more to allay the fears many citizens have that leaving environmental (that is, property) stewardship in the hands of "big business" or "selfish" individuals would result in wholesale destruction of our land, water and air. "Helping a Few, Harming Many" won't do. Government interventions need to be timely and in right proportions and directions, even avoiding its own possible excesses. Government—a planner, promoter, regulator, entrepreneur and consumer—has to do multi-tasking. It is entrusted with power to frame rules and also ensure that the rules are followed by all in a level playing ground. (See Figure 8.4.)

From streets and pavements to buildings, market places, transport and tourist destinations, educational institutions, etc., cleanliness is to be regulated by the government.

Government action and its wings or departments have a vital role each and there cannot be loose ends if public goods are to be properly managed.

The demand for public goods or provision is not static. Many argue that since willingness to pay for a public goods is constrained by ability to pay, how much of a public goods people want changes over time, and depends precariously on budget constraints and to a certain extent on change in taste or outlook. That means that even if we could measure demand for public goods with a high degree of accuracy, it may not have normative significance or public policy implications. Community-based organisations must motivate community demand for adoption of new facilities (behavioural change is often the hardest thing to accomplish), mobilise government initiatives, and assist with technical aspects of

Government Participation	**Community Contribution & Availability of Finances**
• Approval of connections • Makes use of existing government budgets allocated for slums • Operation & maintenance of main infrastructure	• Inculcates a sense of ownership • Results in improved maintenance • Puts pressure on government machinery to deliver • Reduces fiscal burden on government • Willingness of target population to make initial contribution in easy installments which loans from MFIs can enable
Community Awareness & Mobilization	**Engineering Expertise**
• Conscious setting aside of budgets by individual households • Usage & maintenance of services • Increased coverage of slum to maximize health impact	• Need for household infrastructure to be appropriately designed • Need for infrastructure to connect seamlessly to Government's pipeline network

Figure 8.4 Stanford Social Innovation Review

Source: https://ssir.org

construction such as materials sourcing and design, say Urvashi Prasad and Semonti Basu.

NGOs or the Third Sector

Civil society includes the NGOs or voluntary organisations that have to be distinguished from the private sector which exists primarily with a profit motive.

The World Bank defines NGOs as "private organisations that pursue activities to relieve suffering, promote the interests of the poor, protect the environment, provide basic social services or undertake community development".

A voluntary organisation (e.g. SHGs) is a social service and developmental institution motivated to meet the needs of the most disadvantaged in society, either through direct services to the people or through facilitative/indirect services to other voluntary organisations or government, non-profit making, and not undertaken to be fully funded for its maintenance, directly or indirectly by the government. The main objectives and functional areas of NGOs are:

Urban Street Cleaning

Source: https://www.google.co.in

- Enabling for access
- Mobilising resources
- Educating about eco-friendly practices
- Lobbying as a watchdog in relation to environmental projects
- Encouraging local initiatives and participation

Since the mid-1970s, the NGO sector in both developed and developing countries has experienced exponential growth. Today about 15 per cent of total overseas development aid is channelled through this sector.

Picture courtesy: https://www.google.co.in

In India there are thousands of successful NGOs promoting social capital and entrepreneurship building capacities, and combat responses to societal and environmental challenges and problems including sanitation and disaster management. NGOs are known for alternative models and people-empowering strategies in environmental education and governance. The Indian Association for Environmental Management, Nagpur; Madras Naturalists Society, Chennai; Vatavaran, New Delhi; TERI, New Delhi; Green Foundation, Pune; Green Dream, Bengaluru; and Nagarika Seva Trust, Guruvayankere and Danida, Mangaluru, both in DK district in Karnataka, are a few examples. These organisations have been active in bringing a paradigm shift in ecophilosophy and practices such as in the areas of rainwater harvesting, monitoring air and water quality, zero waste management, community sanction improvement and so on.

8.7.2 Community Participation

Environment protection and sustainability are increasingly pressing issues. The environmental challenge will only be met through public participation in decision-making as part of management. People or community participation becomes crucial both legally (right/duty perspectives) and ethically. It sets a series of practical policies and regulations giving wide scope for eco-citizens to participate in the environment protection movement in general and some specific activities (e.g., sanitation) in particular. An eco-citizen waits for no leader, she is proactive.

Community property resources like public goods (e.g., public toilets) have the feature of non-excludability and cannot be sustained or obtained by individual effort. Experts recommend community participation in monitoring and regenerating CPRs.

Community participation is a process wherein members of society involve themselves in the planning, decision-making and carrying out of activities towards the betterment of people's lives and resources. The community participation approach to development and management involves four Ps–People, Process, Products and Performance.

Community participation is cohesive group functionality with a focussed interest and conscious effort for the management of resources for a better life for all. It is a combination of local knowledge, local efforts and local responsibility for local resources. According to Food and Agriculture Organization (FAO) of the United Nations, community or people's participation is the "process by which the rural poor are able to organise themselves and through their organisation are able to identify their own needs, and share in designing, implementing and evaluating the participatory action". Thus, community participation is a self-initiated and common interest approach to CPR management.

The objectives of community participation are:

1. To create awareness about environmental issues, resources, rights and laws
2. To provide information about local resources, and document and disseminate it properly
3. To involve in decision-making to galvanise public opinion and action
4. To give access to legal means for dealing with environmental incidents and grievances
5. To empower the people in terms of eco-sensitisation, and conservation of biodiversity
6. To promote the role of NGOs as active stakeholders in civil society for alternative (Third Sector) intervention
7. To support collaborative approach, i.e., bringing together all stakeholders, and
8. To ensure sustainability i.e., growth with stability and equity.

People's participation in ecological activities can fetch rich dividends provided:

i) It is in the right interest and both people and institutions, including the government, are responsive and responsible.
ii) Environmental information is freely available. People should have the right to voice their opinion about any moves, to criticise, if required, to change, if possible, and profitable.
iii) There is a democratising environment with legal protection to both environmentalist and the environment in a complementary manner with due respect and recognition to assets and avenues.
iv) Cooperation with a sense of love for nature and respect for environmental rights and duties and support to environmental protection organisations become healthy practices.

When we observe days like Earth Day (22 April), World Water Day

(22 March), World Toilet Day (19 November). etc., we must rededicate ourselves to environmentalism with concern and concentrated effort.[3]

Creative and innovative modes and methods should be explored and executed, as for example, portable sanitation. The World Portable Sanitation Day (WPSD) logo symbolises the vital relationships between people, the environment and portable sanitation through the use of a human face, portable restroom, and the colours blue, green and white. The face represents humanity, all of whom can benefit from adequate sanitation. The portable restroom symbolises dignity and safety, two primary needs of every person. The colours blue, green and white represent a clean, healthy environment that is the result of proper sanitary conditions and also symbolise a connection to the Portable Sanitation Association International (PSAI), an organisation dedicated to preservation and protection of human health.

Picture Courtesy: http://psai.org/

Portable Sanitation
Picture courtesy: Portable Sanitation and You
Source: http://psai.org

Experience of free riding and over-exploitation of CPRs has made CPR management by community, important. The advantages of community participation in environmental management are-

1. **Initiation:** Economic development is meaningful and useful if it is for the people and by the people. So also environment management. It should be initiated in the community. The people's collective role is stressed for overcoming the "Tragedy of the Commons".
2. **Empowerment:** Opportunities for participation attract local people towards shared tasks. It enlightens and enables them as they can get the desired outcomes from plans designed by them.
3. **Protection:** Protection by the people is the best protection for local or community resources. They can use their knowledge and rights to protect them for common good.
4. **Flexibility:** Community participation is not bound by rigid rules. According to the changing environment and requirements there is scope for innovation for environment protection.

5. **Proactive:** Community participation does not wait for exogenous help. It makes local people act swiftly and positively. It takes all stakeholders together and does not make anyone subservient to the other.
6. **Service with Quality:** The motto of community-based participatory approach is "service with quality". It is a movement to serve the people without profit for itself. However, it does not compromise on quality of work.

Community-based participatory approach in development, particularly for CPRs, is growing. But certain weaknesses are also getting revealed. They are:

1. **Bad Governance:** Many community organisations are dominated by small groups. Interaction and involvement are concentrated. There is (a) preferential treatment for some, (b) tendency of cornering the benefits, (c) self-exclusion by some members, and (d) closure.
2. **Lack of Co-ordination:** Absence of co-ordination between stakeholders strikes at the root of community participation. There are problems of conflicts, confusion and duplication of work, missed targets and wastage of resources. There is, in short, mismanagement.
3. **Dependency Syndrome:** Overdependency on units and outside agencies results in slow work by the community and poor results.
4. **Resource Constraints:** Communities may also suffer from shortage of funds and trained and full-time working manpower. As a result, many a programme stagnates.
5. **Poor Evaluation:** Evaluation of community work is not done periodically and scientifically. If results are bad they may be swept under the carpet and no action taken. It kills fresh agenda in the womb itself.

We must strengthen community participation in India which is well-known for its cooperative spirit. We should actively participate in the Swachh Bharat Abhiyan (Clean India Campaign) and other national movements. We need clean and green cities and villages and not simply smart cities. Even schools and colleges need to work with local communities to save energy and ensure a clean and healthy environment.

NOTES

1 As per available data, in 1991-2001, in India over 79 per cent of rural households did not have proper sanitation and over 65 per cent did not have proper drainage facilities. This is the vulnerable section of the populace requiring health housing.

2 Money has superseded harmony!

3 Witnessing severe incidence of cholera in the country, which caused a large number of deaths in Ghana, H.E. John Dramani Mahama, president of the Republic of Ghana, has decided to celebrate November 2014 as Ghana's first national sanitation day. And 15 August 2014 marked the inaugural of World Portable Sanitation Day, and kicked off an ongoing campaign to raise awareness and promote change by engaging people from all over the world in expanding access to sustainable sanitation.

Chapter 9

Future of Sanitation

As Søren Kierkegaard said, "Life can only be understood backwards; but it must be lived forwards." No one knows which path the world will take in the next 40 years. But there should remain no doubt that there has been an impressively strong consensus among experts since the 1970s about the major sustainability issues and the broad direction of trends, even though the precise magnitude and dynamics of the future sustainability challenge and improvements in eco-efficiency remain unknown. Not just global issues such as consumerism, climate change and greenhouse effect but even local environmental issues like waste management will for sure occupy central place in growth theories and discussion in the coming decade(s).

The world is transforming in many different ways. These shifts from climate change, to migration, to new technology and urbanisation will have a significant impact on the management of water resources and related services such as sanitation. This impact will be both positive and negative, throwing up a variety of new opportunities and challenges for people and economies.

Sanitation is critical for preventing many diseases including diarrhoea, intestinal worms, schistosomiasis and trachoma which affect millions of people. Ensuring universal access to sanitation in households and institutional settings such as healthcare facilities and schools is essential for reducing disease; improving nutritional outcomes; and enhancing safety, well-being and educational prospects, especially for women and girls. The generations to come must feel and live safely.

Innovation in toilet technology could provide billions of people access to sanitation, while also creating economic opportunities and conserving water. But how can we make the most of the opportunities and face the challenges? While there is no doubt that even a developing/emerging economy like India will not lag behind in making further inroads in

A lavatory-shaped home in Seoul. Photograph: Reuters

Photo Courtesy: Google

social inclusion and high-tech sanitation, the pace, pattern and progress also matter.

9.1 THINGS TO KNOW ABOUT THE FUTURE OF SANITATION

As indicated by the Overseas Development Institute (ODI), here are a few things to watch out for:

- 5.2 billion people will need better sanitation by 2030. The new SDGs are much more ambitious. For sanitation, everyone needs access not only to a toilet, but also to a sanitation system that safely captures and manages waste. Over 60% of the world, 4.5 billion people, currently lack that.
- Poor people will need to be served first. In recent times, even in rural areas, it is the richest who gained access to sanitation faster. Leaving no one behind means actively putting poor people first, not just assuming they will eventually catch up.
- Demand will increase; supply will get more variable. There is

no doubt that future sanitation has to be demand-driven. Yet, increasing demand will put pressure on available resources.

- Quality will matter as much as quantity. It's quality, not quantity, that will limit options in many areas.
- Sanitation, conflict and migration will be increasingly linked. To avoid water-related conflicts of their own, host countries will need help to meet the needs of refugees as well as their own people. Local governments will face a tough time dealing with influx and increased pressure on limited resources.
- Water and sanitation will secure inclusive growth. While ministries of finance have tended to overlook the sector, sanitation offers much more than health benefits to the economy. In India, a latrine for everyone could free up 260 million hours every day, time that people could spend productively instead of trying to find a place to defecate in the open.
- Small cities will drive innovation for billions. It is often assumed that large cities and megacities present the greatest challenge for urban services. Yet, by 2030, it is estimated that 2.3 billion people, more than a quarter of the world's population, will live in towns and cities of fewer than 5,00,000 people. Historically, cities in poorer regions have struggled to extend formal, centralised water and sewerage networks to growing populations living on their edges.
- Joined-up spending will meet the needs of the most vulnerable. Joining up longer-term and emergency water and sanitation would help meet the needs of the most vulnerable people in the world. Over US$700 million was spent on long-term water and sanitation projects in fragile countries and territories in 2015. In the same countries, around US$400 million was spent on emergency water and sanitation. Yet there is little joint planning, even when the money comes from the same source. This results in duplicated effort and contradictory approaches.
- Companies with the long view will prosper. Companies will venture into new areas for profit and prosper using various methods and strategies of marketing: B2B, B2C, etc. CSR will also be an advantage. To get the edge on competitors and win the confidence of investors, companies need to help their suppliers manage water and sewage risks, and engage openly with others—public and private—who rely on the same water resources.

9.1.1 Challenges and Expectations

Sheikh Razak, a slum toilet builder in Mumbai, says, "Like an apartment where there is a kitchen, bedroom and bathroom, people see that they want a bigger house with different rooms for everything. They can't have all that, so they get the big necessity, a toilet."

Grand challenges (and wild expectations too?) seem to be in store. Experiments and explorations must proceed along diverse lines for the future of sanitation and progress of health.

- Suggested areas for innovation to be considered in the sanitation challenge include: Sanitation capture and containment technologies: improvements or alternatives to pit latrines.
- Solutions to menstrual management and safe disposal of child faeces.Extraction and transportation innovations for hauling faecal sludge to transfer or disposal points.
- Advancements in decentralised treatment technology for use at community, apartment block, town and/or city levels.
- Innovations in reuse of waste for agricultural, energy or industrial purposes at community and/or city level.
- Application of innovative technology and emergence of creative business models by social entrepreneurs, say, the "Toil-o-preneurs".
- Improved temporary toilets that do not use chemicals requiring special disposal.
- Low–costcomposting facilities requiring minimal user interaction with composted material.

9.2 INDIAN SCENARIO

The results for the first pan-Indian sanitation survey, Swachh Survekshan 2018, to rank the 7,041 cities and towns of the country, cut will come out soon. The Survey show the impact of sanitation on the lives of about 30 crore people and is the largest of its kind in the world.

Sanitation is a massive problem in India, both in the urban and rural contexts. With increasing population, the problem is growing. Open defecation in rural areas and lack of facilities in the urban regions has created a situation that needs urgent attention. This is one of the largest problems that the country faces, and there are hardly any initiatives tackling the issue. The story of Sulabh International is well-known and it has rendered yeoman service but there must be others also doing similar, if not the same, things. We need division of labour and specialisation for collective good. India is a vast country, it can ill-afford to expect all to be done by one.

Already we can see six initiatives that are doing promising work when it comes to making toilets more accessible:

1. **3S (Sanitation Solutions Simplified):** It was started by Rajeev Kher in Pune in 1999. Currently, the organisation manages 155 million litres of liquid waste, serving more than 1,55,000 people daily.
2. **Basic Shit:** As the name suggests, Basic Shit aims to create a clean and safe environment for public sanitation. Started in 2014 in Dwarka, New Delhi, by Ashwani Aggarwal, Basic Shit builds hygienic, low-cost, portable and biodegradable urinals that can be set up by unskilled labour in public areas where people urinate in the open frequently.
3. **Svadha:** Started by Garima Sahai and K.C. Mishra in 2014 in Odisha, Svadha integrates the entire sanitation value chain. It establishes an army of entrepreneurs to provide access to quality, affordable and sustainable sanitation solutions.
4. **Ekam Eco Solutions:** Based out of New Delhi, Ekam Eco Solutions was started in 2013 by Vijayraghavan Chariar and Uttam Banerjee. It works in the domain of sustainable sanitation, value-added bamboo products and sustainable livelihoods. The company has developed a waterless urinal called Zerodor, which is a completely non-consumable and non-chemical-based mechanical device.
5. **Samagra:** Started by Swapnil Chaturvedi, "Poop Guy" of Pune, Samagra is in the business of making good quality and accessible toilets for the urban poor. Supported by the Bill & Melinda Gates Foundation, the Swachh Bharat Abhiyan and more partners, Samagra works primarily on design and behavioural change to reach a more sustainable future.
6. **Bankabio:** Started by Namita Banka from Telangana in 2012, the company is engaged in promoting and developing innovative environment-friendly products and services for human waste management systems. The company deals with manufacturing,

supplying and installation of bio-tanks for digestion of human waste as a complete solution, rentals and AMC of mobile biotoilets, and so on.

9.3 SANITATION MARKETING

Sanitation marketing is an emerging field that applies social and commercial marketing approaches to scale up the supply and demand for improved sanitation facilities. While formative research is the foundation of any sanitation marketing programme, essential to understanding what products the target population desires and what price they're willing to pay for them, components such as the marketing mix, communications campaign, and implementation are also critical to the design and implementation of an effective programme.

The hygienic disposal of human excreta has been largely achieved through the private sector supplying to individual households. Evidence from what works indicates that development of the market is the only sustainable approach to meeting the need for sanitation in the developing world. This field note explains the marketing approach and suggests that it should be promoted as a central feature of sanitation improvement programmes.

The objectives of sanitation marketing are:

- To ensure that people choose to receive what they want and are willing to pay for
- To make sanitation financially sustainable
- To realise cost-effectiveness and economies of scale
- To go beyond hardware and technology. Sanitation facilities will bring few benefits unless they are used correctly, and this requires changes in behaviour. Marketing of ideas such as through social marketing is to be adopted.

9.3.1 Need for Sanitation Marketing

Sanitation, the hygienic disposal of human excreta, is a basic human need. However, 2.4 billion people, or more than half the population of the developing world, still lack it. To halve that fraction by 2015 was a Millennium Development Goal. Millions of dollars in sanitation programmes have made little impression, especially in Asia and Africa, where the shortfall is greatest. Most progress in access has been achieved by the market of private suppliers supplying individual households. The only sustainable approach to meeting the need for sanitation in the developing world is to support that market. Marketing has been more successful than anything else in changing the behaviour of people when they can see direct personal benefits. Improved health may seem to be the most obvious benefit of sanitation, but other gains are no less important. These include:

- Convenience and comfort
- Privacy and safety for women and girls, avoidance of sexual harassment and assault
- Less embarrassment with visitors
- Dignity and social status.

Because of these other benefits, a large number of people, even very poor people, are willing to pay for basic sanitation.

9.3.2 Will People Buy Sanitation?

If sanitation is so good, why don't people buy it? The short answer is that people do pay for sanitation—in their millions when conditions are favourable. For example, the changes in coverage with different sanitation technologies in Kampala, Uganda, from 1992 to 2003: the extension of coverage, mainly with septic tanks and pit latrines, has more than kept pace with the city's growing population, which nearly doubled in just over a decade. Indeed, the proportion of the population without their own sanitation (who have access only to a shared latrine or to none) fell from three quarters to less than half, although there was no major public programme to build or promote sanitation during that period. Nevertheless, many people in the world continue without sanitation, though they may say they want it badly. Why? One reason is that sanitation is most important to women and children, though it is men who make the investment decisions in many communities, and they may have other priorities. Another is the conflict of interest between landlords and tenants. Landlords often consider it unnecessary to spend money installing sanitation facilities in their properties, if they are not compelled to do so. Poor tenants, with little bargaining power, may fear that if they invest in sanitation themselves, their rent may be increased or they may lose their tenancy, and hence their investment. Another reason is the frequent lack of good home sanitation information, products and services at any price.

Engineers, administrators and bylaws have also impeded sanitation when they prescribe technologies, such as waterborne sewerage systems, that are too expensive not only for the poor but also for local governments. The urgent need today is not for the same technology which is found in the industrialised world. For those who currently have nothing, a simple pit latrine or pour-flush toilet can be a major improvement in public health and far more likely to be affordable.

9.3.3 The 3 Ps of Sanitation Marketing

Product

Latrine designs must respond to what people want, rather than what sanitary engineers believe they should have. In Mozambique, for example, the marketing of a new approach to sanitation began with many visits to existing latrines and consultations with their owners. This "market research" revealed that most people were used to open-air defecation and did not want a superstructure, beyond matting fence for privacy. Their greatest need was for a safe and affordable way of covering the pit.

Usually, a range of different products is needed to suit a variety of pockets and circumstances. The Mozambican programme offered two sizes of slabs, together with bricks to line the pit, if necessary, and a latrine installation service. Selling Sanitation is a joint IFC-WSP initiative that aims to help millions of people across Africa get access to the household sanitation products they want and can afford. The approach is currently being piloted in Kenya, with planned expansion to other African countries by 2014.

Price

This is the hardest part of selling sanitation to those who lack it. The poor, who need it most, can least afford it. Hence the need to keep costs down and market a range of products with various price tags. For example, in one successful programme in Bangladesh, the cost of the latrines varied hugely, from an ingenious design using tin sheeting for the pour-flush pan and a flexible plastic tube for an odour-proof seal, which costs only Tk 15 (US$0.30), to a cement version costing US$500. For comparison, latrine projects elsewhere in Bangladesh typically offer a single model at a subsidised price; this limits the number of latrines that can be built to the size of the subsidy budget.

Place

The product must be delivered to the right place; in particular, a latrine must be installed in the customer's own home. This means that the supply chain has to reach every household.

9.4 WHAT WILL THE GOVERNMENT HAVE TO DO?

With rapid privatisation and withdrawal of public investments, is there much role for the government in sanitation? Not at all. We must not adopt the state versus the market approach but the state and the market approach to get the best of both worlds.

The marketing or privatisation approach does not mean that the government should relieve itself of the responsibility for sanitation and leave it to the local building trade. There is an important role for for the government especially the local government in this approach, but it is very different from the commonly expected one of providing facilities and services. The public sector must:

- Understand the existing demand for sanitation, and what limits it; overcome those limits, and promote additional demand
- Stimulate development of the right products to meet that demand
- Facilitate the development of a thriving sanitation industry and
- Regulate and coordinate the transport and final disposal of wastes

Definitely, the Government of India will talk more and more openly on these issues. Prime Minsiter Narendra Modi's "Mann Ki Baat" radio talk programme is a good beginning.[1] The public sector must talk to consumers, manufacturers/builders/installers of sanitation facilities.

Encouragement is necessary for providers of supporting services, e.g., in emptying pits and septic tanks, other public departments, such as those responsible for urban land tenure, environmental pollution, small business development, etc. Public resources for sanitation also need to be committed to (i) research and development (R&D), (ii) promotion and advocacy, and (iii) training and capacity building.

9.5 TOILETS FOR TOMORROW

In 2011 the Bill & Melinda Gates Foundation raised eyebrows with its announcement that it would fund an initiative to take toilet technology to the next level. In many places now the strategy is to follow a "sanitation edge concept," under which waterborne sanitation is provided where the housing density justifies such infrastructure.[2] The holy grail for the future toilet is one that not only eliminates waste, but also generates wealth.

The toilet's future is analogous to what has happened with telephones over the past two decades. In the same way that mobile phones skipped a generation in the developing world, a similar story could unfold with toilets. Instead of wasteful flush toilets replacing filthy pit latrines, a future commode that uses modern technology could generate economic opportunity across the globe.

The technology to recover waste and energy from human waste exists, but the process requires much refinement. In a world where resources such as phosphorus are becoming limited and expensive, last night's dinner, multiplied by millions and even billions, could offer a wealth of materials that could provide energy, fertiliser and even recycled water. And the technologies involved could include solar, microwaves and nanotechnology.[3]

9.6 CONCLUSION

Hygiene education, especially in primary schools, is a key component of sanitation/water supply plans. How to change habits and long-held beliefs about hygiene? How to discuss sanitation issues where the topic is a taboo? How to achieve the necessary commitment of effort and time, involving children in the process and offering hope for sustainability? As children grow, they will continue to implement better sanitation practices and influence their own children and community to do the same. All the stakeholders, across countries, have their roles cut out, whether practising or propagating good sanitation habits. With SDGs we must have a shared development agenda (SDA) to ensure a world that is clearly much more in line with the world that we all want. It is more sustainable in environmental and social dimensions and promises a decent quality of life for all people. Sustainability must be the key word in our activities, consumption, production and exchange included. As inspiring decision-making is vital in this regard, a functioning science–policy interface must be in place. Law and livelihood should reflect the respect for sanitation culture.

As we have discussed in not less than nine chapters of this book, sanitation culture is a vast and diverse subject. There are many conventional aspects and modern trends. We need to balance both or, as the cliché goes, separate the grain from the chaff. People—children, men and women—wherever they live, villages or cities, hilly terrain or coastal belts, have the right to sanitation in equal respect and in a dignified manner. But, as human civilisation progresses more challenges and complex situations arise and we need to be prepared to change if required or strengthen the existing structures when they become weak. Ideally syntheses of old and new systems are to be considered. After all, being eco-friendly looks like a new mantra but is an old philosophy when man lived close to nature. The ancient Romans used to say, "Back to nature". Perhaps we have turned our backs to nature.

With health and environmental problems arising due to unsanitary conditions in most communities, what are the alternatives for disposing of human waste safely? In providing sanitation systems, what are the essential factors to be considered? In identifying the key considerations for the provision of low-cost sanitation systems in rural communities and urban agglomerations, it is necessary to analyse the environment, community/spatial structure and available services such as water supply, collection of wastewater and solid waste.

The key considerations include environmental factors and community-specific physical, social and cultural factors. Other essential factors affecting the choice of sanitation systems include the available services within the community such as water supply service levels, the means of disposing of wastewater and solid wastes, and the access networks within the community.

When we need to prioritise sanitation facilities, two general stages of selection are recommended. The first stage involves the choice between communal and individual toilets. Communal facilities involve the construction of several toilets built in one location, shared by a number of households, while individual facilities refer to the construction of toilets for each household.

The second stage involves selection of sanitation systems, taking into account the feasibility factor in areas with adverse ground conditions, specifically impermeable and unstable soils with high groundwater; high density areas; areas that do or do not require large equipment for waste collection and transportation. Cost effectiveness cannot be overlooked.

In any sanitation programme, technologies may be identified as appropriate, but if the application does not involve information, training of community members and mobilisation, the project will be a failure. Many sanitation programmes are planned and executed by government bodies, and few are successful due to the failure to convince and educate the people about the importance of sanitation and the need for active cooperation.

Education factors play a very important role because it is only through the basic understanding of the need for sanitation that the people can be mobilised for implementation.

When new sanitation technologies are introduced, planners must find ways to bring the project into balance with community knowledge, attitudes and behaviour relating to health and sanitation.

To identify a demand for improved sanitation is more positive than to initiate a supply of technology that is deemed to be good for communities. The former depends upon cooperation between providers and beneficiaries which comes through dialogue and exchange of information. Individual users are the ultimate decision-makers in the acceptance or rejection of new technology. It is they who determine the success of a project, since the value of the investment depends not only upon community support but, more particularly, on the consent of households and individual users. They need to be convinced that the benefits of improved sanitation, and the new technology with which it is associated, outweigh the costs. Equally, it is for providers to appreciate the social context and the constraints within which individual decisions are made. They must learn from communities about why improved sanitation may elicit negative responses and also the positive features of community values, beliefs and practices which can be harnessed to promote change.

The proposed system should not be too complicated for the user to operate and maintain. It should not require radical behavioural changes that the community will eventually reject it. And most importantly, community training provided will ensure that the skills required to construct and operate the improved facilities are within the local capability. These requirements emphasise that usage and sustainability are critical to the success of sanitation projects. Unless facilities are suitable for the people using them and unless the technologies are affordable and efficient, the facilities will remain unaccepted and underused.

Consideration should be given to the institutions of a political, economic and social nature that are operating at the national and/or local level, such as government, the civil service, religious institutions, schools and colleges, and the family, and to the forms of leadership and authority that are generally accepted by the majority of the people. It is also important to consider the various roles and patterns of behaviour of individuals and social groups, and to determine who is traditionally responsible for such areas as water supply, environmental hygiene, family health and children's defecation habits and so on.

Group and community identity, gender roles, the relative importance attached to different forms of authority and the ways in which it is exercised are all influenced by culture, i.e., all that is passed down by human society including language, laws, customs, beliefs and moral standards. Culture shapes human behaviour in many different ways including the status attached to different roles and what is deemed to be acceptable personal and social behaviour. In many cultures, for example, the elderly command traditional authority and influence within the family and community.

Culture also influences how people interpret and evaluate the environment in which they live. Investments in sanitation seek to improve health by providing a clean physical environment for households. There is a logical series of technical questions that need to be asked in order that acceptable technical solutions can be found. It may be confusing, therefore, when sanitation behaviour is found to vary widely between communities within the same physical environment. Predetermined rules cannot be applied. However, the sanitation behaviour of individuals usually has a rational basis, and people are often aware of the environmental causes of ill health. Many societies have detailed knowledge of the physical environment as a provider of resources for curative and preventive medicine and as a cause of illness. More than this, they have an understanding of the environment, not only in its physical sense, but also in relation to social and spiritual factors. This holistic view of the environment permeates many of the cultural beliefs and customs that impinge on both water use patterns and sanitation behaviour.

NOTES

1. School education and sanitation are the two big mentions in all "Mann Ki Baat" broadcasts, with one episode in February 2016 (before the annual board exams) having 60 mentions of school education and students.
2. Infrastructure is getting more and more importance these days in the realm of development in general and gram vikas in particular. We need to look at its multiplier effect rather than the conventional definition, "the hardware associated with public works" thing. For example, by setting up systems to plan, build and manage alternative water and sanitation systems, the integrated social, institutional and financial structures required to enable a wide range of other developmental objectives are created. Even the wasted resources become new income generators. For details see, Zoe Wilson (2009), pp. 83-87.
3. New technology that turns human waste into odourless charcoal briquettes is already demonstrated by Sulabh International. Scientists have invented a new toilet system that will turn human waste into electricity and fertiliser and also reduce the amount of water needed for flushing by up to 90 per cent compared to current toilet systems in Singapore. Researchers affiliated with Ulsan National Institute of Science and Technology (UNIST), South Korea, have found a new way to convert human w*aste into renewable energy sources.*

Bibliography

Akram, Mohamamd (2015). *Sociology of Sanitation.* New Delhi: Kalpaz Publications.

Bakshi, Rajani (2013, September 16). Can "Toil-o-preneurs" Solve India's Sanitation Woes. Retrieved from http://www.rediff.com/money/report/column-can-toil-o-preneurs-solve-indias-sanitationwoes/20130916.htm

Brown, Lester R. (2001). *Eco-Economy: Building an Economy for the Earth.* NY: W. W. Norton & Co.

Carr, Karen (n.d). Water and Sewage in Ancient China. Retrieved from https://quatr.us/china/water-sewage-ancient-china.htm

Carsberg, Henry C. (2010, August 15). Back to Basics: Sanitation Training and Education. Retrieved from http://www.foodqualityandsafety.com

Centers for Disease Control and Prevention (2017, April 10). Wash Your Hands. Retrieved from https://www.cdc.gov/features/handwashing/index.html

Chikkerur, Shour, Siddharth Bagrecha, and Palash Nandwani (2016). Sanitation in the Indian context–An Environment, Development and Society Perspectives. *Journal of Commerce & Management Thought,* 7(3), pp. 750-767.

Coffey, Dianae (2014, August 14).Culture, Religion And Open Defecation in Rural North India. Ideas for India. Retrieved from http://www.ideasforindia.in/article.aspx?article_id=329

Dankleman, Irene, Joke Muylwijk, Claudia Wendland, and Margriet Samwel (2009, February). Making Sustainable Sanitation Work for Women And Men Integrating a Gender Perspective into Sanitation Initiatives. WECF (Women in Europe for a Common Future). Retrievedfromhttps://genderinsite.net/sites/default/files/WECFGenderandSanitation_final.pdf

Dreibelbis, Robert The Integrated Behavioural Model for Water, Sanitation, and Hygiene: A systematic review of behavioural models and a framework for designing and evaluating behaviour change interventions in infrastructure-restricted setting October 2013BMC Public Health 13(1):1015

Ekanel, Nelson, Marianne Kjellén, Stacey Noel, and Madeleine Fodge (2012). *Sanitation and Hygiene: Policy, Stated Beliefs and Actual Practice: A Case Study in the Burera District,* Rwanda. Sweden: Stockholm Environment Institute.

Elledge, Myles F. (2003 May). *Sanitation Policies Thematic Overview Paper.* IRC

International Water and Sanitation Centre.

Frederick, William C. (2016). Commentary: Corporate Social Responsibility: Deep Roots, Flourishing Growth, Promising Future. In A. Crane, A. Williams, D. Matten, J. Moon, and D.S. Segel (Eds.), *The Oxford Handbook of Corporate Social Responsibility* (pp. 522-531). New York: Oxford University Press, Inc.

Gadkari, Siddharth (2017, August 10). Pune Heroes: Swapnil Chaturvedi. Retrieved from http://punemirror.indiatimes.com/

George, Rose (2008). *The Big Necessity: Adventures in the World of Human Waste*. London: Portobello Books.

Gosh, Arabinda (2017, September). Sanitation in West Bengal Bangladesh Shows the Way, *Economic and Political Weekly* (online), 52 (39), 30-35. Retrieved from https://www.researchgate.net

Hans, V. Basil (2008). Infrastructure for Rural Development–A Comparative Study in Dakshina Kannada District. Unpublished PhD Thesis. Mangalagangothri: Mangalore University.

Hans, V. Basil, and Jayasheela (2010). Environmental Management and Sustainable Development in India: Issues and Challenges. *Journal of Global Economy*, 6(2), pp. 3-14.

Hans, V. Basil (2016, September 6). Sustainable Development Goals and Approaches. Guest Lecture at PG Dept., Mangaluru: St Aloysius College (autonomous).

Hans, V. Basil (2017). Linking Business to Corporate Social Responsibility: The Role of Ethics. *AGU International Journal of Research in Social Science & Humanities*, 5, pp. 150-156.

Hindustan Times (2017, January 25). Bengaluru: How India's "Garden City" Became Garbage City. E-paper.

Hirai, Mitsuaki, Jay P. Graham, and John Sandberg (2016).Understanding Women's Decision Making Power And Its Link to Improved Household Sanitation: The Case of Kenya. JnlWat San Hyg for Dev, February. Retrieved from https://sanitationupdates.wordpress.com/tag/ women/

International Finance Corporation (2017). Catalysing the Market for Household Sanitation in Africa. Retrieved from http://www.ifc.org

Jha, Hetukar. (2015). *Sanitation in India: A Historic-Sociological Survey*. New Delhi: Gyan Publishing House.

Kaye, Leon (2012, October 12). What is the Future of Toilet Technology? Retrieved from https://www.theguardian.com

Lahiry, Samar (2017, January 9). India's Challenges in Waste Management. *Down to Earth*. Retrieved from HYPERLINK "http://www.downtoearth.org.in" www.downtoearth.org.in

Lone, Jon (2004, May 25-27). Ghana, Ceso Tho, And South Africa: Reginal

Expansion of Water Supply in Rural Areas. Retrieved from web.Org/ archive/ website00819C/WEB/PDF/Africa_R.PDF

Malik, Lokendra (2010). Solid Waste Management and Sustainable Cities in India: A Critique. *Nagarlok*, 42(4), pp. 40-48.

Masaon, Nathaniel and Miriam Denis Le Sève (2017, August). 10 things to know About The Future of Water And Sanitation. London: Overseas Development Institute. Retrieved from https://www.odi.org/sites/odi.org.uk/files/resource-documents/11720.pdf

Mehta, Jubin (n.d.). Sanitation Startups in India That Are Creating Impact by Making Toilets Accessible. Retrieved from https://yourstory. com/2017/04/ sanitation-st

Nagla, B. K. (2015). Sociology of Sanitation. New Delhi: Kalpaz Publications.

Nagpal, Tanvi (2009). An NGO in Search of a Business Model (Innovations Case Discussion: Sulabh International). Innovations: Technology, Governance, Globalization, 4(3), 59-64.

Pais, Richard (2015). Sociology of Sanitation. New Delhi: Kalpaz Publications.

Pathak, Bindeshwar (2000). Road to Freedom—A Sociological Study on the Abolition of Scavenging in India. New Delhi: XTreme Office Aids.

———, (2009). Technologies for Human Dignity: The Sulabh Sanitation and Social Reform Movement. Innovations: Technology, Governance, Globalization, 4(3). Retrieved from https://www.mitpress journals.org/doi/ pdf/10.1162/itgg.2009.4.3.43

———, (1995). History of Toilets Exploring History of Sanitation and Hygiene. Paper presented at International Symposium on Public Toilets held in Hong Kong on May 25-27, 1995. Retrieved from http://www.sulabhtoiletmuseum.org/history-of-toilets/

Purushothama K.V. & Hans V. Basil (2012). Solid Waste Management: Trends and Policies in India. In Jayasheela, Ravindra Kumar B., & Vilas M. Kadrolkar (Eds.), Urbanization and Economic Transformation Issues and Challenges (pp. 415-426), New Delhi: Global Research Publications.

Quora. Is Bangalore the Garbage City of India? Retrieved from https://www.quora.com

Ramachandra T. V. (2006). Management of Municipal Solid Waste. New Delhi: Capital Publishing Company.

Rassindren, Marie Joseph Gerard & Hans, V. Basil. (2015) Corporate Social Responsibility–An Evolutionary Outline from an Economic Perspective. NITTE Management Review, 9(2), 54-69.

Rasure, K.A. (2007). Solid Waste Management. In K.A. Rasure (Ed.), Environment and Sustainable Development, Volume I (pp. 297-307). New Delhi: Serials Publications.

Rice. Sanitation Quality, Use, Access and Trends (SQUAT) Survey, 2014. Research Institute for Compassionate Economics. Retrieved from http://

riceinstitute.org/data/squat/

Routray, Parimita; Schmidt, Wolf-Peter; Boisson, Sophie; Thomas; & Jenkins, Marion W. (2015). Socio-cultural and behavioural factors constraining latrine adoption in rural coastal Odisha: an exploratory qualitative study. BMC Public Health, 15: 880.Retrieved from https://bmcpublichealth.biomedcentral.com/articles/10.1186/s12889-015-2206-3

Sanitation India Water Portal (2014 November 22). Grand Challenge—Create the Next Generation of Sanitation Technologies. Retrieved from http://sanitation.indiawaterportal.org

Saxena, Ashish. (2015). Sociology of Sanitation—Themes and Perspectives. New Delhi: Kalpaz Publications.

Science Daily (2012 June 26). New Toilet Turns Human Waste into Electricity and Fertilizer. Retrieved from https://www.sciencedaily.com

Science Daily (2016 May 31). Turning Human Waste into Next Generation Biofuel. Retrieved from https://www.sciencedaily.com

Shetty, Jayakumar A., & Korse, Keshava Hegde (2014).Emerging Business Opportunities in Municipal Solid Waste management: Experience from South Western Karnataka. In A. Dejamma, & Seema Prabhu S. (Eds.), The Green Umbrella: Green Business Opportunities. Proceedings of the UGC Sponsored National Conference, Mangalore: Canara First Grade College.

Sida (n.d.). Women, Water, Sanitation and Hygiene. Gender Tool Box (Brief). Retrieved from https://www.sida.se/contentassets/3a820dbd152f4fca98bacde8a8101e15/women-water-sanitation-and-hygiene.pdf

Sridhar (2018). Dr Bindeshwar Pathak–A Superhero in Sanitation and Waste Management. Wisdom Times. Retrieved from https://www.wisdomtimes.com/blog/dr-bindeshwar-pathak-a-superhero-in-sanitation-waste-management/

Singh, Jagbir & Ramanathan, A.L. (2010). Solid Waste Management—Present and Future Challenges. New Delhi: International Publishing House.

Sinha, Bakshi D. (1996). Environmental Sanitation Health and Panchayat Raj. New Delhi: Concept Publishing Company.

Sulabh Swacch Bharat. Various issues.

The 'f' diagram (n.d.).WEDC (Water, Engineering and Development Centre). Retrieved from wedc.lboro.ac.uk/resources/factsheets/FS009_ FDI_A3_ Poster.pdf

The Hindu (2017, May 24). Mann Ki Baat, Now a Book. Retrieved from http://www.thehindu.com/

Takeo, Santos. (2011) Environment Degradation and Remedies. In Talwar Sabanna Ed.), WTO and Environment Development, (pp. 77- 100). New Delhi: Serials Publications.

United Nations. Visions, Scenarios and Future Pathways towards Sustainable Development. Retrieved from https://sustainabledevelopment.un.org/

content/documents/4239Chapter%204%20 Visions,%20scenarios%20and%20future%20pathways%20towards%2sustainable%20development2.pdf

WaterAid (2009). Towards Total Sanitation: Socio-cultural Barriers and Triggers to Total Sanitation in West Africa. Report, October 2009.

Water and Sanitation Programme (WASP).What is Sanitation Marketing? Retrieved from https://wsp.org/

Water and Sanitation Programme (WASP). The Case for Marketing Sanitation. Available at http://www.wsp.org/

WHO (2011 November). Sanitation and Hygiene. Children's Health and the Environment WHO Training Package for the Health Sector World Health Organization. Retrieved from http://www.who.int/ceh/capacity/sanitation_hygiene.pdf

WHO (2017). Environmental Health in Emergencies. Retrieved from http://www.who.int

Worldbank.org/GWSP (2008). New Sanitation Award Creates Healthy Competition Among Indian Cities. Water and Sanitation Program. Retrieved from https://www.wsp.org/featuresevents/features/new-sanitation-award-creates-healthy-competition-among-indian-cities

Wilson Zoe (2009). Basic Infrastructure for Sustainable Development. Innovations: Technology, Governance, Globalization, 4(3), pp. 83-87. Retrieved from https://www.mitpressjournals.org/doi/pdf/10.1162/itgg.2009.4.3.83

Wikipedia (21 January 2017). Toilet Ek Prem Katha.

World Toilet Organization (2016). World Toilet College India Begins Its Journey. Retrieved from http://worldtoilet.org

Routray, Parimita; Torondel, Belen; Clasen, Thomas; Schmidt, Wolf-Peter (2017). Women's Role in Sanitation Decision Making in Rural Coastal Odisha, India. https://doi.org/10.1371/journal.pone.0178042

Index